Talking About
Sexual
Assault

PSYCHOLOGY OF WOMEN BOOK SERIES

Talking About Sexual Assault

SOCIETY'S RESPONSE TO SURVIVORS

SARAH E. ULLMAN

American Psychological Association • Washington, DC

Published by
American Psychological Association
750 First Street, NE
Washington, DC 20002
www.apa.org

To order
APA Order Department
P.O. Box 92984
Washington, DC 20090-2984
Tel: (800) 374-2721; Direct: (202) 336-5510
Fax: (202) 336-5502; TDD/TTY: (202) 336-6123
Online: www.apa.org/books/
E-mail: order@apa.org

In the U.K., Europe, Africa, and the Middle East, copies may be ordered from
American Psychological Association
3 Henrietta Street
Covent Garden, London
WC2E 8LU England

Typeset in Goudy by Circle Graphics, Inc., Columbia, MD

Printer: United Book Press, Inc., Baltimore, MD
Cover Designer: Naylor Design, Washington, DC

The opinions and statements published are the responsibility of the authors, and such opinions and statements do not necessarily represent the policies of the American Psychological Association.

Library of Congress Cataloging-in-Publication Data

Ullman, Sarah E.
Talking about sexual assault: society's response to survivors / Sarah E. Ullman.
    p. cm.
 Includes bibliographical references and index.
 ISBN-13: 978-1-4338-0741-1 (alk. paper)
 ISBN-10: 1-4338-0741-6 (alk. paper)
 ISBN-13: 978-1-4338-0742-8 (e-book)
 ISBN-10: 1-4338-0742-4 (e-book)
 1. Rape—Research. 2. Rape—Psychological aspects. I. Title.

HV6558.U45 2010
362.883—dc22

           2009032818

British Library Cataloguing-in-Publication Data

A CIP record is available from the British Library.

Printed in the United States of America
First Edition

This book is for survivors and their supporters, and all of those who work tirelessly to respond to, treat, and prevent sexual victimization of women and children.

CONTENTS

ACKNOWLEDGMENTS

I thank my husband, Jason Krause, for his love and support, which helped me write this book, and my family. I thank survivors of sexual assault who speak out on behalf of themselves and other women, and in particular women who have spoken to me over the years about their own experiences. Only by breaking our silence can we stop the crime of rape.

I am grateful for grants from the National Institute on Alcohol Abuse and Alcoholism (AA 13455), the National Institute of Mental Health (MH 57231), and the University of Illinois at Chicago (UIC) Great Cities Institute, which supported some of the research reported in this book. I thank the many colleagues working on issues of sexual assault who have inspired and supported my work in the field over the years. I also thank the graduate students whose collaboration in the Women's Life Experiences Study has taught me so much, including Henrietta Filipas, Stephanie Townsend, Laura Starzynski, LaDonna Long, Susan Long, Gillian Mason, Cynthia Najdowski, and Kelly Kinnison. My colleagues in the criminal justice department at UIC have provided a supportive environment for my work for which I am most grateful. In particular, I am grateful to Lisa Frohmann, Stephanie Townsend, and Mindie Lazarus-Black for giving me advice about conducting and writing up qualitative research and to Greg Matoesian for his support and encouragement to write this book. I extend thanks to Joe Peterson, Dennis Rosenbaum, Edna Erez, and Beth Richie for support of my research, and colleagues in the UIC Interdisciplinary Center for Research on Violence, in particular Paul Schewe. I am grateful to Becki Campbell and Stephanie Riger for their support of my research over the years and expert advice about interviewing survivors of sexual assault. I thank Stephanie Townsend, Nicola Gavey, and Arnie Kahn for helpful feedback and advice regarding revisions, and especially Cynthia Najdowski for her extensive help in finalizing the manuscript. I also thank APA Books editorial staff members Beth Hatch and Susan Reynolds, and in particular Division 35 Book Series Editor Arnie Kahn for encouraging me in this project.

For further information, contact Sarah E. Ullman, Department of Criminology, Law, and Justice (M/C 141), University of Illinois at Chicago, 1007 West Harrison Street, Chicago, IL 60607-7140. E-mail: seullman@uic.edu.

Talking About
Sexual
Assault

INTRODUCTION

In contemporary American society, having a voice reflects empower-ment, whereas those who are silenced are powerless (Reinharz, 1994). Feminist scholars have argued that rape is an act that reinforces women's powerlessness in society (Brownmiller, 1975; MacKinnon, 1987). Talking about sexual assault can be conceptualized as a political act of claiming one's experience in a society that devalues women and their experiences. Disclosure of sexual assault is important for victims for several reasons. On a political level, naming one's experience can help label and resist rape. On a personal level, disclosure can help victims make sense of their victimization and begin the recovery process. Telling others about a sex-ual assault also may lead survivors to feel less distressed (Pennebaker, 1997) and more empowered. Disclosure can enable them to access needed support and services and, in some cases, assist police in apprehending perpetrators.

Although disclosure has the potential to aid in recovery, it can, and often does, add to the trauma of the initial rape when social systems and infor-mal social network members respond in ways that are blaming or unsupport-ive. Unfortunately, negative social reactions such as blame and disbelief are common responses to victims disclosing sexual assault (Ullman, 1999). For example, consider the following actual responses to victims of rape:

- "You should have told him you had AIDS." (said by a sex crimes detective at the scene dusting for fingerprints to a Black 19-year-old survivor of stranger rape)
- "We're very sorry this happened to you, but that doesn't give you the right to talk to us this way!" (said by a mother of a White adolescent survivor of sexual assault)
- "Well that's too bad, but you've got to expect this kind of thing because you're a pretty girl." (said by a professor to a White 25-year-old survivor of acquaintance rape)
- "What were you wearing?" (said by a friend of a White college survivor of rape)
- "At least it wasn't a brutal rape." (said by a friend of a Black teenage survivor of rape)
- "I can't believe you did that. Didn't you know something like that would happen? That's what happens when girls drink. You set yourself up." (said by a friend of a Black teenage survivor of rape)
- "I wonder why this kind of stuff happens to you?" (said by a sister of a White 20-year-old survivor of rape)

Blaming responses generally take two forms. First, people may blame victims overtly by saying something along the lines of "It was your fault" or "You were asking for it." Second, people may implicitly blame victims with questions about their behavior (e.g., their drinking or activities before the assault) or their character (e.g., asking how they could have such poor judgment).

Early research showed that victims are blamed by formal support sources, including police, medical professionals, and especially the legal system (Madigan & Gamble, 1991; Symonds, 1980; J. E. Williams & Holmes, 1981). More recently, researchers have discovered that informal social network members, such as family, friends, and colleagues, respond in ways similar to the formal support sources—they blame the victim for the assault (Ahrens & Campbell, 2000; Ullman & Filipas, 2001b). For example, parents or partners may overtly blame the victim by questioning her behavior or judgment. Friends may accuse the victim of lying about the rape or say they would never have let themselves get into that kind of situation, again implying that the victim's behavior must have caused the assault.

These types of blaming reactions have been called the *second injury* (Symonds, 1980), the *second assault* (Martin & Powell, 1994), or *secondary victimization* (Campbell & Raja, 1999; L. S. Williams, 1984). Although there are no prevalence estimates from nationally representative samples about how often survivors receive these social reactions, research suggests that one third to two thirds of survivors may experience one or more of these negative responses (Ahrens, Campbell, Temier-Thames, Wasco, & Sefl, 2007; Starzynski, Ullman, Townsend, Long, & Long, 2007).

PURPOSE OF THIS BOOK

I wrote this book to highlight the knowledge uncovered by researchers about how women talk about sexual assaults they experience and the responses they receive from others in American society. I discuss current research that shows how such reactions affect survivors' recovery. I argue that both *actual* negative social reactions and *anticipated* negative social reactions emanate from broader social norms and attitudes about rape (e.g., rape myths). Furthermore, these responses to victims must be taken into account to understand how to effectively treat and prevent sexual assault and its consequences.

In addition, I wrote this book to show how support providers experience disclosure, as well as factors that influence how they respond to the disclosing survivor. To improve responses to disclosing victims, it is important to understand the perspective of both formal support providers (e.g., psychologists, rape victim advocates, police, doctors) and informal support providers (e.g., friends, family, intimate partners). By being aware of providers' perspectives, potential support providers will be better able to understand the risk of secondary trauma and transference and how to deal with their own emotional reactions when responding to a victim. Organizations will also be able to "help the helper" deal with victim disclosures.

The book's discussion of secondary trauma and transference may be particularly important for rape victim advocates, who, unlike licensed mental health professionals, typically do not have advanced clinical training on how to deal with secondary trauma and transference. Still, trauma-related training is not required in many psychology graduate training programs, so knowledge about and experience working with survivors of sexual assault (common among advocates) may be lacking in mental health professionals who encounter victims. The provider perspectives can also help community-based prevention efforts address the emotional barriers that bystanders face to intervening to stop assaults from occurring, commonly known as *bystander interventions* (Banyard, Moynihan, & Plante, 2007). When providers are supported and able to prevent secondary trauma and transference, they can also engage in activism against violence against women and encourage survivors to do the same. This agenda fits well with broader efforts to address violence against women using an ecological perspective (Centers for Disease Control and Prevention, 2004; Grauerholz, 2000).

Because social attitudes affect how people respond to victims, I also review studies of social attitudes toward rape, including experimental and survey research on people's beliefs and judgments toward victims of rape (Ward, 1995). I focus on how these social attitudes are manifested in daily life through the behaviors of ordinary people as well as professionals in society. By showing the consequences of rape myth acceptance and how rape myths are manifested in responses to survivors, I hope to motivate people to support individual women who disclose sexual assault, to recognize the problem of rape, and to join efforts to combat this widespread social problem. This is important, because many survivors suffer alone in silence that is due to a fear of how others may respond to them if they talk about their assault experiences. It is unlikely that we will reduce the prevalence of sexual assault and its impact on survivors without changing the social environment or rape culture that continually manifests itself in harmful reactions toward women who disclose rape.

My aim is to reach individuals who may encounter survivors, including helping professionals (e.g., mental health professionals, rape victim advocates, criminal justice personnel, health care professionals), educators, researchers, policymakers, and students interested in violence against women (including survivors of sexual assault and their social support networks). Survivors and the people who encounter them may benefit from a synthesis of research-based knowledge about social reactions to sexual assault survivors' disclosures and recovery from trauma.

Although my primary focus is on adult sexual assault, I also address the related area of social reactions to child sexual abuse survivors, because there are many parallels between these two forms of victimization and society's response to the survivors. In addition, because most of the studies in this area of research focus on women, and most survivors of sexual assault are women victimized by men (85%; Bureau of Justice Statistics, 1984), I focus primarily on women as victims/survivors and men as perpetrators. I have not extensively reviewed the research on prevalence, psychological impact, treatment, or prevention of rape/sexual abuse, because such reviews have appeared elsewhere (e.g., Bachar & Koss, 2001; Breitenbecher, 2000; Foa & Rothbaum, 1998; Gidycz, Dowdall, & Marioni, 2003; Resick, 1993; Russell & Bolen, 2000; Schewe, 2002).

BACKGROUND: DEFINITIONS, RECENT PROGRESS, AND LIMITATIONS

Recognition of rape as a social problem and a crime has evolved over time, and definitions have varied historically and continue to do so even to this day. There is no single agreed-on definition of *rape*, and definitions vary depending on whether they are legally based, and thus can also vary on the basis of locality, or used for other purposes, such as research or treatment. Definitions of sexual assault typically include the following: nonconsensual sexual penetration of an adolescent or adult obtained by physical force; threat of bodily harm; or at such a time when the victim is incapable of giving consent by virtue of mental illness, mental retardation, or intoxication (for a review, see B. S. Fisher & Cullen, 2000). Depending on the type of sample (college or general population), anywhere from 17% to 24% of women have been raped in their lifetime (Brener, McMahon, Warren, & Douglas, 1999; Tjaden & Thoennes, 2000).

An early response to victim blame and negative reactions to survivors of rape was the rape crisis movement that began in the 1970s as part of the second wave women's movement. (The first wave was the women's suffrage movement of the late 19th and early 20th centuries.) Rape crisis centers were formed to provide victims with a supportive place to recover from the trauma of rape. Feminists also fought for rape law reforms and for improved medical, police, and mental health responses to survivors (Campbell & Martin, 2001). The rape crisis movement has had positive effects, including enhanced awareness of the problem of sexual assault through education, forums for victims to speak out about their experiences, advocacy for victims dealing with the medical and legal systems, and counseling for at least some victims (for a review, see Campbell & Martin, 2001). However, rape crisis centers are still among the most rarely contacted formal sources, with community studies showing that only 5% to 10% of victims of sexual assault indicating that they went to this source (George, Winfield, & Blazer, 1992; Golding, Siegel, Sorenson, Burnam, & Stein, 1989). In addition, the high prevalence of sexual assault and its documented negative impact on women do not appear to have diminished (Russell & Bolen, 2000). Thus, it is likely that need for services and activities performed by rape crisis centers still far outstrips their availability in many communities. National data show that rape still remains prevalent and that many women experience rape every year (Kilpatrick, Resnick, Ruggiero, Conoscenti, & McCauley, 2007). Thus, rape crisis centers have not achieved all of their goals, including early activist goals of stopping rape, and thus they will probably always be essential resources for sexual assault survivors.

Despite some progress in responses to individual survivors, we still live in what has been termed a *rape culture*. This term refers to the fact that U.S. society often holds women responsible for being raped, frequently ignores or excuses rapists, and fails to support victims afterward (Buchwald, Fletcher, & Roth, 1993). This pathological social environment in effect condones rape.

One reason that there has been limited success in changing the rape culture is that most research, clinical work, and prevention programming dealing with sexual assault operates from a narrow individualistic framework.

Trauma disclosure research and theory about the impact of sexual assault disclosure on health outcomes has largely ignored the social context. For example, experimental research on the benefits of disclosing stressful life events in college students (Frattaroli, 2006) shows positive health benefits for students randomly assigned to write about traumas compared with those assigned to write about neutral events. In contrast, similar studies in clinical populations have shown smaller positive effects (Frisina, Borod, & Lepore, 2004). It is important to note that these studies were focused on anonymous disclosures in which participants were writing in a laboratory with no social response from others. When such contextual factors are assessed, such as in real-life trauma disclosures, the results may differ. For example, Lepore, Ragan, and Jones (2000) showed in an experiment that if a confederate gave invalidating feedback in a laboratory setting to a participant disclosing trauma, the disclosure had negative effects on the participant. In addition, the few existing studies of actual victims of sexual trauma randomly assigned to write about their victimization or a neutral event in a laboratory setting have shown either negative or neutral effects of disclosure, suggesting that type of trauma and social context of the trauma may be important to assess (Antal & Range, 2005; Batten, Follette, Hall, & Palm, 2002; E. J. Brown & Heimberg, 2001; Crawford et al., 2008). Thus, it is important to consider the responses women receive to disclosures. These experimental studies show that disclosure of sexual assault and abuse may actually have negative or neutral effects, in contrast to studies of trauma disclosure in general.

Clinical approaches are also based on research that has not adequately examined social factors. For example, state-of-the-art treatments for posttraumatic stress disorder in victims of rape focus on changing individuals' emotional responses (e.g., feelings of fear), such as prolonged exposure treatment, or on changing their cognitions (e.g., self-blame) and behaviors (e.g., avoidant forms of coping) related to their assaults, such as cognitive behavior therapy (Foa & Rothbaum, 1998; Follette & Ruzek, 2006; Resick & Schnicke, 1992). Neither of these approaches addresses the harmful reactions victims often experience from their social networks and from formal support sources, or the ways in which these responses may emanate from the larger patriarchal society.

Prevention programs typically attempt to change people's rape-supportive attitudes (e.g., rape myths) using educational curricula in the hope that changing people's attitudes will eventually reduce the occurrence of rape. Although such programs attempt to reduce victim blame, they may not always be able to comprehensively address the broader social environment that gives rise to such blame. This is because such programs attempt to change individuals' attitudes rather than changing the systems and environments that give rise to those attitudes. One common goal of prevention programs is to change attitudes precisely in order to reduce victim-blaming responses that people make when a friend or family member discloses to them. Some programs that conduct outcome evaluations acknowledge that educational programs are not successful at primary prevention; however, many of them contend that their evaluations succeed at secondary prevention, because they may lead participants to be more supportive of survivors, which helps to ameliorate long-term effects of the assault (Schewe, 2006; Townsend & Campbell, 2008). Even when prevention programs spend substantial time trying to change victim-blaming attitudes and teach people how to effectively respond when friends or family disclose, however, they are limited in impact. Program effects on victim-blaming may be substantially diminished because programs are very short (typically 1–2 hours) and do not address the broader social environment that condones sexual violence and blames victims (Townsend & Campbell, 2008).

U.S. society has yet to adequately address and attack the rape-supportive culture. This rape culture affects how we are socialized and how we respond to victims of sexual assault in everyday situations. This book addresses this gap by providing information about the disclosure and help-seeking experiences of survivors of sexual assault and the experiences of informal and formal support sources who are faced with responding to victims following assaults.

SURVEY AND INTERVIEW RESEARCH APPROACH

Although this book integrates a wide variety of qualitative and quantitative studies, much of the book derives from three extensive studies that I directed: (a) one interview study on the experiences of clinicians and advocates who respond to rape disclosure (Ullman & Townsend, 2007, 2008), (b) one mail survey study on the experiences of rape survivors (e.g., Ullman, Filipas, Townsend, & Starzynski, 2007; Ullman, Townsend, Filipas, & Starzynski, 2007), and (c) one follow-up interview study with rape survivors who had responded to the mail survey study. Quotations from the survey and interviews appear throughout the book, so it is worthwhile to briefly describe the studies here.

The first study, the clinician and advocate interview project, was called the *Mental Health Provider Interview Study* and was conducted from 2002 through 2003 with support of the University of Illinois at Chicago Great Cities Institute Faculty Scholar Program. The sample comprised 30 women who were mental health professionals or current or former rape victim advocates, working in a variety of settings, including rape crisis centers, mental health and other social service agencies, and private practice in the Chicago metropolitan area. Participants were recruited using multiple methods, including mailing letters to mental health professionals listed in the yellow pages and to advocates listed as participants at a recent conference on sexual violence. In addition, former advocates were recruited by getting referrals from advocates who had already participated in interviews.

Participants completed in-person interviews at a time and location convenient for them, mostly at their work offices. Semistructured interviews ranged from 45 minutes in length to 1 hour and 20 minutes and asked about women's training and work experience with survivors of sexual assault as well as other relevant work experience, how disclosures of sexual assault tended to occur, how interviewees typically respond to disclosures, difficult and rewarding aspects of working with survivors, barriers to working with survivors and to survivors' obtaining services, and solutions that might improve services to this population. Participants were also asked about their own approach to treatment and their views about the role of mental health professionals in working with sexual assault survivors. Findings have been published in Ullman and Townsend (2007, 2008).

The second study, the survivor survey project, was funded by the National Institutes of Health and was called the *Women's Life Experiences Survey*. This Chicago-based project involved two mail surveys, 1 year apart (2002–2004), sent to survivors who responded to newspaper advertisements; signs in the community and on local university campuses; and fliers in mental health and social service agencies, including rape crisis centers. Over the course of a year, 1,084 women completed the mail survey, which collected information about women's sexual assaults, traumatic life experiences, psychological symptoms, drinking problems, coping strategies, attributions of blame and perceived control, and social reactions received after disclosing their assaults to others. The main point of the survey was to collect information about the women's assaults and how the women dealt with them. We gave women a list of local rape crisis centers and other community mental health agencies and paid them for participation. We also included a postcard asking whether they would be willing to participate in a 1-year follow-up survey and/or in-person interview. Findings from this survey project have been published in various articles (e.g., Ullman, Filipas, Townsend, & Starzynski, 2007; Ullman, Townsend, Filipas, & Starzynski, 2007).

The third, study, the survivor interview project—called the *Women's Life Experiences Interview Project*—was also part of the Women's Life Experiences Study funded by the National Institutes of Health. Approximately 60% of women who responded to the survey indicated on returned postcards that they would be interested in doing an interview. We had funding to interview only about 10% of the sample, which we had estimated to be 600 rape survivors—in other words, 60 interviews. Whereas the mail survey was intended to test a theoretical model of the relationships of social reactions to coping, attributions, and recovery outcomes (symptoms of posttraumatic stress disorder, drinking problems), the follow-up interviews were to be more exploratory in nature and designed to obtain more information about women's experiences talking with others, especially mental health professionals, about their assaults. This was important because previous research had shown that women underutilize mental health professionals and, when they do go to them, have mixed experiences (Golding et al., 1989). Thus, the interviews were designed to build on information from the mail survey by asking more about help-seeking experiences in depth and reactions they got from others, including both informal and formal sources (especially mental health professionals). The interviews were conducted from 2003 through 2006, and results have not yet been published.

These three studies have collectively provided a rich basis of knowledge about the experience of rape disclosure, from both the survivor's perspective and the clinician/rape victim advocate's perspective. Furthermore, the survivor interview study prompted me to examine my own experience responding to rape disclosure—in this case, as a researcher conducting interviews with survivors. After all, despite the research purpose of the interviews, my responses to the survivors could nonetheless affect survivors' chances of recovery. Thus, my experiences conducting the survivor interviews are also discussed in the book. Multiple perspectives—from all who experience rape disclosure—are critical for considering the entire social context of rape and rape disclosure.

ORGANIZATION OF THIS BOOK

This book contains seven chapters. In chapter 1, I provide background on the recent social historical context of rape and attitudes toward rape, including the second wave women's movement and how that has framed our understanding of talking about rape. I explain how societal attitudes can frame our understanding of and affect women's experiences of disclosing assault. In chapter 2, I review theories of rape and women's disclosure, including sociological, feminist, psychological, and ecological theories, and I introduce an ecological model of help-seeking. An understanding of theories of rape disclosure and help-seeking shows how existing knowledge has been arrived at to date. In chapter 3, I review research on disclosure of sexual assault, responses to disclosure, and factors related to the social reactions survivors receive from others. I explain why women disclose assaults and how others respond to them. In chapter 4, I discuss studies of social reactions and their effects on survivors, and I show how negative social reactions are harmful to survivors.

I argue that research should go beyond survivors' perspectives on seeking help to also include perspectives of helpers, both formal (e.g., rape crisis advocates, clinicians, and other formal providers) and informal (e.g., family, friends, intimate partners). In this way, we can better understand how the social context of rape impacts support providers' ability to respond to survivors and the effects that hearing survivors' stories has on helpers. Thus, in chapter 5 I report on advocates' and clinicians' perspectives on helping survivors, and in chapter 6 I discuss my own experience of conducting interviews with survivors, the effects it had on me, and how I coped with those effects. I believe that my experience conducting this research has direct parallels with emotional reactions people have when hearing victims discuss their assaults. Because my research has involved interviews with survivors about their experiences disclosing sexual assault to others, it is directly relevant to my understanding of the impact of hearing about survivors' disclosure experiences.

Finally, in chapter 7, I consider how knowledge gained from research grounded in a feminist social ecological model can help us to understand and dismantle the pathological social environment, or rape culture, by changing social attitudes and societal responses to sexual victimization (e.g., macro level) and interactions with survivors (e.g., micro level).

1

THE SOCIAL CONTEXT OF TALKING
ABOUT SEXUAL ASSAULT

Two decades of research have consistently shown that approximately 15% to 30% of women experience attempted or completed sexual assault in adulthood (for a review of prevalence studies, see Russell & Bolen, 2000). Sexual assault is most common among younger women and adolescent girls, with over half of all first rapes of women occurring before age 18 (Tjaden & Thoennes, 2000). Women assaulted either in childhood or adolescence (Messman-Moore & Long, 2000) also have a significantly greater risk of sexual revictimization in adulthood.

In recent years, there has been increased public awareness of and societal responses to issues of violence against women and children. However, since the 1980s we have experienced a political and social backlash of sorts in response to the gains won by the second wave of the women's movement in the 1960s and 1970s regarding various social issues, including sexual assault (see chap. 2, this volume, for more detailed definitions of first-, second-, and third-wave feminism; Conte, 2002; Eliasson, 2002; Faludi, 1991; Hammer, 2002). It is important to be aware of this because what is considered *rape* is still hotly contested in U.S. society. In addition, rape stereotypes are quite prevalent and affect survivors' decisions of whether to disclose rape as well as how people react to survivors' disclosures. Therefore, one cannot truly understand the topic of sexual assault without first having knowledge of the broader societal context of rape. In this chapter, I review the social phenomena that maintain a rape-supportive environment, including simultaneous acknowledgment and denial of rape in society, the "real rape" stereotype, and rape myths; the silencing effect of these phenomena; the variables that influence individual attitudes and beliefs about rape; and the question of whether disclosure really empowers women.

SOCIAL PHENOMENA THAT MAINTAIN A RAPE-SUPPORTIVE ENVIRONMENT

It is important to begin with some background about social phenomena underlying disclosure of traumatic events, including sexual assault. These factors include societal beliefs about rape, such as stereotypes and myths, as manifested in the media, societal response to rape cases, and socialization practices.

Simultaneous Acknowledgment and Denial of Rape

In American society, women's sexuality is still subject to numerous stereotypes. Both the objectification and victimization of women continue to be glorified in the media and societal institutions (American Psychological Association, 2007). Proliferation of the sex industry, including pornography (Paul, 2005) and sex trafficking in women and girls in the United States and abroad (Barry, 1979), sets the larger stage for sexual assault in our society. In this context, all forms of sexual victimization (from child sexual abuse to adult sexual assault) have seemingly been acknowledged and denied, sometimes simultaneously.

On the one hand, U.S. society acknowledges that sexual assault is wrong on media talk shows and in public statements about rape by societal agents such as police, prosecutors, social service and public health administrators, and some religious leaders. We encourage and expect victims to come forward so that we can catch and prosecute offenders and provide treatment to victims. On the other hand, rape is still effectively condoned, as evidenced by responses of institutions such as the criminal justice system and the media. We revictimize survivors who report rape by questioning their accounts, and we provide justice to only a few "legitimate" victims. Estrich (1987) labeled these *real rape* victims—namely, those who are attacked by strangers and who have not engaged in any potentially blamable preassault behavior. All of this occurs in a context in which few rapes are reported; of those that are reported, attrition of cases due to weeding out based on extralegal characteristics (e.g., alcohol) is extremely high, resulting in a "justice gap" in cases of sexual assault (Temkin & Krahe, 2008).

Treating some victims as illegitimate (i.e., responsible for their rape) is also a bad practice of the media, as evidenced by the recent priest abuse scandal and high-profile college rape cases (Finkelhor, 2003; Leonard, 2007). For example, in the priest abuse scandal, some prelates of the Roman Catholic Church supported and protected accused priests with financial backing in the face of numerous sexual abuse claims while victims' stories were silenced, disbelieved, and generally less represented in the media (Dokecki, 2004). Yet even when sexual assault is showcased in the media and through victim accounts of their experiences on talk shows, this may do little more than titillate viewers and reinforce stereotypes about rape and its victims than to enlighten people about rape or to provide any real assistance to victims—either those portrayed or those in the viewing audience (for recent analyses of the media and rape, see Ehrlich, 2001; Moorti, 2002). For example, television shows often portray victims as stupid or naïve in stories about incest or rape by known, trusted men. Girls or young women are typically questioned in ways that imply blame by incredulous talk show hosts, who may, for example, ask victims how they did not know that the rape/abuse was wrong. Mothers are frequently asked why they did not realize that the rape/abuse had happened or was going on. This is especially likely in intrafamilial cases. Such victim-blaming responses are another way in which society denies the validity of victims' experiences and contributes to many women's inability to acknowledge and speak about their experiences.

The "Real Rape" Stereotype

The most dominant stereotype of rape is that of an unknown man, often Black, jumping out of an alley and assaulting a White, middle-class, conservatively dressed woman. The woman has not consumed alcohol or engaged in any other "suspect" behaviors. She resists him by kicking, grabbing, scratching, and screaming, but her attempts to get away fail. He rapes her. This common stereotype is often viewed as the only situation in which the victim is blameless, or "legitimate." When rapes do not fit this stereotype—for example, if the man is White, if the woman is a member of an ethnic minority group, if the man is at the woman's home, if the woman has been drinking, if the woman does not physically resist after telling the man "no"—the rape is often seen as not being a "real" rape. The rape and its victim are not deemed legitimate.

Societal beliefs about sexual assault often dismiss women of lower socioeconomic status (SES; A. Y. Davis, 1978/1981; Estrich, 1987) and women of color (A. Y. Davis, 1978/1981; Estrich, 1987; Pierce-Baker, 1998; Washington, 2001) as not being "real victims." Several writers and researchers in the 1980s showed that the scope of "real rape" is not in fact limited to the racist yet ever-present stereotype of the Black male stranger in an alley with a knife.

Rape is in fact most likely to be committed by acquaintances and intimate partners (80% of cases) of the same race (Estrich, 1987; Koss, 1985; Russell, 1982). Despite this information, U.S. society still takes less seriously assaults perpetrated by men known to their victims, even though such assaults are neither less violent nor less likely to lead to psychological distress (Koss, Dinero, Seibel, & Cox, 1988; Ullman & Siegel, 1993).

Given that stranger rapes are more legitimate and fit with society's stereotypes, victims of these assaults are likely to be less stigmatized, disbelieved, or blamed. In fact, such victims are often viewed as heroes and honored for their strength in speaking out. These victims may be easier for people around them to deal with because they fit our stereotypes. In addition, we can usually distance ourselves by believing that stranger rape is unlikely to happen to us, which is accurate from a statistical perspective. In addition to the stereotype of "real rape," other false beliefs about rape exist.

Rape Myths

Despite significant social changes over the past several decades in societal awareness about rape in American society, persistent social beliefs known as *rape myths*, or false beliefs about rape, are still widespread (for reviews of these studies, see Pollard, 1992; Ward, 1995). Rape myths serve to deny and justify male sexual aggression against women (Lonsway & Fitzgerald, 1994). Burt and Albin (1981) originally grouped rape myths into four categories: (a) Nothing happened: Women make false allegations against men; (b) No harm was done: Rape is "just sex"; (c) She wanted it: Women say "no" when they mean "yes"; and (d) She deserved it: Women ask for rape. Exhibit 1.1 includes common rape myths as assessed in frequently used rape myth acceptance scales (Payne, Lonsway, & Fitzgerald, 1999). Although most researchers do not report the percentages of people who endorsed individual rape myths (only mean scores on rape myth acceptance scales), Lonsway and Fitzgerald (1994) reported in their review of research studies that up to 35% of college students endorsed at least one rape myth, perhaps in part because rape myths are commonly expressed in media accounts of rape cases (Franiuk, Seefelt, Cepress, & Vandello, 2008).

THE SILENCING EFFECT OF RAPE-SUPPORTIVE SOCIAL PHENOMENA

U.S. culture expects women to tolerate and reconceptualize sexual assault as something other than sexual aggression in which victims may experience difficulty talking about private matters involving sexuality and violation. Our

EXHIBIT 1.1
Common Rape Myths From the Illinois Rape Myth Acceptance Scale (IRMAS)

SA-3[a]   1. If a woman is raped while she is drunk, she is at least somewhat responsible for letting things get out of control.

WI-5[a]   2. Although most women wouldn't admit it, they generally find being physically forced into sex a real "turn-on."

MT-3   3. When men rape, it is because of their strong desire for sex.

TE-5[a]   4. If a woman is willing to "make out" with a guy, then it's no big deal if he goes a little further and has sex.

LI-4   5. Women who are caught having an illicit affair sometimes claim that it was rape.

FI-1   6. Newspapers should not release the name of a rape victim to the public.

LI-3   7. Many so-called rape victims are actually women who had sex and "changed their minds" afterwards.

WI-1[a]   8. Many women secretly desire to be raped.

DE-5   9. Rape mainly occurs on the "bad" side of town.

DE-4   10. Usually, it is only women who do things like hang out in bars and sleep around that are raped.

FI-2[a]   11. Most rapists are not caught by the police.

NR-1[a]   12. If a woman doesn't physically fight back, you can't really say that it was rape.

DE-2[a]   13. Men from nice middle-class homes almost never rape.

TE-1   14. Rape isn't as big a problem as some feminists would like people to think.

SA-2   15. When women go around wearing low-cut tops or short skirts, they're just asking for trouble.

LI-2[a]   16. Rape accusations are often used as a way of getting back at men.

NR-5   17. A rape probably didn't happen if the woman has no bruises or marks.

WI-4   18. Many women find being forced to have sex very arousing.

SA-4   19. If a woman goes home with a man she doesn't know, it is her own fault if she is raped.

MT-5   20. Rapists are usually sexually frustrated individuals.

FI-3[a]   21. All women should have access to self-defense classes.

DE-3[a]   22. It is usually only women who dress suggestively that are raped.

WI-2   23. Some women prefer to have sex forced on them so they don't have to feel guilty about it.

NR-3[a]   24. If the rapist doesn't have a weapon, you really can't call it a rape.

SA-6   25. When a woman is a sexual tease, eventually she is going to get into trouble.

TE-3   26. Being raped isn't as bad as being mugged and beaten.

DE-7[a]   27. Rape is unlikely to happen in the woman's own familiar neighborhood.

DE-1   28. In reality, women are almost never raped by their boyfriends.

TE-2[a]   29. Women tend to exaggerate how much rape affects them.

MT-2   30. When a man is very sexually aroused, he may not even realize that the woman is resisting.

LI-1[a]   31. A lot of women lead a man on and then they cry rape.

FI-4[a]   32. It is preferable that a female police officer conduct the questioning when a woman reports a rape.

LI-5   33. A lot of times, women who claim they were raped just have emotional problems.

NR-2   34. If a woman doesn't physically resist sex—even when protesting verbally—it really can't be considered rape.

DE-6   35. Rape almost never happens in the woman's own home.

SA-5[a]   36. A woman who "teases" men deserves anything that might happen.

(continued)

SA-8[a] 37. When women are raped, it's often because the way they said "no" was ambiguous.

TE-4   38. If a woman isn't a virgin, then it shouldn't be a big deal if her date forces her to have sex.

MT-1[a] 39. Men don't usually intend to force sex on a woman, but sometimes they get too sexually carried away.

FI-5   40. This society should devote more effort to preventing rape.

SA-1[a] 41. A woman who dresses in skimpy clothes should not be surprised if a man tries to force her to have sex.

MT-4[a] 42. Rape happens when a man's sex drive gets out of control.

SA-7   43. A woman who goes to the home or apartment of a man on the first date is implying that she wants to have sex.

WI-3   44. Many women actually enjoy sex after the guy uses a little force.

NR-4   45. If a woman claims to have been raped but has no bruises or scrapes, she probably shouldn't be taken too seriously.

Note. All items are from the IRMAS. Item label prefixes refer to the subscale corresponding to the item: SA = *She Asked for It;* WI = *She Wanted It;* MT = *He Didn't Mean To;* TE = *Rape Is a Trivial Event;* LI = *She Lied;* FI = filler item (not scored); DE = *Rape Is a Deviant Event;* NR = *It Wasn't Really Rape.* From "Rape Myth Acceptance: Exploration of its Structure and its Measurement Using the Illinois Rape Myth Acceptance Scale," by D. L. Payne, K. A. Lonsway, and L. F. Fitzgerald, 1999, *Journal of Research in Personality, 53,* 27–68. Copyright 1999 by Elsevier. Reprinted with permission.
[a]IRMA-SF (short-form) item.

society expects victims to speak up in a timely manner about sexual assault, but only if they are "legitimate" rape victims. Ultimately, there is only a narrow path to being considered a legitimate rape victim in both the criminal justice system and society in general. If women fit into a narrow rape stereotype, they can sometimes be acknowledged as victims and even viewed as heroic. However, if a woman does not report rape quickly after it occurs; have a spotless character; and fit notions of race, class, and gender that lend a given assault to fitting into rape stereotypes; and/or if she has engaged in any "suspect" behavior prior to assault, her legitimacy as a rape victim is usually questioned (P. H. Collins, 2004; Neville & Pugh, 1997). Such victims may be silenced if they speak out about rape and claim to be rape victims.

It is noteworthy, for example, that published memoirs about rape to date have focused exclusively on stereotypical stranger rapes (Brison, 2002; Francisco, 1999; Meili, 2003; Pierce-Baker, 1998; Raine, 1998; Scherer, 1992; Sebold, 1999; Winkler, 2002; Ziegenmeyer, 1992). The lack of memoirs on rapes perpetrated by known men, which are more common than those committed by strangers, is likely due to women's realistic fear of not being believed, much less being honored or viewed as heroes in such cases. Victims of these rapes may believe societal stereotypes about rape and often do not label or acknowledge their unwanted sexual assaults as rapes at all (for a review, see Littleton, Rhatigan, & Axsom, 2007). Even victims who identify these assaults by intimate partners, dates, acquaintances, and other men known to them as rapes are likely to be disbelieved. Speaking about them threatens survivors' relationships and social networks, as well as men's right to sexual access to women they know (MacKinnon, 1987). This is why much of the current backlash against rape victims is focused on date and acquaintance rape. Some writers still disagree that such assaults should count as rapes, as do rapes by strangers (e.g., see Gilbert, 2005; Roiphe, 1993).

Over 20 years ago, Koss (1985) coined the term *hidden* rape victim to refer to those who acknowledge experiencing acts meeting legal definitions of rape (i.e., sex obtained by threats, force, or incapacitation; typically, acquaintance rape victims) but respond "no" to questions about whether they have ever been raped. Today, for a woman to self-label as a rape victim still carries social costs, such as the stigma of identifying oneself as a victim. This may be why lack of acknowledgment of this victim identity is still common in U.S. society. Anywhere from one half to two thirds of women do not self-label as rape victims (Littleton et al., 2007), despite having experienced assaults that meet the legal definition of rape. Conservative writers have used many women's lack of self-labeling as rape victims to argue that the women are not actual rape victims (Gilbert, 2005; Roiphe, 1993). However, there are valid reasons for women to distance themselves from such acknowledgment both to themselves and to other people. Many women believe rape stereotypes that limit the rape label to certain types of incidents and/or mistakenly believe that not self-labeling may protect them from the consequences of coming to grips with being a victim of sexual assault (Koss et al., 1988; Ullman & Siegel, 1993).

Silencing is a process that occurs before and after rape disclosures. Survivors often anticipate receiving negative reactions. If they do disclose, receipt of actual negative social reactions can serve to reinforce self-blame and feelings of delegitimation as a rape victim (Ahrens, 2006). Thus, many women do not disclose their sexual assaults and remain silent, fearing censure or being delegitimized, blamed, and/or stigmatized should they identify themselves as rape victims. These forms of silencing and judgments are ways in which victims are revictimized (e.g., a form of *secondary victimization*, or negative reactions to victims after rape) for speaking about rapes perpetrated by known men, assaults involving alcohol, and incidents not fitting the crime stereotype. Silencing of women and general silence about the reality of sexual assault in society reflect a larger silencing of women's voices in society. In fact, rape victims have been called an *invisible community* whose members need to find ways to come together to end their pain and isolation in dealing with sexual assault alone (Campbell, Sefl, Wasco, & Ahrens, 2004). Such communal forms of disclosure may occur in private settings, such as support groups. Public arenas, such as rape speak-outs/take-back-the-night marches or online forums, also provide outlets for political, collective disclosures/discourse working for social change.

VARIABLES THAT INFLUENCE INDIVIDUAL ATTITUDES AND BELIEFS ABOUT RAPE

Rape myths are widespread, with many people endorsing false beliefs about rape across a variety of research studies (for a review, see Ward, 1995), and these myths have serious consequences. For example, rape myth acceptance is also related to negative evaluations of survivors of rape, greater blame of victims of rape, lower conviction rates for accused rapists, and shorter sentences for convicted rapists in mock jury trials (K. Anderson, Cooper, & Okamura, 1997; Finch & Munro, 2005; Lonsway & Fitzgerald, 1994). However, there are individual-difference factors that have been shown to relate to the extent to which people endorse them.

Gender

Research shows that women endorse rape myths significantly less often than men (Lonsway & Fitzgerald, 1994). Research also shows that rape myth acceptance is related to greater acceptance of interpersonal violence, hostility toward women, greater gender role stereotyping, and more conservative attitudes toward women (Acock & Ireland, 1983; Baron & Straus, 1989; Burt, 1980; Ward, 1995). Rape-supportive attitudes are common in male college students and are related to greater use of pornography (Allen, Emmers, Gebhardt, & Giery, 2006), and a significant proportion of male college students agree that there is some likelihood that they would rape a woman if they could get away with it (Bohner, Jarvis, Eyssel, & Siebler, 2005; Check & Malamuth, 1985; Malamuth & Check, 1985). Males growing up in patriarchal families in which traditional gender roles are reinforced are more likely to be taught that sexual aggression is an acceptable way to show male dominance (Malamuth & Dean, 1991).

Age

In general, older adults have more rape-supportive attitudes. For example, R. F. Rich and Sampson (1990) surveyed 450 Chicago residents about their conceptions of rape and found that older people were more than twice as likely to believe that rape was caused by the way women dress and act.

Older adults were also less likely to see rape as an act of violence or to endorse feminist interpretations of rape or legislation against marital rape.

Race/Ethnicity

Race/ethnicity also is an important correlate of rape myth acceptance. J. E. Williams (1979) studied 1,000 residents of San Antonio, Texas, and found that Whites were more likely to define situations as rape and less likely to blame victims than were Blacks or Latinas. However, demographic variables of age, education, and income had different relationships to rape attitudes within each ethnic group. Research suggests that Latinas, who tend to adhere to more traditional gender roles, have greater rape myth acceptance than Whites (Jimenez & Abreu, 2003). Assimilated Latina women, however, are more rejecting of date rape than their less assimilated Latina counterparts (G. J. Fisher, 1987). Asians are also more accepting of rape myths than Whites (Lee, Pomeroy, Yoo, & Rheinboldt, 2005). In both interracial and intraracial date rape scenarios, participants with greater rape myth acceptance were more tolerant of the rapist and less tolerant of the victim regardless of race (Varelas & Foley, 1998). This suggests a lack of evidence for adherence to stereotypes of the Black rapist–White victim scenario and supports other research showing that women are more sympathetic toward victims and more negative toward offenders in all scenarios (Varelas & Foley, 1998) compared with men. However, Donovan's (2007) recent experimental study found that male, but not female, participants were influenced by perpetrator and victim race when making attributions about victim promiscuity and perpetrator culpability in rape situations. She suggested that women's vulnerability to rape might have led them to identify with the victim regardless of her race, whereas the risk of rape was not present for men, which perhaps made race/racial attitudes more salient in their judgments. Donovan also reported that White men viewed Black victims as more promiscuous than White victims when the perpetrator was White but did not judge victims of different races differently when the perpetrator was Black. She interpreted this finding as support for the *Jezebel stereotype*, which defines Black women as sexual temptresses (see also Washington, 2001). It is striking that Donovan also reported that 58% of White men and 63% of White women incorrectly chose White women as the most likely victims of Black rapists. This finding provides evidence of White participants' adherence to the stereotype of the Black male sexual predator of White women. Howard (1988) studied a random sample of 14- to 17-year-old teens in Milwaukee, Wisconsin, and found that race differences in attitudes toward rape disappeared when education and SES were controlled, suggesting that structural, not cultural, factors explain attitude differences.

Socioeconomic Status

SES indicators, such as income and education, appear to be related to more sympathetic attitudes toward rape victims. For example, individuals with higher incomes appear to have more positive attitudes toward victims of sexual assault (Nagel, Matsuo, McIntyre, & Morrison, 2005), and more highly educated persons are more rejecting of rape myths (Burt, 1980; R. F. Rich & Sampson, 1990). These findings may be due to a greater likelihood of acceptance of nontraditional gender roles in people of higher SES. Some research shows that lower income families are more traditional and patriarchal in their attitudes (Hagan, Simpson, & Gillis, 1987) and that patriarchal attitudes are related to greater rape myth acceptance (Orcutt & Faison, 1988; Sheldon & Parent, 2002). Thus, gender role attitudes may vary according to SES and actually account for more negative attitudes toward rape victims. These negative attitudes may translate into more blaming of victims in more disadvantaged SES groups.

Occupation

Occupational groups also vary in their attitudes toward rape victims. Studies have shown greater adherence to rape stereotypes in medical students (Best, Dansky, & Kilpatrick, 1992) and in certain professionals, such as police officers, medical staff, and clergy (Sheldon & Parent, 2002). Conversely, mental health professionals have less negative attitudes toward rape victims (Field, 1978; Ward, 1988), and rape crisis counselors have more positive attitudes (Blake, Heesacker, & Marks, 1993) than other groups. Some of these differences may be affected by or interact with the gender of persons in specific occupational groups. For example, recent research shows that male medical students have more negative attitudes toward rape victims than female medical students (I. Anderson & Quinn, 2009). In addition, some evidence suggests that male and female police officers may not differ in their actual treatment of rape cases (Alderden, 2008; Jordan, 2002), despite experimental evidence that female officers are more positive in their evaluation and treatment of these cases (Schuller & Stewart, 2000).

Geographic Region

Furthermore, there is geographic regional variation, with individuals of some parts of the United States (e.g., the South) more conservative in their attitudes toward rape than residents of other regions (Baron & Straus, 1989; Bourque, 1989; J. E. Williams & Holmes, 1981).

Interactions of Demographic and Other Factors

When looking at beliefs in relation to demographic factors and judgments of rape we must also look at these complex interrelationships to avoid overly simplistic explanations for sexual assault judgments. For example, although gender may be a stronger predictor of rape myth acceptance (although it is lower for women) than race, these two factors appear to interact to predict beliefs (Giacopassi & Dull, 1986); specifically, Black women are less accepting of rape myths than are White women (Kalof & Wade, 1995), whereas some data from college students show that Black men are far more accepting of rape myths than are Black women (Sapp, Farrell, Johnson, & Hitchcock, 1999). In addition to gender role attitudes, attitudes about sexuality that likely reflect gender role beliefs may also affect rape myth acceptance. For instance, men's greater rape myth acceptance is associated with greater homophobia and victim-blaming behaviors and attitudes (Kassing, Beesley, & Frey, 2005; White & Kurpius, 2002), such as the belief that women want or deserve to be raped. In experimental research on rape scenarios, if victims could be construed as being attracted to perpetrators (e.g., heterosexual women attacked by men, lesbians attacked by women, or gay men attacked by men), participants were likely to endorse rape myths and blame victims (Ford, Liwag-McLamb, & Foley, 1998; Wakelin & Long, 2003).

Influence of Situational Factors

Other research shows that situational factors also affect beliefs about the justifiability of rape. For example, college students see date rape as more justifiable when a woman goes to a man's apartment or initiates a date and when a man pays for a date (Muehlenhard, Friedman, & Thomas, 1985). Most recently, Frese, Moya, and Megias (2004) showed in an experimental study that degree of rape myth acceptance affects the influence of situational factors on attributions of victim blame made by college students. In their study, undergraduate students read rape scenarios and then made judgments about blame. They found that students' judgments of the "blameworthiness" of the victims were best explained by an interaction between the degree to which they believed in rape myths and situational cues in the rape scenario. Although people with greater rape myth acceptance were more likely to blame victims to a greater degree, situational factors also affected these attributions, even for those low in rape myth acceptance; specifically, the less stereotypic the rape situation was, the greater the influence of students' attitudes toward rape on their attributions of blame. This is important because it suggests that both people's pre-existing characteristics and attitudes and factors related to victims' experiences influence the likelihood that victims will be blamed for rape. Given the problem of rape myth acceptance and the harmful effects of these beliefs, it is not surprising that the problem of rape is both acknowledged and denied in contemporary American society.

IS DISCLOSURE EMPOWERING?

Can disclosure be empowering in a society that sends conflicting messages about rape? The meaning of women's disclosure and the notion that it is a positive or empowering act is an assumption that should be questioned in a victim-blaming society focused on the individual. Speaking out about rape was an early activist approach of women's early attempts to fight rape collectively in the 1970s feminist movement. For many women, this was an empowering act to publicly call their perpetrators to account and name the victimization so often hidden in shame and silence.

Although "legitimate" victims are applauded for speaking up about rape and working through their trauma, they are nonetheless encouraged to do so in the confines of individual therapy (Maracek, 1999). For example, popular daytime talk show icons such as Oprah Winfrey and Dr. Phil both personally model and have their guests talk about their personal problems, including incest, rape, and domestic violence. Such programs take place in a context in which guests are presented as speaking out for their own benefit as well as for others like them. In fact, they are often said to have contacted the show for help or responded to an invitation for guests on a specific topic. Often, there is an offer of follow-up therapy or some kind of support services to guests disclosing personal traumas, although this is not always the case. Guests typically are thanked for speaking out and praised for seeking help and coming forward on behalf of others like them. However, rape is typically presented as a personal problem and almost never presented in social–political terms that emphasize disparate power relations or structural causes (e.g., gender inequality) of their plight. These portrayals generally encourage people to seek help through therapy or to use self-help strategies to cope with their problems, which can be effective at the individual level. However, broader critical analyses of traditional gender role socialization, media portrayals of victimization of women, and how corporations benefit financially from industry's exploitation of female victims (e.g., pornography, the sex industry) are not presented. Thus, modeling disclosure of trauma and allowing space for survivors to speak out can be viewed as positive in that they counter a culture that encourages the silencing of sexual victimization and survivors; however, such portrayals may or may not be liberating or therapeutic for survivors or for viewers of these programs.

Commercialized forms of public talking about and disclosure of rape also occur in the form of individual accounts written in published memoirs about rape (e.g., Raine, 1998; Sebold, 1999) as well as on Web sites such as the Voices and Faces Project (http://www.voicesandfaces.org; Ream, 2004), a nonprofit national survivor network that was created to give voice and face to survivors of sexual assault. The project's aim is to provide solidarity among survivors willing to stand up and speak out about sexual assault. The Web site provides a space for women to tell their stories in their own words of sexual assault online in order to enhance public awareness. It also has information about community events that publicize and help to fight against sexual assault. Finally, survivors can provide information about their experiences via an online survey hosted by the site and can choose to allow Voices and Faces to publicize their story/face on the site or request that their information be kept confidential. Such material has the potential to bring survivors of rape together in empowering ways while protecting the anonymity of those who are unwilling or unable to speak out publicly about their experiences. However, such public disclosures are more common among more empowered women (e.g., White, middle-class women) and among those who fit rape stereotypes.

Although talking about rape may increase healing in many cases, some scholars have argued that talking about such traumatic experiences will not be healing if it is unaccompanied by actions to deal with them, such as joining with other survivors to take part in collective action against perpetrators (Hobfoll et al., 2007; Mardorossian, 2002). Talking without action may help individual survivors who are fortunate enough to find a safe haven in friends or therapists to whom they disclose, but this does nothing to stop rape and/or challenge myths and social attitudes that perpetuate both rape and secondary victimization of rape victims. Both rape prevention and treatment of individual survivors may flourish if safe communities for disclosure are nurtured that also encourage taking action for survivors who are willing and able to do so, as well as others in the community who wish to end rape. Although certainly second-wave feminists encouraged women to raise their consciousness and recognize how their personal experiences were political (Morgan, 1970), it must also be acknowledged that not all survivors of sexual assault will be willing or able to speak up for various reasons, including differing ways of coping, mental or physical health functioning, and/or unwillingness to sacrifice themselves for the larger cause. As with any social change movement, those who speak out and advocate often do so on behalf of themselves and others like them. By stating this I do not mean to encourage or reinforce a stereotype of the helpless, silenced victim or to add to the burden of rape victims by reinforcing society's expectation that they speak up. It is important to acknowledge the individual differences among women and survivors of sexual assault in how they respond to being victimized, because these differences are likely to affect their ability and willingness to talk about it and to come together to engage in activism.

It is also important to note that theories about disclosure must take into account the fact that *disclosure* may mean different things to different victims. From a sociological perspective, just as not all women face equal risk of being raped, the costs of disclosure may vary by race, age, SES, sexual orientation, disability, and other dimensions. Early work on representative adults in the community suggested differences by gender and ethnicity in sexual assault experiences (Sorenson & Siegel, 1992). Qualitative data and some newer quantitative data show that reactions to rape victims are worse for those in discriminated-against subgroups, such as women who are members of sexual minority groups, women of color, women of lower SES, disabled women, and mentally ill women (Campbell, 1998; L. Long, Ullman, Starzynski, Long, & Mason, 2007; S. Long, Ullman, Long, Mason, & Starzynski, 2007; Ullman & Filipas, 2001b; Ullman & Townsend, 2007). Therefore, women may choose not to disclose because they believe that their minority status makes them more subject to negative social reactions.

CONCLUSION

Situating the meaning of rape in the recent social and historical context of society enhances an understanding of how women talk about sexual assault. The women's movement and subsequent changes in how rape and female victims are viewed, including rape myths and social attitudes toward rape in U.S. society, provide needed context for exploring the meaning and experiences of women who disclose sexual assault. There is now a large body of research on rape myths and social attitudes about rape that has used both nonexperimental and experimental research methods. However, less is known about how these attitudes relate to actual behaviors people engage in toward survivors of sexual assault they encounter in daily life. It is not known whether what people *say* they think and believe in a survey or experiment reflects how they *really* think and behave. For example, some people may have positive attitudes toward victims and say they would help them in a hypothetical scenario; however, it may be much more difficult to do so when faced with a real-life victim who is distressed. Also, sexual assault disclosures may be shocking and upsetting to the support provider and make that person less able to respond empathically if he or she is caught up in his or her own reactions. This may occur because people are not always aware of or willing to acknowledge their attitudes, especially if those attitudes are negative, such as endorsing discriminatory beliefs about rape. Also, people often want to maintain positive views of themselves and have others view them positively (Taylor & Brown, 1988), and they may be unwilling to admit having negative views of victims (e.g., social desirability bias).

Support persons may be unfamiliar with sexual assault and have misconceptions about it. They may also be unprepared for such a disclosure and unsure of what to say or do in the immediate situation. Therefore, it is important to look at what people actually say and do when survivors disclose sexual assaults, not only from the perspective of support providers but also from the survivors themselves. Research has emerged from the social attitudes/rape myths literature in recent years that documents supportive and unsupportive responses or reactions that survivors experience when disclosing sexual assault. In chapters 3 through 6, I examine what is known about disclosure and how people actually react to survivors of sexual assault. First, however, I discuss different theories of rape and women's disclosure. The theories described in chapter 2 reflect the social context I have described in this chapter.

2

THEORIES OF RAPE
AND WOMEN'S DISCLOSURE

Various theories have been posited regarding women's disclosure of sexual assault. These theories can help guide research, prevention, and treatment of sexual assault. In this chapter, I review the early theory of rape disclosure to police, which emphasized economic and sociological theories, including rational choice and social disorganization, respectively; feminist theories; and psychological theories. I then critique the depoliticization of rape, which resulted in part from changes in the women's movement and in feminist theory, which led to an increased emphasis on psychological theories. Finally, I describe an integrated, ecological model of help-seeking that both repoliticizes rape and considers a confluence of social and individual factors.

RATIONAL CHOICE, SOCIAL DISORGANIZATION,
AND RAPE DISCLOSURE TO POLICE

The study of rape disclosure has historically focused on rape reporting to police. *Rational choice theory* and *social disorganization theory* have been applied to victims' reporting of crime, including victims' reporting of sexual assault to police (Greenberg & Ruback, 1992; for a review and discussion of this literature, see Menard, 2005). Rational choice theory is a framework for understanding and often formally modeling social and economic behavior and is the dominant theoretical paradigm in microeconomics (G. S. Becker, 1968). This theory was adopted by other social sciences, including criminology in the 1980s, and is based on the *expected utility principle* in economic theory, which states that people will make rational decisions based on the extent to which they believe those choices will maximize benefits and minimize costs. According to rational choice theory, a victim would be more likely to report to police if the expected benefits (e.g., ability to get services, justice) outweighed the costs (e.g., shame/stigma, blame, disbelief or lack of response from authorities; Block, 1974).

Social disorganization theory was developed in studies of crime by sociologists at the University of Chicago in the 1920s and 1930s (Shaw & McKay, 1942). Social disorganization theorists assert that disorganized communities result in crime because informal social controls break down and criminal cultures emerge. This theory has received renewed attention in recent years as scholars have argued that socially disorganized communities lack collective efficacy to fight crime and disorder (Bursik & Grasmick, 1993; Sampson, 1995). Lack of collective efficacy may also be related to a lack of individual efficacy, which may also lead to lower rates of crime reporting. According to social disorganization theory, social norms or shared beliefs that women should not report rape may informally reduce victims' likelihood of reporting (Bursik & Grasmick, 1993). For example, rape myths in U.S. culture, such as the myth that only assaults by strangers constitute "real rape," may discourage reporting of acquaintance rape. In such cases, the rational choice may be to not report if doing so violates social norms, will be frowned on by social network members, and lead to negative social consequences.

Menard (2005) suggested that both rational choice theory and social disorganization theory play a role in victims' decisions to report; that is, the decision to seek help from the police "is affected by the normative influence of consulted others" (p. 95). This argument is supported by research showing that informal social networks influence the reporting of rape. However, Menard also contended that these theories do not account for the fact that rational choices and social norms may vary by geographic location. She argued further that a social ecology perspective is needed to incorporate micro- and macro-level influences of social control; specifically, victims' decisions to call police are affected by advice they receive (e.g., social norms) and the larger social context (e.g., community type, availability of services). For example, on the one hand, a victim may report a rape to police if her family or friends encourage her to do so and if she lives in a community where residents have a positive relationship with the police. On the other hand, a victim may not report the rape if she is discouraged by those around her who are less aware about rape and if her community has an adversarial relationship with police. Menard's theory is useful for integrating context (urban vs. rural county) into understanding police reporting by victims of sexual assault, even though her study did not explicitly address the broader reality of women's disclosure or nondisclosure of sexual assault to various informal sources. Unfortunately, neither the rational choice theory of decision making nor social disorganization theory takes into account the larger societal context of decision making (e.g., rape culture); neither have these theories been applied to the study of disclosure of crime more broadly to various support sources beyond police.

FEMINIST MOVEMENT WAVES AND FEMINIST THEORIES

First-Wave Feminism

First-wave feminism refers to a period of feminist activity during the 19th and early 20th centuries in the United Kingdom and the United States. It focused on officially mandated inequalities, primarily on gaining women's suffrage (the right to vote). The term *first wave* was coined many years after the movement, in the 1970s. Major theorists included Mary Wollstonecraft (1792/1967) in the United Kingdom and Margaret Fuller in the United States. Starting in the mid-1800s, Lucretia Mott, Elizabeth Cady Stanton, and Susan B. Anthony all campaigned for the abolition of slavery before pioneering women's right to vote (for a review, see Rossi, 1973). The end of this wave is often linked with the passage of the 19th Amendment to the U.S. Constitution in 1920, granting women the right to vote.

Second-Wave Feminism

In contrast to rational choice and social disorganization theory, second-wave feminist theory did consider the larger social context of rape and did consider disclosure more broadly than just police reporting. The second wave of feminism began with *radical feminism*, which occurred during the late 1960s through the mid-1970s and featured key figures such as Shulamith Firestone, Ti-Grace Atkinson, Kathie Sarachild, and Valerie Solanas (see Echols & Willis, 1989, for a review; Firestone, 1970). Radical feminism is a philosophy that emphasizes the patriarchal roots of inequality between men and women, or, more specifically, the social dominance of women by men. Radical feminism views patriarchy as dividing rights, privileges, and power primarily by gender and, as a result, oppressing women and privileging men. Radical feminists tend to be more militant in their approach and oppose the existing political and social organization in general because it is inherently tied to patriarchy. Thus, radical feminists tend to be skeptical of political action within the current system and instead support cultural change that undermines patriarchy and associated hierarchical structures.

During the early part of the second wave of the feminist movement, talking about rape took place in the context of the larger political struggle for women's liberation. Radical feminists viewed men as collective oppressors of women in society (Russell, 1974) and claimed that all sex between men and women was tantamount to rape because consensual sex cannot take place between people who are socially unequal (MacKinnon, 1987). In the context of acknowledging sexist oppression, talking about and speaking out about rape were viewed as political acts of resistance against the system of male dominance. However, calling attention to sexist oppression also had some negative unintended side effects, such as reifying the labeling of men as aggressive and of women as uniquely vulnerable (Gavey, 2005; Hollander, 2002; McCaughey, 1997). These are essentialist ideas about gender that view men as inherently violent perpetrators and women as helpless victims. Furthermore, the dualistic notion that in the context of heterosexual relationships, all men were inherently rapists and all women inherently victims of rape did not help to explain various facts, such as that some women are more vulnerable to rape, men vary in their likelihood to perpetrate rape, both men and women can be perpetrators or victims, and rape can occur in same-sex relationships.

Because of racial bias of second-wave White feminists, rape was framed as a political problem based on gender, without a critical analysis of racial oppression and how it intersects with gender oppression to contribute to rape. In addition, the history of institutionalized rape of Black women by White slave owners, racist sexual stereotypes of women of color, economic circumstances that make women of color more vulnerable to sexual assault in their communities, and blaming reactions were not addressed (P. H. Collins, 2004; A. Y. Davis, 1984; Getman, 1984). The voices of women of color and their concerns were excluded, and survivors of color were not acknowledged or represented as "legitimate" victims of rape; instead, the "legitimate" victims of rape were typically White, middle-class women. To this day, most police-reported stranger rape, like other violent crimes, is committed by Black men against Black women (Rennison, 2002). However, some data suggest that White detectives are less likely to take these cases seriously and make a decision that they are legitimate (e.g., make a positive *founding decision*), so they can move forward in the criminal justice process (Alderden, 2008).

Because it failed to acknowledge these issues, the White feminist movement has framed rape in terms of White, middle-class women's concerns. In the 1980s, when a national prevalence study found that 1 in 4 college women had experienced sexual assault (Koss, Gidycz, & Wisniewski, 1987), rape awareness became focused on privileged, predominantly White, middle-class college women. Meanwhile, concerns of women of color and poor women have received far less attention in research and policy related to sexual assault.

Third-Wave Feminism

Third-wave feminism began roughly in the 1990s and is still largely in effect. A key figure in this movement was Rebecca Walker (1992). Third-wave feminism seeks to challenge or avoid what it deems the second wave's "essentialist" definitions of femininity, which often assumed a universal female identity and overemphasized experiences of upper-middle-class White women. A poststructuralist interpretation of gender and sexuality is central to third-wave ideology. Third-wave feminists often focus on micropolitics and challenge the second wave's paradigm as to what is, or is not, good for women. Third-wave feminism allows women to define feminism for themselves by incorporating their own identities into the belief system of what feminism is and what it can become through their own perspective. Third-wavers are proactive in issues and often engage in activist pursuits. Baumgardner and Richards (2000) wrote the book *Manifesta: Young Women, Feminism, and the Future*, which introduced the idea of third-wave feminism by making the connection that feminism can change with every generation.

The issues of race, social class, sexual orientation, and other factors that necessarily complicate the picture of what constitutes rape became part of the agenda of third-wave (also called *postmodern*) feminists (A. Y. Davis, 1978/1981; hooks, 1981, 1984), who challenged the racism in the earlier feminist movement and the framing of rape in terms of gender alone without discussing race (Moraga & Anzaldua, 1981) or class.

During the social movements of the late 1960s and early 1970s (including second-wave feminism), structural inequality and power were the major explanations of social problems such as rape (Mardorossian, 2002). Thus, it seemed inevitable that, following the 1970s, American society would return to its strong individualistic roots. Rape was quickly reinterpreted with explanations focused on the psychology of perpetrators (typically viewed as either mentally ill or out of control) and victims (typically viewed as asking for it or helpless). Despite postmodern critiques that have challenged scholars to attend to differences based on race, class, gender, and other identities emerging from the third-wave feminist movement (P. H. Collins, 2004; Richie, 2000), rape has continued to be viewed as an individual problem. "Talking about rape" has been reconstructed as "disclosure of trauma," often in the private context of therapy or within one's informal social network.

PSYCHOLOGICAL THEORIES

Social science experts have tried to address rape to at least some extent. For example, psychologists have sought to help treat individual victims and perpetrators. This approach was fueled by development of a discourse of psychological harm in which posttraumatic stress disorder (PTSD) became formally recognized as a psychiatric disorder in the *Diagnostic and Statistical Manual of Mental Disorders* (American Psychiatric Association, 1980). This disorder was shown to be strongly associated with a history of child sexual abuse and rape and is rightly acknowledged to be one of the various harmful impacts of sexual assault for many women. In fact, sexual assault stands out from a range of traumas as being most highly associated with PTSD, in addition to combat. This knowledge led to development of some helpful psychological treatments for victims (Foa & Rothbaum, 1998). However, the PTSD framework has also been critiqued for pathologizing female victims (Gilfus, 1999; Mardorossian, 2002; Wasco, 2003). Rape has thus effectively moved from the sociopolitical domain, where it had been strongly situated during the feminist antirape movement (Matthews, 1994) to the individual domain, as exemplified by the psychotherapeutic culture in which rape is a problem of individual women who need treatment for symptoms (for a critical discussion of gender, empowerment, and the psychotherapeutic culture, see D. Becker, 2005). Although therapy is sometimes (but not always) intended to empower women (e.g., feminist therapy qualifies as an example; Ballou & West, 2002), most treatments are individualized approaches to the victim of rape that do not typically involve collective political action and may not be adequate to empower women as a group (D. Becker, 2005; Riger, 1993).

Traditional psychological theories, such as stress and coping theory (Lazarus & Folkman, 1984), have been applied to rape and yielded knowledge that has provided some, but not enough, corrections to individualized clinical models of rape and recovery (Burgess & Holmstrom, 1974). According to this theory, people respond to stressful life events by engaging in various cognitive and behavioral efforts or coping strategies to try to manage and reduce the negative effects of these stressors (Folkman & Moskowitz, 2004). Such models typically have not generally acknowledged gender or the broader contexts in which rape and victims of rape are situated.

Psychological theories continue to dominate and inform the therapeutic trauma disclosure paradigm (e.g., that asserts that disclosing trauma has positive health benefits) pioneered by health psychologist James Pennebaker and colleagues (Pennebaker, Kiecolt-Glaser, & Glaser, 1988) and the PTSD paradigm, which began when *rape trauma syndrome* was first identified by Burgess and Holmstrom (1974) to describe phases of reactions that victims of rape go through following assault. Although useful at an individual level, these theories have yet to explicitly acknowledge gender or the social level at which traumatic experiences occur.

CRITICISM OF FEMINIST AND PSYCHOLOGICAL THEORIES: THE NEED TO REPOLITICIZE RAPE

Current feminist and psychological theories of rape have been criticized for focusing too much on individual-level factors rather than society-level factors, which effectively depoliticizes rape. In particular, Mardorossian's (2002) groundbreaking essay in *Signs* articulated the lack of feminist theorizing about rape by postmodern feminists and the problems with some accounts (e.g., W. Brown, 1995; Marcus, 1992) that she viewed as unwittingly consistent with backlash popular press books that emerged and framed the public discourse about rape (e.g., Paglia, 1991; Roiphe, 1993; Sommers, 1994). She described the problem whereby contemporary feminist theory has turned from outward critiques of society and male domination to inward critiques of women and their behavior/psychology. She explained that criticisms of essentialism in second-wave feminist theory led to critiques in third-wave feminism that tended to focus on media constructions of rape and/or language. She also criticized feminist psychology for focusing on women's trauma and individual responses to rape, which effectively contributed to depoliticization of the problem. It is clear that a theory is needed that focuses on the social context of rape in order to correct the tendency to focus solely on individual women and their responses.

Theoretical approaches based on ecological/community psychology and the sociology of mental health (Horwitz, 2002) hold promise for both repoliticizing women's rape disclosures and society's reactions to them. Such theories may help to develop solutions at the community level to stop rape and its deleterious consequences, such as restorative justice approaches to sexual assault (see Koss, 2000). These theories focus on how individuals' mental health is affected by contextual factors such as neighborhoods and communities and by larger social structural factors, such as poverty, urbanicity, and gender inequality.

In general, the field of traumatic stress is also recognizing the need to refocus on social and ecological contexts in which violence and our responses to it are embedded (Heise, 1998; Kaniasty, 2005; Liang, Goodman, Tummala-Narra, & Weintraub, 2005; Neville & Heppner, 1999; F. H. Norris, Foster, & Weisshaar, 2002). This focus is warranted because empirical research shows that social support and network responses are important buffers of the effects of trauma exposure, especially rape. Social support is actually one of the strongest protective factors associated with reduced risk of PTSD in general (Brewin,

Andrews, & Valentine, 2000; Charuvastra & Cloitre, 2008; Guay, Billette, & Marchand, 2006; Ozer, Best, Lipsey, & Weiss, 2003).

It is important to facilitate the collective responsibility of all men and women in society, including survivors of sexual assault, to speak out against rape, in support of survivors. This can help to create an environmental context that is conducive to supporting victims to disclose and have positive experiences doing so, instead of negative reactions and blame that are currently common and result from the culture of stereotypes and myths about rape.

We must repoliticize rape and talk about it in an active, political manner so that women (and men) can join together to fight against rape (Gavey, 2007). Part of this process entails speaking out about and refusing to tolerate rape and other forms of violence and oppression that suppress women as a group on the basis of gender, race, and social class inequalities. This kind of public collective speaking out and refusal to condone rape does not mean that women should not also privately disclose their experiences, whether to family, friends, and/or in support groups or therapy; in fact, healing from personal trauma and recovery is very important in its own right and can occur in tandem with collective efforts to stop rape. Ideally, individual, personal, and collective political empowerment should go together. However, contemporary efforts still remain far too limited and underfunded. Without this level of attention to the ecological context, rape is unlikely to go away, and responses to victims are unlikely to improve.

AN INTEGRATED ECOLOGICAL MODEL OF HELP-SEEKING

Liang and colleagues (2005) presented a theory to explain how individual, familial, economic, and cultural influences affect women's decisions to seek help in response to intimate partner violence. The theory posits several stages of seeking help, including problem recognition and definition (including self-labeling), deciding to seek help, and choosing where to seek help. All of these processes are influenced by individual, interpersonal, and sociocultural factors (Liang et al., 2005). This integrated model of help-seeking can explain not only the low rate of support seeking for sexual assault but also who is told and why formal sources, such as police, are very unlikely to be notified (see Figure 2.1 for a heuristic model of disclosure of and responses to rape).

Phase 1 of Liang et al.'s (2005) ecological model involves *woman's recognition and definition of the problem*. Many women do not self-label or use the word *rape* to describe their experiences. A recent study of college women showed that almost two thirds had had experiences the met legal criteria for rape (i.e., sex obtained with force or threats for force without the woman's consent) disavowed that label (B. S. Fisher, Daigle, Cullen, & Turner, 2003a; Koss, 1985).

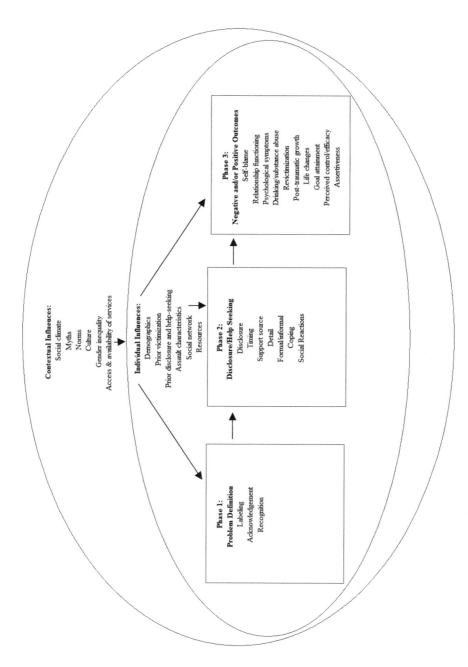

Figure 2.1. Adaptation of Liang et al.'s (2005) feminist social ecological model to sexual assault disclosure and help-seeking outcomes.

It is not surprising that rates of sexual assault disclosure are lower among women who do not self-label as victims (e.g., acknowledge their victimization), both for survivors of child sexual abuse and adult sexual assault (Bottoms, Rudnicki, & Epstein, 2007; Littleton, Axsom, Breitkopf, & Berenson, 2006). Because so many women do not disclose these assaults as rapes to others, it is difficult to fully study the impact of assault disclosure. The failure of women to self-identify as victims may contribute to the fact that women sometimes do not even disclose on anonymous surveys (Lyon, 2009).

Not labeling oneself a victim may also be due to a tendency to engage in cognitive avoidance or denial. Lack of self-labeling may also occur if women feel ashamed about the experience or that somehow the assault will "not count" or be seen as legitimate (e.g., because of contextual factors, such as a date rape, or an assault in which alcohol, which is known to affect judgments of victims, was used; J. Norris & Cubbins, 1992; Richardson & Campbell, 1982). The costs of acknowledging the experience as a rape may simply be too high for many women because of a fear of being stigmatized or blamed by others or a fear of reprisals from the offender or others. Shame may directly or indirectly contribute to women not acknowledging their rapes to themselves and others, which may lead to nondisclosure of assault. For example, Vidal and Petrak (2007) studied 25 female victims of sexual assault from a sexual health service in London and found that most women (75%) felt ashamed of themselves after the assault. Prior sexual assault, physical consequences, self-blame, concealing the assault, and being assaulted by a known assailant were each related to greater feelings of shame. These findings suggest that shame is not only common but also is related to greater self-blame; nondisclosure; and experiencing known-offender assaults, which are much more likely to be unacknowledged (Koss, 1985). Thus, many barriers to acknowledging oneself as a victim of rape should be addressed to facilitate victim help-seeking.

Problem definition affects both the decision to seek help and the person from whom a victim decides to seek help. If a victim does not recognize and define her situation as problematic, she probably will not think it is something she needs help for and thus will not seek help from or disclose the assault to others. For example, in many cases of acquaintance rape the first step of problem recognition/definition is often not taken by victims (e.g., *unacknowledged* or *hidden* victims; Koss, 1985) because their assaults do not fit rape stereotypes. In such cases, victims may not believe that seeking help, especially from formal sources such as police or medical or mental health professionals, is appropriate, either because they blame themselves or do not view the assault as a crime.

Interpersonal influences may exacerbate victims' failures to define the experience as an assault if social network members (i.e., friends and family) do not believe the victim, suggest that the assault was a misunderstanding, or blame the victim for the experience. Sociocultural influences (e.g., social class, culture, socioeconomic status) may also shape survivors' understanding of an assault, thereby influencing whether they define a violent incident as a problem and/or whether they believe their experiences warrant help from others. For example, individuals from cultures or religions that value the family or collective over the individual may discourage help-seeking from any source following rape because they do not want to shame their families. This may be especially true in the context of intimate partner violence or family relationships, in particular if sexual assault is stigmatized and seen as shameful by the victim and/or her family (Bletzer & Koss, 2006; Kastigurirangan, Krishnan, & Riger, 2004).

Phase 2 of Liang et al.'s (2005) ecological model is *disclosure/help-seeking*. Whether a victim seeks help is affected by Phase 1 (problem definition) as well as the same social and individual factors that influence Phase 1. Even when women identify their experiences as rape and acknowledge the impact it has had on their psychological well-being, they do not always seek mental health services. Factors such as recognition of need and the availability and accessibility of services may explain why some people seek mental health or medical care but others do not. These factors have been considered for women coping with a wide range of issues and their use of mental health services in general (K. S. Collins et al., 1999; Padgett, Harman, Burns, & Schlesinger, 1994). For example, research has examined crime victims' service-seeking, including the role of informal social support (see Kaniasty & Norris, 1992; F. H. Norris, Kaniasty, & Scheer, 1990).

Although little research has tested these factors comprehensively in samples of victims of sexual assault (for a review of research on factors associated with mental health service-seeking by victims of sexual assault, see Ullman, 2007b), Logan, Evans, Stevenson, and Jordan (2005) found numerous barriers to help-seeking among victimized women in general, including lack of available, affordable, accessible, and acceptable services, and some distinct barriers for rural and urban victims, suggesting that community context is important. In particular, poor women of color may lack telephones, access to transportation, and money needed to seek formal help. In addition, they may not have informal networks of individuals who are willing or able to support them in getting help from medical, legal, or mental health professionals. In a now-classic example, Fine (1983) vividly described a young Black rape survivor who did not seek help because the assault was only one of many other major life stressors (e.g., poverty, caring for children as a single mother) she had to cope with daily. Those other stressors superseded her ability to devote space, time, and resources to coping with and responding to rape. In fact, such stressors may lead some women to block out these assaults and engage in avoidance coping, which is related to greater psychological symptoms of PTSD (Ullman, Filipas, Townsend, & Starzynski, 2007).

Phase 3 of Liang et al.'s (2005) ecological model is *negative and/or positive outcomes (e.g., psychological, physical, social functioning) of the disclosure/help seeking process.* This phase represents the final state of the victim, that is, whether or not she has recovered from the sexual assault. Each phase of the help-seeking process is integral and dependent on the other processes, such that all must work together for a victim to decide to seek help, to receive effective treatment, and to recover (Liang et al., 2005). This model highlights the importance of stepping back to look at the broader social context of women's disclosure of sexual assault.

CONCLUSION

Although early theories of rape disclosure focused on police reporting, second-wave feminists encouraged women to speak out to everyone about sexual assault. Previously secret rape experiences were brought to light and destigmatized. This was a necessary step to effect social change and helped to call attention to sexist oppression of women, garner resources for victims, develop strategies for preventing perpetration, and bring cases into the criminal justice system.

Third-wave feminism broadened the second-wave White middle-class feminists' focus to include women of color, lower class and/or inner city women, and women who are members of sexual minority groups. Differences among women were emphasized at the expense of commonalities, which helped to make feminist theory more applicable to all women. Unfortunately, decreased social and political activism generally beginning in the late 1970s led rape to be reframed as a personal, individual issue rather than a public, political one. The resulting disproportionate emphasis on treating victims for symptoms of PTSD reflected the depoliticization of rape.

Liang et al.'s (2005) ecological model integrates individual factors with social factors to explain how individual, familial, economic, and cultural influences affect women's decisions to seek help in response to intimate partner violence. The model considers how these factors interact at every stage of the help-seeking process to ultimately influence victims' final positive and/or negative outcomes. This model may also be helpful to begin to better understand various factors related to sexual assault disclosure and help-seeking, including contextual factors, such as social reactions from informal and formal support sources, which are all topics I address in the chapters that follow.

3

WHY, HOW OFTEN, AND TO WHOM DO WOMEN DISCLOSE, AND WHAT FACTORS INFLUENCE WHETHER DISCLOSURE IS HEALING?

Before considering the effects of social reactions to victims of rape, it is important to step back and consider what we know from empirical research about women's disclosure of sexual assault. Although in chapter 2 I discussed various theories and models for disclosure, it is important to listen to women to understand their decisions about disclosing. This may reveal why women often decide not to talk about rape and what actually happens when they do disclose to others. Such investigation can provide critical information about the societal context that needs to be addressed to improve rape prevention and treatment. There are significant data that address why women do and do not talk about and report sexual assault to others, including formal authorities. In this chapter, I review several topics, including women's reasons for disclosing or not disclosing, prevalence of disclosure, factors related to likelihood and timing of disclosure, and the effects of disclosing sexual assault.

WHY DO WOMEN NOT DISCLOSE SEXUAL ASSAULT?

Why women do not disclose is a fundamental question that should be studied by researchers, because as a society we often question why victims do not talk about and report this crime. There are many good reasons not to report, given the U.S. culture's victim-blaming climate. In general, research on reasons for telling and not telling about sexual assault is consistent with literature on this subject in the area of crime victimization. Several national surveys of women have reported relevant findings about why many victims do not disclose rape. In the National Violence Against Women Survey (NVAWS), a representative telephone survey of American women, 42% of women reported fear, shame, and anticipated negative social reactions such as disbelief and blame as reasons for not reporting a sexual assault to police (Tjaden & Thoennes, 2006). In the National Women's Study, a second national telephone survey study, women cited a fear of being blamed and of others finding out their identity as reasons for not reporting rape (Kilpatrick, Edmunds, & Seymour, 1992). More recently, Kilpatrick, Resnick, Ruggiero, Conoscenti, and McCauley (2007) conducted two national telephone surveys of the general population and the college student population to study forcible rape and incapacitated/drug-facilitated rape (e.g., assaults that occurred when victims were too intoxicated to consent because of either voluntary or involuntary alcohol and/or drug consumption prior to assault) and found that four of the major reasons women gave for not disclosing rape to police included (a) not wanting family or other people to know about the assault; (b) lack of proof; (c) fear of reprisal by the assailant or others; and (d) fear of being treated badly by police, lawyers, or the criminal justice system in general. In victim surveys and interviews that my colleagues and I have conducted, women said the following about their decisions not to disclose:

- "I never felt like anyone ever cared about what I had to say. As a young girl growing up, I felt less valued, able to speak, or be heard in my family. Coming from that early experience, why would I have ever thought that anyone would care to hear about my experiences, especially something stigmatizing, embarrassing, and personal like sexual assault?" (43-year-old White female survivor of sexual assault)
- "I haven't told anyone close to me. Instead I just stopped dating." (Victim of date rape)
- "I essentially worked through this myself. I didn't want to discuss it with anyone. I felt it was too personal to share with anyone close to me. Perhaps I had feelings of guilt. I've never really been comfortable talking about it." (Survivor of acquaintance rape)

- "I never told my family or reported it to officials because I didn't think they would believe me since I was involved with the person." (Victim of romantic partner rape)
- "I didn't tell my family about my experience because you are not considered to be a victim of rape or sexual assault if it was by someone you know. Acquaintance rape is not acknowledged in the Latina community. This is an American concept. I myself had no idea this existed until I went to college." (Survivor of acquaintance rape)
- "I have attempted to seek counseling several times but decided against it because I'm afraid of what people will think." (Survivor of acquaintance rape)

Other reasons may underlie low rates of rape reporting, including awareness of low criminal conviction rates (Campbell, Wasco, Ahrens, Sefl, & Barnes, 2001) and the fact that victims who report are subjected to procedures that are unsupportive and blaming and result in unwanted publicity (Koss, 2000). It is common for victims' behavior and accounts of rape to be questioned and disbelieved, and despite the ethical obligation of journalists to protect victim privacy (i.e., not publish their names in newspapers or name them publicly), the press sometimes reveals the identities of women who report rape. In addition, in a multiethnic community sample of victims of rape in Los Angeles, contact with the police or authorities was related to initial and lasting negative consequences (e.g., Wyatt, Notgrass, & Newcomb, 1990). Other reasons for low reporting rates to local and campus police are varied. Studies, including the National Crime Victimization Survey (NCVS), the National Women's Study, and national college data, indicate that the six most frequently cited reasons for not reporting are (a) victims' perceptions that the incident was not serious enough; (b) uncertainty over whether a crime or harm was intended; (c) not wanting others, including family, to know; (d) lack of proof that the incident occurred; (e) fear of reprisal by the assailant or others; and (f) beliefs that police would not view the incident as serious enough (see B. S. Fisher, Daigle, Cullen, & Turner, 2003b; Kilpatrick et al., 1992).

Finally, victims may believe that if they do not talk or think about the rape, they will recover (Resick, 1983). Furthermore, they may fear that the rape would be seen as their fault: An analysis of sexual assault and physical assault reporting of female college students (Thompson, Sitterle, Clay, & Kingree, 2007) showed that victims of sexual assault cited fears the assault would be seen as their fault 28% of the time. In summary, there are many valid reasons for not disclosing or disclosing sexual assault, which are important to understand in order to reduce barriers and enhance women's willingness to talk about their assaults.

WHY DO WOMEN DISCLOSE SEXUAL ASSAULT?

For women who do disclose, four common reasons for doing so to police include wanting to (a) get help/medical care, (b) prevent further crime against themselves or others, (c) catch or punish the offender, and (d) report the crime (Kilpatrick et al., 2007). Characteristics of the assault affect how victims interpret the incident and influence disclosure, which is more likely if women interpret the incident as a rape, assault is completed, the offender is a stranger, injury or emotional distress results, and self-blame is low (Boudreaux, Kilpatrick, Resnick, Best, & Saunders, 1998; Golding, Siegel, Sorenson, Burnam, & Stein, 1989; Starzynski, Ullman, Filipas, & Townsend, 2005; Ullman, 1996b). Cultural and societal factors also may influence perceptions of the rape and subsequent disclosures. For example, sexualized media images of women may lead victims to question whether the assault is rape or to minimize it and thus not acknowledge it as rape.

Survivors reach out when it will make them feel better, get needed aid, or result in justice (Bachman, 1993; Feldman-Summers & Norris, 1984; Golding et al., 1989). Victims disclose to get support, not advice (Frazier & Burnett, 1994), and to seek support from those they think will be most helpful (Golding et al., 1989).

HOW OFTEN AND TO WHOM DO SURVIVORS DISCLOSE SEXUAL ASSAULT?

Qualitative interview research shows that disclosure is not a one-time, all-or-none event. The nature and extent of disclosure can vary over time, and one may tell different people at different times after the assault, all of which may affect recovery (Ahrens, 2006). For adult sexual assault, research shows that most women tell more than one person and that disclosures range from minor references to fully verbalized accounts.

It is impossible to know how many women have been raped, for several reasons: silence and stigma surrounding sexual assault; the fact that many women delay telling others for months or years after the assault, especially if they were attacked by someone they know (Ullman, 1999); some victims never acknowledge it to themselves; and some victims never disclose. Given this limitation, representative community studies in which researchers ask people whether they have had this experience are the best source of information. Such studies indicate that only one half to two thirds of adult women disclose their sexual assault experiences to someone at some point in their lives (Golding et al., 1989; Koss, 1985).

Community samples are the best source of data for prevalence rates because only one third to one half of sexual assaults are reported to police (Bureau of Justice Statistics, 2003; Rennison, 2002), a figure consistently lower than that of other violent crimes. Data from the NCVS indicate that, from 1992 to 2000, only 36% of rapes, 34% of attempted rapes, and 26% of other sexual assaults were reported to police. Other research suggests that only 5% to 30% of sexual assaults in college and community populations are reported to police (B. S. Fisher et al., 2003b; Kilpatrick et al., 1992; Koss, Gidycz, & Wisniewski, 1987; Tjaden & Thoennes, 2000, 2006). Furthermore, research shows that, despite extensive reforms made to rape laws, neither rates of sexual assault nor reporting of this crime have significantly changed (see Bachman, 1993; Clay-Warner & Burt, 2005). Rape remains a disproportionately underreported crime.

A similar pattern of underreporting is also the case for child sexual abuse. Some representative samples of adult women show that only 7% to 12% reported child sexual abuse at the time of the abuse to police or other authorities (J. Anderson, Martin, Mullen, Romans, & Herbison, 1993; Hanson, Resnick, Saunders, Kilpatrick, & Best, 1999).

Some research suggests that reporting rates to other formal sources are higher. For example, Kilpatrick et al.'s (1992) telephone survey of a representative sample of 4,008 American women (the National Women's Study) showed that only 16% of victims of sexual assault told police, and 26% told doctors, about their assaults. In Kilpatrick et al.'s (2007) national study, less than 18% of victims reported to the police. Although only approximately 20% of victims sought medical care, over 60% sought mental health care related to the assault. However, reporting to each of these sources was lower for women victimized by incapacitated/drug-facilitated rape (in contrast to forcible rape) in both the community and college samples. In the NVAWS about one third of women injured during their most recent rape since age 18 sought and received medical care.

Unfortunately, most recent national studies (e.g., Kilpatrick et al., 1992; Tjaden & Thoennes, 2006; but see B. S. Fisher et al., 2003b) have not reported results about which of a variety of specific support sources women told about their assaults. Two thirds of victims who disclose typically tell someone other than the police because they may want to avoid some of the negative outcomes associated with reporting to formal authorities and because they seek social support (B. S. Fisher et al., 2003b). Although victims are least likely to disclose to formal support providers (e.g., police, physicians, rape crisis centers; Ahrens & Campbell, 2000; Ullman, 1996b, 2000), they are more likely to disclose to family members or romantic partners and most likely to disclose to friends (88%; B. S. Fisher et al., 2003b). Young women are especially likely to disclose to their friends.

IS DISCLOSURE HIGHER IN SPECIAL VICTIM SERVICE PROGRAMS AND RAPE CRISIS CENTERS?

Special victim service programs and rape crisis centers are designed to be more supportive than traditional providers. Thus, one might think that disclosure rates would be higher in these environments. Multicrime victim service programs must address the needs of all violent crime victims, not just survivors of sexual assault, so research assessing service-seeking in these contexts typically has not differentiated victims of sexual assault from victims of nonsexual assault (e.g., Sims, Yost, & Abbott, 2006). Even so, it appears that victim service programs reach few victims and appear to be less effective than informal support sources. For example, although specialized victim advocates and crisis counselors are sometimes available through victim services in prosecutors' offices, these resources are available only for the minority of victims who report their assaults to police. Even for victims who do use such services, the usual short-term crisis intervention services are not enough to alleviate their long-term psychological symptoms (R. C. Davis, 1987).

Rape crisis centers that developed from the second-wave feminist movement provide counseling, advocacy, and education about rape. Rape crisis centers are uniquely situated to respond to the physical, emotional, and social needs of victims. Their services focus on three main areas: (a) 24-hour crisis hotlines, (b) individual and group counseling (often on a short-term basis only), and (c) legal and medical advocacy (Campbell & Martin, 2001). These services do not require victims to report the assault to police. Research has shown that 5% to 10% of victims seek help from such services (George, Winfield, & Blazer, 1992; Golding et al., 1989). This rate is low either because victims do not know about these services or they perceive that such help is only for stereotypical stranger rapes. Rape crisis centers have been rated most positively overall compared with various other support sources in studies of victims (Campbell & Raja, 1999; Filipas & Ullman, 2001; Golding et al., 1989).

Although there have been few explicit studies on the benefits of receiving rape crisis services, there is evidence that rape crisis center advocates do help victims obtain services from the legal, medical, and mental health systems. In a study of survivors' postassault experiences, survivors who worked with a rape crisis center advocate experienced significantly less distress than those who did not (Campbell, 2006). Thus, more work is needed to help rape crisis centers reach more survivors, especially those with less stereotypical sexual assaults. Such centers help to legitimize victims of rape and increase their access to sensitive support and needed services following assault.

FACTORS RELATING TO THE LIKELIHOOD AND TIMING OF DISCLOSURE

Various factors such as victim demographics and assault characteristics are related to likelihood and timing of rape reporting. Several of these are discussed in the following paragraphs.

Age

In an analysis of data from the NVAWS, Chen and Ullman (in press) found that older victims were more likely than younger victims to immediately report rapes to police. Other studies have reported that one third of people disclose soon after an incidence of child sexual abuse (e.g., days or weeks afterward), whereas two thirds delay months or years before telling anyone (Arata, 1998; Lamb & Edgar-Smith, 1994; Roesler & Wind, 1994). In an analysis of childhood rapes before age 18 identified from the National Women's Study (D. W. Smith et al., 2000), 28% of women had never disclosed before the survey, whereas almost half (47%) did not disclose to anyone for more than 5 years after the rape.

Race, Ethnicity, and Culture

The NVAWS has shown that immediate reporting is more likely for White victims. An exception to this may be among White adolescents, who often do not seek help for serious problems, such as depression and suicidal thoughts (Dubow, Lovko, & Kausch, 1990), so they may be less likely to report these problems related to sexual assault.

In a study of female college students, non-White victims of sexual assault were more likely than White victims of sexual assault to say they did not report the assault because of fear of blame and because they did not want police involved (Thompson et al., 2007). The study authors argued that this finding suggests that racial discrimination influences reporting. Washington (2001), who studied the disclosure patterns of Black female victims of sexual assault, found that their lower likelihood of disclosure might be due to specific beliefs about Black female identity. These beliefs include the myth of the superwoman, racial loyalty to Black men, lack of knowledge and appropriate sexuality socialization, cultural prohibitions regarding revealing personal problems and information to others, and expectations of support they would receive from institutions such as criminal justice. Bryant-Davis, Chung, and Tillman (in press) echoed this idea, arguing that nondisclosure might result from stereotypes about Black female sexuality as well as a perceived cultural mandate to protect Black male perpetrators, given their unfair treatment by the criminal justice system.

In a study of male and female NCVS respondents, Rennison (2007) found that Latinas were much less likely to report completed rape and sexual assault to police than Whites overall. The reason for this discrepancy may be that Latinas are more likely to blame themselves because of a greater belief in rape myths. They may also face more negative social reactions from family as well as from formal support providers, who may not be biculturally sensitive (for a review, see Low & Organista, 2000). Finally, the cultural value of *marianismo*, the Latin American feminine ideal of divine self-sacrifice entailing passivity and sexual purity based on the Virgin Mary, may be used to hold women responsible for men's sexual aggression. Also, unlike most research showing that severity of violence predicts greater reporting, this pattern was not true for Latina, Native American, and Asian victims.

S. G. Smith and Cook (2008) described how help-seeking behaviors vary across cultures and how cultural norms affect adult disclosures. Research on cross-cultural influences on adolescent help-seeking (Cauce et al., 2002) shows that some Blacks may rely on willpower to overcome difficult situations (Broman, 1996). Some Asian Americans handle problems by choosing not to dwell or focus on them (Cheng, Leong, & Geist, 1993) and have negative attitudes about seeking mental health help out of fear of disclosing personal problems, seeing this as shameful and perhaps as dishonoring their families (Cheung & Snowden, 1990; Sue, 1994). Negative cultural attitudes toward victims of sexual assault are common in Asian American communities (Mori, Bernat, Glenn, Selle, & Zarate, 1995), and significant in-group social pressure on victims may lead survivors to remain silent instead of seeking help (Dussich, 2001). Underreporting is also serious for Native American survivors, who have the highest rates of sexual assault of any ethnic group yet the lowest rate of reporting to authorities (Greenfield & Smith, 1999). This may be due to mistrust of White agencies and helpers, fear of ostracism by families, and shame and guilt, as well as concerns about confidentiality and jurisdictional confusion (Gonzales, 1999).

In addition, cultural norms often dictate dating practices about when and whom girls are allowed to date, which may also influence disclosure. Young women raped by someone of a different ethnicity may experience shame and not disclose the rape because they fear blame from their family and others within their culture. Cultural and religious views about sex (e.g., that it is shameful, natural, for procreation only) are also important. Promotion of abstinence for prevention and religious purposes may leave women uncomfortable or ashamed about discussing sexual experiences, including coercive ones.

Acculturation

Acculturation (i.e., modification of groups' and individuals' behavior, culture, values, and beliefs by borrowing from or adapting to other cultures), language, and immigration status are also likely to be important in understanding disclosure of sexual assault. Although early research found lower rates of sexual assault reported by Latinas to interviewers in the Los Angeles Epidemiologic Catchment Area study (Sorenson, Stein, Siegel, Golding, & Burnam, 1987), there might be other factors that explain varying disclosure rates. For example, Garcia, Hurwitz, and Kraus (2005) interviewed women at public health clinics in Los Angeles and found that Latina victims were more likely to report intimate partner violence (including sexual assault) if they were more acculturated than if they were less acculturated. Similarly, Rennison (2007) found that more educated Latinas were more likely to report and suggested that this might be due to greater acculturation or English language proficiency.

Gender

Although the present volume is focused on women's disclosure, sexual assault is a "gendered" crime, and researchers cannot fully explore disclosure of sexual victimization without examining potential gender differences in these experiences (Tang, Freyd, & Wang, 2007). Such differences are less apparent in the adult sexual assault literature because men perpetrate most adult sexual offenses against women (90%; Bureau of Justice Statistics, 1984), and research has accordingly focused on women. We do know, however, that women are more comfortable than men with disclosing: Men are less likely to disclose a sexual assault to police (Menard, 2005) or to anyone in their lives (Widom, 1997). Thus, much less is known about this even more hidden portion of the sexually victimized population. To fill this gap, recent studies have compared men's and women's adult sexual assault experiences (see Elliott, Mok, & Briere, 2004; Kimerling, Rellini, Kelly, Judson, & Learman, 2002; Sorsoli, Kia-Keating, & Grossman, 2008). Although neither Elliott et al. (2004) nor Kimerling et al. (2002) examined disclosure experiences or social reactions from others, Sorsoli et al.'s (2008) qualitative study revealed various barriers to disclosure for male survivors of childhood sexual abuse, including personal (e.g., lack of cognitive awareness, avoidance, emotional readiness, shame), relational (e.g., fear of negative repercussions, isolation), and sociocultural (e.g., lack of acceptance for men to experience or acknowledge victimization) factors. This research suggests that gender differences need to be explored to better understand the unique meanings of experiencing and talking about sexual assault. There are likely to be overlapping issues for men and women, such as psychological symptoms, shame, and self-blame; however, there are likely to be differences in what these experiences mean to men and women about their gender identity, sexuality, and relationships.

Interactions Between Race and Gender

Although S. G. Smith and Cook (2008) argued that cultural and ethnic norms may be more influential than gender in disclosure, other research suggests that race and gender interact to influence victims' disclosure. In a recent national study of 4,023 adolescents of both genders (ages 12–17), researchers found both race and gender differences in child sexual abuse disclosure (Hanson et al., 2003). Overall, two thirds of youth told someone about their abuse. Sexually abused boys, Black youth, and victims of fathers or nonrelatives were less likely to disclose than were girls, Whites, or victims of nonfather relatives, respectively. For girls, life-threatening abuse was related to more disclosure, whereas physical injury and knowing the offender reduced likelihood of disclosure. Researchers also reported that, for Whites, life-threatening assaults and those without physical injury were related to disclosure. Conversely, for Blacks, being female and experiencing penetration forms of abuse were related to telling others.

Social Class

Data on social class and rape disclosure are clearly lacking (Donovan & Williams, 2002; McNair & Neville, 1996). Social class may intersect with race, culture, and gender in affecting disclosure and social reactions from others (West, 2006). For example, low-income Black women may face unique barriers to disclosure, such as stereotypes of Black women as promiscuous, having greater blame for the assault, having their credibility questioned, and having their experiences trivialized (Neville & Pugh, 1997), especially if they are poor and/or marginalized (Ullman & Townsend, 2007).

Conformity to Rape Stereotypes

Empirical studies have shown that, unless an incident involves characteristics that conform to stereotypical rape (e.g., stranger perpetrator, physical force, or physical injury), victims may not define a situation as rape and therefore not report it or may delay reporting it (Bachman, 1998; Chen & Ullman, in press; DuMont, Miller, & Myhr, 2003; Greenberg & Ruback, 1992; Lizotte, 1985; Stewart et al., 1987; Vicary, Klingaman, & Harkness, 1995; L. S.

Williams, 1984). This is particularly true among police disclosures: Most rapes reported to police fit the stereotype of rape (Menard, 2005), yet stranger rape is also more often reported to informal support sources (Starzynski et al., 2005). In Menard's (2005) review of research on police reporting of sexual assault, greater assault severity was related to greater police reporting.

Results from the NVAWS suggest that women may be less likely to report a rape if they were drinking or engaging in risky or suspect behavior prior to the incident (Tjaden & Thoennes, 1998). Other studies also have shown that victims who experience rape while drinking and/or under the influence of drugs may be less likely to acknowledge their experiences as rape and to report to police (Kilpatrick et al., 2007; Littleton, Grills-Taquechel, & Axsom, 2009). Menard's (2005) review of research on police reporting of sexual assault showed that absence of alcohol intoxication prior to assault was related to greater police reporting. Drinking victims tend to be judged more harshly, as evidenced by data showing they receive more negative social reactions from others than do nondrinking victims (Ullman & Filipas, 2001a), and they may be judged to be less credible in legal settings (Schuller & Wall, 1998; Wall & Schuller, 2000). Conversely, victims may be more likely to disclose rape quickly if the perpetrator was drinking (Rickert, Wiemann, & Vaughan, 2005). Using the NVAWS data, Chen and Ullman (in press) found that immediate reporting of rape increased when offenders used substances at the time of the incident as well as when offenders were strangers and victims sustained injuries.

History of Abuse

An analysis of women with a history of childhood rape before age 18 from the National Women's Study (D. W. Smith et al., 2000) revealed that women were more likely to delay disclosure if they were younger at the time of the rape, if the perpetrator was a family member perpetrator, and if they had experienced a series of rapes. Receiving negative responses to early disclosure of childhood sexual abuse likely decreases one's likelihood of disclosing adult sexual assaults. Furthermore, when adult victims do disclose, their prior victimization experiences may affect the social reactions they receive from others (Ullman, 2003).

Psychological Distress and Self-Blame

Psychological distress is generally associated with increased help-seeking, which may be more likely in stereotypical rapes that typically involve greater perceived life threat (Ullman, 1999). In support of this idea, Chen and Ullman (in press) found that women in the NVAWS were more likely to report a rape to police if they perceived that their life had been in danger during the assault. In addition, Starzynski et al. (2005) reported that victims who reported greater behavioral self-blame (e.g., "The rape occurred because of my behavior") were less likely to tell informal or formal support sources.

Parental Communication About Healthy Sexual Behavior

Factors such as parents' comfort in discussing and educating their daughters about healthy sexual behavior likely affect young women's willingness to talk to them about unwanted sex, especially given that parents may not discuss sexual topics with their adolescent children (Jaccard & Dittus, 1991). Data on adolescent girls suggest that unless they already have an open dialogue with parents regarding sexuality (which is uncommon), they may not recognize that they have been assaulted and/or disclose sexual assault to parents (Sudderth, 1998; Washington, 2001). As a result, many young women may not have the opportunity to discuss important sexual topics when they are most likely to encounter sexual situations. Sudderth (1998) suggested that, without appropriate settings for young women to discuss sexuality, dialogue about sexual coercion is silenced as well. S. G. Smith and Cook (2008) contended that this lack of communication and education may leave women lacking sufficient knowledge to distinguish between consensual and nonconsensual sex. This fact, in conjunction with these other influences, may reduce their ability to protect themselves from rape, recognize it when it occurs, and discuss it with other people.

Social Expectations to Seek Help

A study of 179 victims of rape showed that social expectations of friends and family (e.g., advice, pressure to seek help) influenced help-seeking from police and social service agencies (Feldman-Summers & Norris, 1984). In Kilpatrick et al.'s (2007) recent national study, more than half of victims were encouraged by others to report assault to the police, and less than half were encouraged to do so in incapacitated/drug-facilitated cases.

Methodology Used to Assess Disclosure

In surveys, women are less likely to disclose sexual assault when interviewed by telephone than in face-to-face interviews (Gordon & Riger, 1989), and anonymous mail surveys may enhance disclosure of sexual assault (Koss, 1993). Web surveys are also an increasingly popular way to collect data on sexual assault by researchers; they appear to be especially effective in college populations (Littleton & Henderson, 2009; Parks, Pardi, & Bradizza, 2006), with similar disclosure rates of sexual assault in Web versus paper mail surveys. However, some victims do not disclose even on anonymous surveys, contributing to the problem of underestimating true prevalence rates (Lyon, 2009).

HOW DOES TALKING ABOUT SEXUAL ASSAULT
AFFECT SURVIVORS?

Studies of adult survivors of sexual assault and child sexual abuse show little effect of disclosure per se on psychological symptoms. Despite these findings, many women in victim surveys that my colleagues and I have conducted felt that talking about their rape with us helped them recover:

- "Your survey has helped me a little. I was able to talk about it, meaning write a little about it. Thank you."
- "This survey has forced me to remember something I thought didn't bother me as much as it seems to. Yet it also has helped me to make me feel better too. I know I will talk about it with my friend again sometime soon."
- "It seems that when I talk about it, it's almost as if I'm talking about someone else . . . it seems easier that way—dissociate yourself and it will not matter, it will go away and in time it is like it happened to someone else."

Researchers and mental health professionals also tend to assume that telling about traumas and working through them is therapeutic and even necessary for recovery to occur. This assumption is largely based on studies of ordinary stressful events, often conducted on samples of college students who come to the laboratory. Participants are randomly assigned to write about a traumatic event or a neutral event and are assessed before and after this procedure on their psychological and physical symptoms (Pennebaker, 1997; Pennebaker, Kiecolt-Glaser, & Glaser, 1988). These studies have shown significant positive effects on physical health and mental health measures of writing about traumas in these anonymous disclosure situations; however, a recent meta-analysis of studies of clinical populations showed that expressive writing was more effective for ameliorating physical health symptoms than mental health outcomes (Frisina, Borod, & Lepore, 2004). Whether positive outcomes will occur for disclosure of sexual assault in the laboratory setting remains to be seen. Most studies have not focused on this specific trauma or have had too few cases to compare trauma types. A few experimental studies have actually shown that adult and child survivors of sexual assault got worse or showed no improvement relative to a control group when writing about their victimization (Batten, Follette, Hall, & Palm, 2002; E. J. Brown & Heimberg, 2001; Crawford et al., 2008; Freyd, Klest, & Allard, 2005).

It is likely that the nature and content of the writing task affect whether writing about trauma is helpful. Although not specifically focused on sexual victimization, in a recent study college students were asked keep a journal about a traumatic experience of their choosing. They were then randomly assigned to focus, while writing, on emotions only, cognitions and emotions, or facts related to the trauma (Ullrich & Lutgendorf, 2002). The results showed that writers who focused on cognitions and emotions had greater awareness of positive benefits of the event than the other two groups, possibly because of greater cognitive processing (e.g., thinking through) during writing. Writers who focused on emotions alone reported more severe illness symptoms than the other group, which appeared to be due to a greater focus on negative emotional expression during writing. More recently, experimental researchers have studied the mechanisms by which writing about trauma (not sexual assault specifically) may facilitate recovery, perhaps by helping trauma victims make meaning of their experiences (Park & Blumberg, 2002). It is clear that more work is needed to ascertain when and what type of writing about sexual traumas may be helpful.

It is also important to determine whether such anonymous disclosure is therapeutic in both the laboratory study situation as well as in real-life situations. This is especially true for sexual victimization, which is commonly not discussed with other people, making it likely that many survivors need access to recovery methods they can use on their own, such as journaling. In fact, journal writing is a common recovery tool for survivors of trauma. However, research is needed to determine whether written disclosure in laboratory studies is analogous to journal writing in a naturalistic situation. The context of one's own spontaneously initiated writing about trauma in a journal in the privacy of one's own home or another comfortable location is quite different from an experiment in which one is randomly assigned to write about one's sexual assault experience on the spot in the laboratory. Thus, it is probably important to actually assess and control for these contextual variables (e.g., voluntariness, privacy of setting), which could confound experimental results focused on survivors. Such factors have nothing to do with the experimental writing condition, and they could actually contribute to even greater positive outcomes than seen in the laboratory. However, they could also lead to less positive outcomes because victims may be able to be more themselves and feel as bad as they want to in the privacy of their own homes.

It does appear that withholding disclosure, or not telling about abuse or assault when one wants to tell, is related to worse psychological symptoms (Kellogg & Huston, 1995; Sinclair & Gold, 1997), as is delayed disclosure (Arata, 1998; Ruggiero et al., 2004; Ullman, 1996c; Ullman, Townsend, Filipas, & Starzynski, 2007). The related response of *avoidance coping*, which can include withdrawal from others or avoiding talking about assault, is also associated with worse psychological symptoms in both child and adult survivors of sexual victimization (Coffey, Leitenberg, Henning, Turner, & Bennett, 1996; Koss, Figueredo, & Prince, 2002; Santello & Leitenberg, 1993; Ullman, 1996a; Valentiner, Foa, Riggs, & Gershuny, 1996). Why avoiding or withholding disclosure is harmful remains unclear, although suppressing unwanted thoughts of traumatic memories appears to be harmful in victims of rape (Shipherd & Beck, 1999). It is possible that more distressed survivors are more likely to try to block out or avoid talking about their assaults. However, it is also possible that holding in one's traumatic experiences (e.g., not telling others) means that they cannot be cognitively or emotionally processed. Cognitive appraisals (e.g., thoughts and feelings about the assault), as well as self-labeling or acknowledgment of one's experience as sexual assault and changes in these factors, may affect symptoms of posttraumatic stress disorder (Dunmore, Clark, & Ehlers, 2001; Fairbrother & Rachman, 2006; Layman, Gidycz, & Lynn, 1996) and are also likely to be affected by talking to others (Littleton, Rhatigan, & Axsom, 2007; Resick & Schnicke, 1992).

FACTORS THAT INFLUENCE WHETHER DISCLOSURE IS HEALING

Who Initiates the Disclosure

In a series of in-depth interviews, Ahrens, Campbell, Temier-Thames, Wasco, and Sefl (2007) found that some assaults were discovered by other people on the scene or were quickly revealed by survivors who were visibly distressed and asked by others what was wrong. In fact, more than one third of disclosures were not initiated by survivors themselves, and, consistent with other studies, most were disclosed to informal sources (75%). Analysis of the data revealed an interesting interaction showing that women who actively sought help from informal sources, such as friends and family, were more likely to receive positive than negative reactions. In contrast, survivors who actively sought help from formal sources, such as police or doctors, were more likely to receive negative than positive reactions. This finding was interpreted as being due to the fact that formal sources generally make more negative responses to survivors than informal sources (Campbell, Wasco, et al., 2001; Filipas & Ullman, 2001; Ullman, 1996b). It is interesting, though, that when formal sources initiated the sexual assault disclosure by asking about the assault survivors received only positive reactions. This may suggest that the power differential between the discloser and the support source, and who initiates the disclosure, may affect whether the survivor receives positive or negative responses. Professionals such as police, doctors, and mental health professionals have roles that involve asking less powerful people they are helping sensitive questions. They may feel comfortable initiating asking survivors about their experiences, which may lead to positive reactions. However, if victims initiate disclosure, this may challenge the power dynamic. Professionals may not want to deal with and/or know how to respond to victimization. Thus, in addition to professionals being socialized to be in control of their interactions (e.g., with the public for police, with patients for doctors, and with mental health clients for clinicians), they may also vary in the extent to which they feel it is appropriate (e.g., their role) and comfortable for them to deal with victims of sexual assault. For example, many doctors and health care professionals do not screen for violence against women, even though major organizations recommend such screenings (Stevens, 2007).

Level of Detail in the Disclosure

More detailed disclosures appear to be related to better psychological functioning in adult survivors of sexual assault (Ullman, 1996c; Ullman & Filipas, 2001b) and in adult male and female child sexual abuse survivors (Ullman & Filipas, 2005). More detailed disclosures may lead to greater *cognitive processing* of the trauma, which refers to successful working through of distressing thoughts and feelings associated with a trauma. Such cognitive processing is known to relate to fewer psychological symptoms (e.g., depression, anxiety; Resick & Schnicke, 1992; Resick et al., 2008). In addition to cognitive processing, disclosures may result in positive responses from other people that may promote healing. Both of these hypothesized mechanisms should be tested in future research to better understand the relationship of disclosure to psychological outcome.

Social Reactions

Most important, the effect of disclosure on individuals who disclose may depend in part on receiving a positive, empathic response from the person told. Lepore, Ragan, and Jones (2000) recently found that talking alone or talking to a supportive confederate after being exposed to a stressful stimulus in a laboratory setting appeared to facilitate adjustment compared with not talking. In contrast, the benefits of talking were diluted when the participant talked to an unsupportive confederate. Negative reactions may reinforce silencing, which in turn decreases the chances of future disclosure (and any healing effects that could result from it). For example, in a victim survey conducted by me and my colleagues, one survivor responded, "After I told my boyfriend and he abandoned me, I didn't tell anyone else that this happened to me until a few years ago."

CONCLUSION

Research shows that, regardless of age or race, victims commonly disclose sexual assault. Despite this, a majority of women wait months or years before telling, and most tell informal support sources such as friends and family but rarely report assaults to formal sources, such as police or doctors. Stereotypical stranger assaults are much more likely to be disclosed than acquaintance or romantic partner rapes, in particular to formal support sources. Less is known about the process or meaning of disclosure of sexual assault for various subgroups of women who vary in race/ethnicity, social class, and sexual orientation. Nondisclosure may be more likely for Black women, who may also experience more unsupportive responses when they disclose to others (Wyatt, 1992). This is not surprising given the devaluation of Black female victims of rape and stereotypical constructions of Black women's sexuality in general (Washington, 2001). Campbell, Wasco, et al.'s (2001) study of survivors of sexual assault found that Black survivors were less likely to disclose sexual assault to formal sources such as police and medical providers. In addition, nondisclosure is more likely for nonstereotypical rapes (e.g., nonstranger assaults when the victim has been drinking). More research is needed to fully understand why, how, and under what circumstances various groups of women talk about/disclose sexual assault to informal and formal support sources. Victims who are less likely to disclose and more likely to face greater negative reactions when they do seek help and victims of assaults that are deemed less legitimate (e.g., alcohol-related acquaintance assaults) need much more investigation to improve rape treatment and prevention efforts.

4

SOCIAL REACTIONS AND THEIR
EFFECTS ON SURVIVORS

In this chapter, I discuss the conceptualization of and empirical research on social reactions to victims of sexual assault. First, I review the development of the construct of social reactions as distinct from social support. Next, I describe the Social Reactions Questionnaire, a research measure I developed to assess social reactions to victims of sexual assault. Each type of positive and negative social reaction assessed by this measure is presented, with examples from research with survivors who reported receiving each reaction. Then, I discuss the responses that survivors *wish* they had received. Finally, I discuss the effects of social reactions on recovery of survivors.

SOCIAL REACTIONS VERSUS SOCIAL SUPPORT

In the traditional research literature on social support, most attention has been paid to assessing the general characteristics of one's *social network* (e.g., frequency of contacts with others, size and composition of support

This chapter draws on material from "Barriers to Working With Sexual Assault Survivors: A Qualitative Study of Rape Crisis Center Workers," by S. E. Ullman and S. M. Townsend, 2007, *Violence Against Women, 13*, pp. 412–443. Copyright 2007 by Sage. Adapted with permission.

networks), *perceived social support* (which refers to perceptions of available support from others, e.g., the belief that help is available if needed), and *received support* (i.e., actual instances of help one has experienced from others; for a review, see Taylor, 2007). However, social, clinical, and health psychologists have demonstrated that people have interactions with members of their social support networks that can be positive and negative. Such responses do not fit into these conceptualizations of social support and thus have been labeled *social reactions* (e.g., Herbert & Dunkel-Schetter, 1992; Rook, 1984). Some have also termed these *social interactions*, and they have been observed in various populations of persons experiencing stressful events (e.g., health conditions, abortion, AIDS, loss of a loved one, victimization).

Whereas *social support* generally refers to ongoing availability of help, *social reactions* are specific responses to disclosure or knowledge of the event or condition. Social support is necessarily positive, but researchers and clinicians have observed that victims, especially those with a stigmatized condition or who have experienced a threatening event, often receive both positive and negative reactions from others that are distinct from social support (Herek, 2009; Lanza, Cameron, & Revenson, 1995; Major, Zubek, Cooper, Cozzarelli, & Richards, 1997).

Researchers have identified a variety of positive and negative reactions experienced by sexual assault survivors, but it is important to understand that the concept of social reactions includes both social responses received by victims as well as the absence of particular responses (e.g., lack of social support, absence of negative or positive social reactions). The absence of these responses is important to assess and evaluate because victims may perceive them as a positive or negative reaction from the support provider. For instance, anecdotal data suggest that victims report the absence of negative reactions, such as being blamed, as a positive reaction from others (Ullman, 1996b). This implies that women are actually expecting to be blamed and then feel fortunate if they do not receive those responses. Similarly, some data suggest that if survivors receive no response at all from someone they tell about an assault, this lack of acknowledgment of their victimization is perceived to be a negative reaction and can lead to a silencing of the survivor (Ahrens, 2006).

THE SOCIAL REACTIONS QUESTIONNAIRE

It is important to understand the effects of positive social support as well as positive and negative social reactions in relation to adjustment to sexual assault. Therefore, researchers have developed specific scales to assess social responses or reactions in different populations (e.g., R. C. Davis, Brickman, & Baker, 1991; Ingram, Betz, Mindes, Schmitt, & Smith, 2001; Lanza et al.,

1995; Maercker & Muller, 2004). In earlier work, I developed a measure of these reactions to women who tell others about their sexual assaults called the *Social Reactions Questionnaire* (SRQ; Ullman, 2000). Although this measure was developed for research purposes, it may also be used by clinicians who wish to assess victims' experiences with their social networks. However, it has been validated to date only as a research measure and is not intended to be used as a clinical assessment tool specifically.

The SRQ was developed from an initial checklist of positive and negative social reactions experienced by victims identified in a literature search and pilot tested with victims of sexual assault (Ullman, 1996b). This measure of social reactions was constructed to measure specific types of positive and negative reactions that would go beyond past measures that simply examined general supportiveness or unsupportiveness of peoples' responses to victims or did not assess social reactions relevant to all types of victims of sexual assault (e.g., R. C. Davis et al., 1991). The theoretical basis for the SRQ came from the literatures on social support and social reactions to victims (Herbert & Dunkel-Schetter, 1992; House, 1981). The SRQ was conceptualized as encompassing several types of supportive behavior or positive social reactions commonly studied in the social support literature: *instrumental support* (i.e., actions or tangible aid), *emotional support* (i.e., expressions of love, caring, and esteem), and *information support* (i.e., advice or information; House, 1981; Turner, 1983). Items were developed to tap each of these conceptual domains. Review of the victimization literature also revealed that being believed and validated were helpful reactions, so I added the positive domain of Validation/Belief distinct from Emotional Support. Five types of negative social reactions were identified from the literature: (a) taking control of a victim's decisions, (b) victim blame, (c) treating the victim differently, (d) distraction, and (e) egocentric response.

I conducted a preliminary pilot study of a 40-item checklist (Ullman, 1996b). Participants were recruited by means of newspaper advertisements, posted flyers, and public service announcements for a study of "threatened or forced sexual intercourse or other sexual experiences since age 14." Participants from community, student, and mental health agency samples were recruited. They called about the study and completed a brief confidential mail survey about their experience, were paid $10, and received a list of medical and mental health resources in the community and/or on campus (for students). Students were resurveyed 8 weeks later and again paid $5 so that we could assess test–retest reliability of the measure.

The pilot measure was organized with items in a randomized order and administered in the context of a survey on sexual assault, with items asking participants about an incidence of sexual assault, their experiences following that assault, whether they had disclosed the assault to anyone, to whom they disclosed, and whether the person or persons to whom they had disclosed had been helpful. Each item on the scale is phrased as a statement (e.g., "Told you you were loved"), and respondents indicate how often they received each reaction after telling someone about their assault on a 5-point scale ranging from *never* to *always*. The following instructions preface the measure:

> The following is a list of behaviors that other people responding to a person with this experience often show. Please indicate how often you experienced each of the listed responses from other people by placing the appropriate number in the blank next to each item. (1 = never to 5 = always). This questionnaire assesses both positive and negative reactions a woman receives from people when she tells them that she was assaulted.

The results of the pilot study led to modifications of the measure and selection of the most discriminating items for each domain (for a detailed description of the development of the current SRQ from the initial checklist measure, see Ullman, 2000). For example, factor analysis revealed that validation/belief responses actually belonged with the Emotional Support domain (Ullman, 2000). Examples of the reactions that comprise the subscales of the SRQ, as well as additional reactions identified in a validation study of the SRQ from open-ended written comments of survivors, are shown in Table 4.1 (Filipas & Ullman, 2001). This measure has also been adapted for use with victims of child sexual abuse and domestic violence, as well as for support providers reporting on reactions they made to victims (Ullman & Filipas, 2005; Outcault, Dilalla, & Weston, 2006). Each type of reaction is described in detail in the following sections.

Positive Social Reactions

Positive social reactions to assault disclosure include three major types of responses: (a) emotional support, (b) tangible aid, and (c) information support. They are quite common, with research showing that the majority of survivors receive one or more positive reactions from others (Ullman, 1999). Positive reactions likely result from those responding directly to victims' disclosures and/or to the victims' own reactions to and/or coping with their assaults. Such responses likely represent people's attempts to comfort and provide support to victims in the hope of making them feel better and getting them needed assistance. In the following sections, I discuss each of these in detail and include illustrative examples from interviews with survivors.

Emotional Support

Studies show that emotionally supportive responses are the most common of positive reactions, with as many as 80% of survivors who experienced positive reactions experiencing emotional support (Filipas & Ullman, 2001;

TABLE 4.1
Social Reactions Assessed by the Social Reactions Questionnaire

Social reaction	Sample quotes from survivors
Positive	
Emotional support	"He (boyfriend) said he was here for me in whatever way I needed him and that we didn't have to have sex unless I wanted to."
	"My close friends were the only people that knew so they were the most helpful by listening to me and comforting me."
Tangible aid	"My partner took me to go get tested for sexually transmitted diseases."
	"[My romantic partner] accompanied me to an abortion clinic."
Information support	"My counselor at college provided information and resources during my years in session with her."
Negative	
Victim blame	"My father and mother said that the way I dressed and the friends I chose provoked the incident. They blamed me for the first 2 months after the incident."
	"[An acquaintance] mentioned that I should have never been talking to him and I should have fought harder—that I should have known what he wanted."
	"The woman detective said, 'Why did you have him in your apartment if you weren't going to have sex with him?'"
Egocentric response	"He asked too many questions, asked for too many details; things I didn't want to share at the time."
	"My father said, 'If it really happened I'd like to kill the guy.'"
Stigmatizing response	"Someone made it into a joke."
	"My biological mother disowned me and ignored the situation."
Distraction	"My mom just wanted me to forget."
	"The person I was talking with became uncomfortable and tried to say a couple of words like, 'Oh that's awful' or 'What a jerk' and quickly changed the subject."
	"My mom is very uncomfortable any time the subject comes up. She always changes the subject. This hurts her badly. I don't talk with her about it because I don't want to hurt her, but she's the one I most want comfort from."
Controlling responses	"My father treated me as if I was 5 years old instead of 25."
	"He (romantic partner) wanted to physically harm the perpetrator and got very angry when I first told him. This upset me because I had to calm him down."

Ullman, 1996b). The following responses, reported by survivors who told others about their assaults, also appear to exemplify emotional support:

- "My boyfriend held me and listened to me cry as long as I needed. He reassured me that even though I had been drinking, it was not my fault over and over." (16-year-old White survivor of acquaintance rape)
- "Believed me and clarified that what happened was actually rape and not my fault, put the anger on the perpetrator instead of suspecting I caused it (as I believed)." (18-year-old Black acquaintance rape survivor)
- "She said to my boyfriend (ex after the incident) that his friend raped me. To have that spoken out loud affirmed what I couldn't accept myself." (18-year-old Black acquaintance rape survivor)
- "He loved me and married me in spite of it all. And didn't hold me responsible." (Black survivor of romantic acquaintance rape at age 24 on her husband's response)
- "No one can offer the same degree or quality of empathy, support, courage, and compassion as another woman who has been raped and healed from the experience." (White adolescent acquaintance rape survivor on the response of women in her support group)
- "She listened to me discuss the experience in detail and how it has affected me and how I have felt about it and reassured me that my reactions and feelings were normal, reasonable, natural, and that she could accept and handle everything." (White adolescent acquaintance rape survivor on friend's response)
- "Allowed me to talk about it without judging me." (26-year-old stranger rape survivor on friend and family member)

Survivors' reports indicate that it is important that they receive emotional support and validation not just in response to the rape incident itself but also regarding their psychological reactions to it and their ways of coping with the assault. Consider the following statements from survivors:

- "People were supportive of the decisions I made, even when they wouldn't do the same thing themselves." (16-year-old Latina romantic partner rape survivor on romantic partner, friend, and family member responses)
- "He asked me to talk about it, just held me, and listened to me." (16-year-old Latina survivor's romantic partner response).

It is important to note that sometimes attempts to be emotionally supportive are not perceived as such by survivors. Some survivors may appreciate empathic responses that reflect the survivor's reaction and show understanding; however, expressions of sympathy (e.g., saying, "You poor thing," or showing pity) may make victims feel stigmatized, weak, or like objects of disdain. For example, one 16-year-old White acquaintance rape survivor appreciated that her friend did not show pity: "The most helpful was my friend just listening to me without passing judgment or trying to sympathize." Thus, support providers may need to think carefully about how their responses will be received, even if they have good intentions.

Tangible Aid

Tangible aid consists of actions or assistance provided by others to the survivor. Such instrumental support may include spending time with the survivor, taking her to police or medical providers, giving her a place to stay, or giving her resources following an assault. These responses were reported by 60% of victims (Ullman, 1996b). This type of support is most commonly offered by formal support providers, but it also can be offered by informal social network members. Survivors have stated the following about tangible aid:

- "People (friends, family, partner) had slept over at my apartment after the attack and walked me from my parking lot to my apartment for months after the attack." (Adolescent victim of White stranger rape)
- "My estranged husband stood by me—was with me with the police and in the hospital emergency room. Then he let me stay at his house for several days, (letting me) sleep in his bed while he slept in the living room like a guard dog. Also, my brother came from another city to spend the night on my first night back home. Third, an older woman who had been raped sat with me in the hospital holding my hand and empathetically listening to me. My best friend told me the same man raped her two months before. She helped the police and now he's in jail." (34-year-old Black stranger rape survivor)

These supportive responses from others may buffer effects of trauma exposure on posttraumatic stress disorder (PTSD) in general in female victims (Glass, Perrin, Campbell, & Soeken, 2007). However, such informal help may not always be available to survivors who have fewer resources or have been sexually victimized in the context of violent relationships (R. C. Davis, 2007). In fact, the lack of tangible support (i.e., financial resources) for some victims may lead them to seek help from formal sources. Davis suggests that such victims have fewer resources in their support networks, which makes them unable to secure the help they need following victimization. More research is needed to identify needs and develop interventions for high-risk subgroups of victims, such as sexually victimized women in violent relationships of lower socioeconomic status.

Information Support

Information support is a third class of positive reactions that includes giving useful resources, such as books, to survivors or educating them about rape and its effects. This form of support is often reported by survivors, with some research showing that as many as 90% of victims receive this type of response from others (Ullman, 1996b). The following survivor statements demonstrate information support:

- "A friend of a friend (who was not helpful, was blaming) told my boyfriend to shape up and gave us both Linda Ledray's *Recovering From Rape*, which articulated so many of my feelings and aftereffects—it let me know I wasn't alone or crazy." (23-year-old Asian American survivor of acquaintance rape)
- "My friend spoke of empowering one's self. She provided books and literature about and by women that reshaped my values and my own perception of women. She taught me a great respect for women and as a result respect for myself as well. This was a focal point of my healing process." (White adolescent survivor of acquaintance rape)

Negative Social Reactions

Other responses have been termed *negative social reactions* (e.g., victim blame, disbelief), which can be further distinguished from lack or absence of positive social support (R. C. Davis et al., 1991; Ullman, 1996b). As mentioned earlier, these negative social reactions can be purposeful attempts by support providers to harm victims or unintentional harmful responses that were actually meant to be supportive by support providers (Herbert & Dunkel-Schetter, 1992). For instance, a well-meaning family member may tell a victim to put the assault behind her and go on with her life, but such a response may be perceived as insensitive by the victim. Dunkel-Schetter and Skokan (1990) theorized that victims' distress and maladaptive coping may lead to awkward or ineffective support attempts by other people who respond assertively because of their own discomfort in response to survivors' distress. As with positive reactions, negative social reactions may in part result from judgments not of the victimization itself but of survivors' reactions to it. This may occur when survivors are very symptomatic or engage in maladaptive coping, but support providers feel that enough time has passed and the victim should be "getting over it." Distress that support providers feel in response to seeing survivors with these problems may lead them to respond in negative ways, even if this is unintentional.

The SRQ assess five types of negative reactions: (a) victim blame, (b) distraction, (c) stigmatizing response, (d) egocentric response, and (e) controlling response. I now discuss each of these reactions in detail and provide illustrative examples from interviews with survivors.

Victim Blame

Victim blame is the classic form of negative social reaction and is commonly received from formal and informal support sources. Studies show that 70% to 80% of women who disclose a sexual assault receive these reactions (Filipas & Ullman, 2001; Ullman, 1996b). These reactions encompass overt statements that the assault is due to the survivor's behavior (e.g., "You were not careful") or her character (e.g., "You are a weak person"). The following survivor statements demonstrate victim blame:

- "My dad said that I got myself in that situation and that it was not his responsibility to pay the medical bill." (20-year-old White victim of acquaintance rape on her father's response)
- "I had someone tell me it was somewhat my fault; that all the warning signs were there, but that I was too stupid at the time to notice them." (Teenage White victim of romantic partner rape)
- "[They said] I can't believe you did that. Didn't you know something like that would happen? That's what happens when girls drink. You set yourself up." (20-year-old Black rape survivor on her family and romantic partner's responses)

The first quote reflects blame of the victim's behavior, which the father uses to justify his lack of tangible aid to his daughter. The second quote actually appears to involve both behavioral blame (i.e., the victim's partner says there were warning signs that the victim should have recognized) and characterological blame (i.e., the victim's partner says she was stupid). The third quote expresses a reaction that the survivor's drinking put her at risk, which exemplifies behavioral blame.

Distraction

Another form of negative reaction is *distraction*, or discouraging the victim from talking about the assault, which 58% to 80% of victims have noted in past studies (Filipas & Ullman, 2001; Ullman, 1996b). Survivors have stated the following:

- "Someone told me if I dwell on this, the person who did this to me is winning." (20-year-old White acquaintance rape survivor)
- "My boyfriend at the time told me to forget and stop talking about it." (17-year-old White victim of acquaintance rape)
- "All the men who say when issues of sexual victimization are brought up, 'I don't need to hear this, I've never raped anyone.'" (16-year-old White victim of stranger rape)

These responses may be harmful because they imply that the victim is overreacting to the event; not coping adequately; and/or burdening the support provider, who does not want to hear about it. Such responses may actually be self-serving on the part of support providers, even though they are made in the guise of helping the victim "get her mind off the assault." This may be especially difficult and invalidating when providers respond in such ways because they are trying to be helpful. Such responses may preclude victims from labeling the behavior as hurtful and expressing their feelings about the rape and need for support in order to cope with it.

Stigma

Stigmatizing responses that treat the victim differently or like damaged goods after the assault are also common. Eighty percent of victims received these verbal and behavioral responses from others to whom they disclosed assault (Filipas & Ullman, 2001). Survivors have stated the following:

- "My biological mother disowned me." (15-year-old victim of rape perpetrated by a relative)
- "[My friend] didn't return my calls and blew me off." (17-year-old Black victim of acquaintance rape)
- "My brothers who I told in general handle me like I'm about to break." (41-year-old Black victim of stranger rape)

These responses reflect blatant rejection of the survivor that is due to the stigma of rape in U.S. society. They also show that survivors can and do lose relationships with significant others, including family and friends, who stigmatize them and then distance themselves by breaking off the relationship with the victim. The last example, in which the victim states that her brothers treated her as fragile, may reflect the brothers' belief that a victim of rape is somehow broken, or on the verge of breaking down, and that they feel they might say or do something that could push her over the edge. This fear may lead family and friends to tiptoe around the victim for fear of making her "worse." Although such a response may emerge from positive and self-serving intentions, the victim may end up feeling stigmatized and judged by such responses. She may view them as evidence that her family does not think she can handle the assault and/or is coping poorly. Such judgments are not as bad as outright rejection when victims are cut off completely by others in their lives, but these responses may reinforce a sense of weakness and helplessness that victims already feel as a result of the rape. As a result, this may thwart the survivor's ability to feel and believe in one's own inner strength and ability to recover.

Egocentric Reactions

Egocentric responses involve support providers responding in a selfish way that reflects their concern about the effect of the victim's assault on themselves. Although such concerns are real and legitimate, these responses may effectively deny the victim's immediate needs and the assault's effect on her by focusing attention on how the support provider is reacting to the assault. Eighty percent of survivors have cited these responses (Filipas & Ullman, 2001), and they appear to be especially common from romantic partners and family members:

- "My partner at the time took it too personally. He felt more violated than I did." (26-year-old Black stranger victim on her romantic partner's response)
- "He wanted to physically harm the perpetrator and got very angry when I first told him. This upset me because I had to calm him down." (20-year-old "other race" acquaintance rape survivor on her romantic partner's response)

First, these responses can be stressful for the survivor because they take the focus off of her and her needs and focus instead on the support provider and his or her reactions and needs. This may impede the victim's capacity to get the types of support she needs, because the provider is caught up in his or her own reaction/response to the rape. Second, the survivor may feel a greater loss of control beyond that caused by the rape itself if a supporter is now seeking revenge on the perpetrator. Such responses may simply reinforce feelings of fear, helplessness, and loss of control over potentially escalating consequences of one's victimization that are clearly out of the survivor's control. Third, the survivor may feel she must calm the person down and help him or her with his or her reaction at a time when she is the one in need of support, which constitutes an added burden on an already-stressed individual. Although these kinds of reactions have potentially negative consequences for victims, they illustrate that support providers are affected by rape disclosures and indicate that research is needed to improve both victims' and support providers' disclosure experiences.

Controlling Responses

The last type of negative reaction on the SRQ is *controlling responses:* trying to take control of the victim or the situation following the assault. It is estimated that at least 80% of victims who disclose their assaults to others receive such controlling responses (Filipas & Ullman, 2001; Ullman, 1996b). One survivor stated, "Two people wanted to seek revenge. The last thing I wanted was to see myself or someone I cared for in jail for a payback" (White 24-year-old romantic partner rape survivor on her family and romantic partner's responses).

Either informal or formal sources may give controlling responses. Often, postassault medical care providers and/or police/legal personnel revictimize survivors by taking control away from them. One survivor stated, "The whole ER deal made me feel victimized all over again. They didn't care about me. They just wanted evidence"(White adolescent victim of stranger rape on hospital personnel).

Even attempts to help by specialized rape victim advocates may be perceived as reinforcing the victim's lack of control and her sense of shame and stigma:

> Rape counselors who come to the ER need more training. I think it would be better for them to be there as supportive listeners, standing up for our rights (especially at a time when we are in shock and not thinking correctly) and not shoving pamphlets in our face and telling us we might get AIDS. That, in itself, is telling us that we are being punished. It adds one crime to another. It would be kinder if they acted more as a compassionate friend instead of a crazed information machine. (Survivor on a victim advocate's response)

ADDITIONAL SOCIAL REACTIONS IDENTIFIED FROM QUALITATIVE DATA BUT NOT ASSESSED ON THE SOCIAL REACTIONS QUESTIONNAIRE

Additional qualitative data have identified other reactions that are not assessed by the SRQ. Although they appear to be less frequent responses and may in some cases be subcategories of existing SRQ categories, further research is needed to examine them and to determine whether the SRQ should be updated to include them. This would be particularly important if such reactions were found to have a significant impact on victims' recovery. These additional reactions are summarized in Table 4.2.

Positive Social Reactions

Additional positive reactions identified from our qualitative data include belief/validation, non-blame, listening, reassurance, and sharing experiences.

TABLE 4.2
Additional Social Reactions Assessed by Survey Respondents' Open-Ended Comments

Social reactions	Sample quotes from survivors
Positive	
Belief/validation	"A close friend that I helped with her flashbacks from a similar experience classified it as a rape. She helped put the experience into perspective."
Non-blame	"The therapist kept reinforcing that the incident was not my fault. It did not occur because of any poor judgment on my part."
Listening	"[My romantic partner] listened and was proud of how I handled it."
	"[My friend] gave me a chance to talk and didn't question me like an authority."
Reassurance	"Any male (friend) that shows me he can be trusted and I feel comfortable trusting him helps me from thinking all guys are assholes."
Sharing experience	"Every time I talk to another rape survivor (at speak-outs) I get a special boost—like someone else really understands and knows what I'm feeling and I love it when someone else talks publicly."
Negative	
Rape myths	"The first person I told was my brother's girlfriend. She knew I really liked the guy and asked me how I liked it."
	"(My mom's boyfriend told me) you have no business going out looking like that."
Trust violation	"My younger sisters just blurted it out to the kids. I'll never forgive them."
	"My friend that I first told went and told her boyfriend. I wanted it to be personal and now more people know. It is like the grapevine effect."
Minimizing response	"An acquaintance told me that I didn't have it as bad as some other victims."
Revictimization	"A guy I was friends with who I talked to about it tried to rape me."
Disbelief/denial	"The first person I told (a nurse at the hospital) said it wasn't rape."
	"A friend who was with me at the time stated that it didn't really happen—that I must be mistaken."

Belief/Validation

Some survivors indicate that they had received responses of *belief and validation* from those to whom they disclosed. For example, one survivor said, "A close friend that I helped with her flashbacks from a similar experience classified it as a rape. She helped put the experience into perspective." Another survivor said, "My counselor told me what happened to me was an assault and validated my experience as a rape."

Non-Blame

Not being blamed and receiving expressions of non-blame from others are also mentioned by survivors as positive reactions. For example, one survivor said, "The therapist kept reinforcing that the incident was not my fault. It did not occur because of any poor judgment on my part." Another survivor said, "My friend told me that the incident was not my fault and nothing I did caused it to happen." These responses may be viewed as positive because survivors anticipate that others will blame them given how common blaming of victims of rape is in society. It may come as a relief to receive responses that actively counteract blame.

Listening

Listening is another positive response that some survivors mention. One survivor remarked that "[My romantic partner] listened and was proud of how I handled it." Another survivor said "[My friend] gave me a chance to talk and didn't question me like an authority." Listening may help by allowing victims to be heard and taken seriously.

Reassurance

Survivors also mention being *reassured* by others they told about the assault as positive. One survivor mentioned, "Any male (friend) that shows me he can be trusted and I feel comfortable trusting him helps me from thinking all guys are assholes." Reassurance may help victims feel comforted and know that others will be there for them.

Sharing Experiences

Finally, *having other survivors share their assault experiences* is seen as positive. Such reactions may be helpful because a victim knows that another survivor truly understands what he or she is experiencing. One survivor said, "Every time I talk to another rape survivor (at speak-outs) I get a special boost—like someone else really understands and knows what I'm feeling and I love it when someone else talks publicly."

Negative Social Reactions

Several additional negative reactions identified from our qualitative data include expressing rape myths, trust violation, minimizing responses, revictimization, and disbelief/denial.

Expressing Rape Myths

Responses that reinforce *rape myths* include statements such as "What were you wearing?" "Did you struggle?" "Why did you dress so sexy?" and "How did you like it?" These statements imply that women invite rape, enjoy it, and are responsible for rape because of their dress or behavior.

Trust Violation

People to whom survivors disclose sometimes *betray the survivor's trust* by going behind the survivor's back and telling others about her victimization:

- "A friend told my children that I had been raped by my neighbor." (35-year-old Black acquaintance rape survivor)
- "My partner a few years ago told some other people about my experience, when I was not there and without my permission. This was a real violation of my privacy." (White victim of stranger rape assaulted at age 14)

Minimizing Response

Responses that minimize the trauma of rape and/or pathologize survivors' reactions and coping following rape are also quite harmful:

- "My best friend didn't understand what I was going through, nor did my family. They all thought I was acting crazy. In fact, I was reacting normally to a traumatic event. I wish they had been better able to understand instead of writing me off as going off the deep end." (18-year-old Black victim of acquaintance rape)
- "The staff psychiatrist said I didn't have it as bad as some other victims." (26-year-old White victim of stranger rape)
- "[The college dean said] 'Well, since it wasn't your first sexual experience, it's not that bad of a thing.'" (18-year-old White acquaintance rape survivor)
- "An ex-boyfriend who I'm still close with said that I have sex with everyone anyway, so by this time sex really didn't mean too much to me anymore, and therefore I wasn't too offended or violated by the rape at the time." (Adolescent White victim of acquaintance gang rape)

Revictimization

Revictimization was a more infrequent, yet surprising response noted by a few survivors who said the had disclosed a sexual assault (Filipas & Ullman, 2001); specifically, some men respond to disclosures of sexual assault by perceiving that the woman is somehow a legitimate target and then attempt to rape her again. One survivor said the following: "A guy I was friends with who I talked to about it tried to rape me" (20-year-old "other race" victim of acquaintance rape).

Disbelief/Denial

Survivors also experienced responses from others of *denial and disbelief* that they said were unhelpful:

- "My friend didn't believe it really happened and told me it couldn't really be true." (White victim of date rape)
- "My parents denied it had occurred and refused to talk about it again." (18-year-old Latina victim of acquaintance rape)

IMPACT OF SOCIAL REACTIONS ON SURVIVORS

Although various positive and negative social reactions have been identified in quantitative and qualitative studies, researchers have also started to examine various effects of these reactions on survivors. Next, I review the effects of social reactions on mental health and victims' future disclosures as well as factors that influence the impact of social reactions on these domains.

Impact on Mental Health

Several studies using the SRQ and other measures have found that women who receive negative reactions when telling others about sexual assaults have more psychological symptoms of depression and posttraumatic stress and even poorer perceptions of their health (Andrews, Brewin, & Rose, 2003; Campbell, Ahrens, Sefl, Wasco, & Barnes, 2001; R. C. Davis et al., 1991; Ullman, 2000; Ullman & Siegel, 1995). Studies that have assessed positive reactions show that they either do not affect the survivor's symptoms significantly or they relate to slightly fewer symptoms, suggesting that they enhance recovery somewhat (Ullman, 1999).

Interviews with 105 victims of sexual assault seeking help at a victim services agency in New York City showed that unsupportive behavior from significant others was related to more psychological distress for victims, whereas supportive behavior was not significantly related to adjustment

(R. C. Davis et al., 1991). A survey of 155 female sexual assault survivors from college, community, and mental health agencies in Los Angeles showed that negative social reactions were related to poorer self-rated recovery, more psychological symptoms, and poorer perceived health (Ullman, 1996a; Ullman & Siegel, 1995).

Several more recent studies have used the SRQ to examine the relationship of social reactions to mental health of victims. A survey of 323 sexual assault survivors in Chicago revealed that negative social reactions were related to greater PTSD symptoms (Ullman & Filipas, 2001b). Campbell, Ahrens, et al. (2001) used a modified version of the SRQ in an interview study of 102 victims of rape in Chicago and found that negative social reactions were related to greater posttraumatic stress symptoms.

In a rare longitudinal study, negative responses from family and friends shortly after violent crimes (including sexual assault), assessed with a more general measure of perceived supportiveness of others' responses, were related to greater PTSD symptoms 6 months later (Andrews et al., 2003). Research also shows that when sexually assaulted female veterans received negative responses from legal and medical providers, the victims felt guilty, depressed, anxious, and distrusting of others, and they were reluctant to seek further help (Campbell & Raja, 2005). In a recent longitudinal study, victims who received more negative social reactions from those they told about assault were more likely, over time, to blame their character for the assault (Ullman & Najdowski, 2009).

Impact on Silencing of Survivors

Despite the need for interventions to encourage disclosure of sexual assault, there is reason to believe that the negative reactions discussed here further silence survivors and keep them from seeking help in general. To document this process, Ahrens (2006) analyzed qualitative narratives of eight rape survivors who initially disclosed the assault and then stopped talking about it for a significant period of time. Ahrens uncovered three routes to silencing. First, negative reactions from professionals led victims to question whether future disclosures would help. Second, negative social reactions reinforced victims' self-blame, which led to self-silencing. Third, negative reactions from either formal or informal sources reinforced survivors' uncertainty about whether their experiences qualified as rape. This work suggests that even when victims do disclose sexual assault they may not get the help that they need and may even decide that it is too risky to continue to speak about their victimization, because of negative responses they have already faced. In general, this research suggests that negative social reactions originate from the social climate that both inhibits sexual assault disclosure initially and discourages victims who do disclose from continuing to talk about their assaults and seek professional help.

FACTORS THAT AFFECT THE PROVISION AND IMPACT OF SOCIAL REACTIONS

Support Provider Type

Research suggests that the impact of social reactions on victims may vary as a function of which support provider makes the response. Little research has examined this possibility, and it is complicated by the fact that victims often tell multiple sources and receive multiple different reactions from different sources and sometimes even from the same source.

Who Provides the Most Supportive Reactions to Survivors?

Women consistently rate friends as most supportive (Golding, Siegel, Sorenson, Burnam, & Stein, 1989; Ullman, 1999) following sexual assault. Female peers are most likely similar to survivors and may have also experienced sexual assault or at least understand the fear of rape, which is common among women. It makes sense that women would go to female friends for support in disclosing sexual assault. In a study of the effect of female friends on victims of rape, friends reported reacting positively, did not blame the survivor, were not distressed, felt their helping efforts were effective, and believed their friendships grew closer (Ahrens & Campbell, 2000). Similarly, studies have found that survivors rated female friends as most supportive, followed by rape crisis centers (Golding, Stein, Siegel, Burnam, & Sorenson, 1988; Ullman, 1996b; Ullman & Filipas, 2001a), out of a range of potential support sources.

Gender of support provider was also significant; specifically, victims said that female significant others' unsupportive behavior toward victims did not differ between sexual versus nonsexual assault but that male significant others were more likely to be unsupportive to victims of sexual assault than to victims of nonsexual assault. This shows that who is asked about responses to victims does affect what is reported, especially for negative behaviors, and that victims of rape are more subject to these negative behaviors than victims of nonsexual assault, in particular by male significant others. This conclusion is supported by qualitative research on couples following sexual assault. Connop and Petrak's (2004) work shows that male partners' anger and blame about the assault and toward the perpetrator were sometimes displaced onto their female partners in the form of attributing responsibility and/or blame to the women. Male partners often described their reactions as emerging from their own emotional reactions that conflicted with their rational/logical beliefs that the woman was not to blame for the assault.

Mental health professionals are the next most supportive group, according to survivors (Campbell, Sefl, et al., 1999; Golding et al., 1989; Ullman, 1996b, 2000), as are family members. Both of these two support sources are mixed, however, with survivors reporting both positive and negative interactions with them.

Who Provides the Most Unsupportive Reactions to Survivors?

Support providers consistently rated by survivors as most unhelpful or unsupportive in their responses to sexual assault survivors' disclosures include police/legal personnel, physicians, and clergy (Ullman, 1999). In addition, studies that have asked these groups directly (e.g., medical students, police, prosecuting attorneys) about their attitudes toward victims of rape reveal negative attitudes, as well as adherence to rape myths (Best, Dansky, & Kilpatrick, 1992; Sheldon & Parent, 2002; Ward, 1988). A study of clergy's attitudes toward victims of rape showed that most clergy blame the victim and adhere to rape myths, in particular if they are more fundamentalist and more sexist in their beliefs (Sheldon & Parent, 2002). Police also can be problematic in their response to rape cases. Jordan (2004) argued that low police reporting is due to skepticism with which police respond to women's claims of rape. Her data show that police viewed such cases similarly to people in general. Stereotypes about women's demeanor, intoxication, and conceal-ment (e.g., willingness and the way in which the victim talks about the assault) are taken into account in judging women's credibility. Victims also often perceive the legal system in a negative way. For example, Frazier and Haney's (1996) study of 990 criminal rape trials showed that most victims believed that rapists had more rights, the system was unfair, victims' rights were not protected, and that they were deprived of information about and control over the handling of their cases. A recent in-depth examination and review of the so-called "justice gap" for victims of rape by Temkin and Krahe (2008) revealed significant barriers in the legal system for the few victims of rape whose cases ever enter the system.

What Is the Impact of Support From Different Sources on Recovery?

Few studies have evaluated the impact of different types of support from different support sources on recovery. In one study, victims who received positive reactions (e.g., listening) from friends had better recovery than those who reported such reactions from other sources (Ullman, 1996b). In another study, the SRQ was administered to 517 female college victims of sexual assault for both informal (e.g., family, friends, partners) and formal (e.g., medical, mental health, police) support sources told about the assault (Borja,

Callahan, & Long, 2006). This study was valuable in that it isolated the types of social reactions made by each type of source as well the differential impact of those reactions by each type of source. Positive reactions from both formal and informal sources were related to perceived benefits following assault, whereas negative reactions from informal sources only were related to more PTSD symptoms. No social reactions were related to general psychological distress in that study.

Victims' Appraisal of Social Reactions

Some research suggests that some social reactions, such as distraction and having others take control, may be perceived either positively or negatively by different victims (Campbell, Sefl et al., 1999; Filipas & Ullman, 2001). This suggests that subjective appraisals of reactions may also affect the impact of social reactions. For example, Uji, Shono, Shikai, and Kitamura (2007) studied 532 Japanese female college students who had had negative sexual experiences, some of which were adult sexual assaults. They found several results that conflicted with previous studies. First, women did not necessarily regard it negatively when the incident was viewed less seriously or when they were criticized by people to whom they disclosed. In addition, instrumental support was not always viewed as a supportive response. However, this study focused on mostly less serious unwanted sexual experiences perpetrated by strangers, most of which occurred in childhood or adolescence, not adulthood. Sexual assault was not assessed with a standardized measure, and the authors acknowledged that the study likely underestimated the prevalence of sexual assault. In addition, it is possible that the results reflect differences in how social reactions are viewed cross-culturally.

Other Factors

In the Women's Life Experiences Study, more than 1,000 sexual assault survivors were surveyed using media recruitment, including posted fliers and advertisements at universities, mental health agencies/rape crisis centers, and in the community (see Introduction, this volume, for details). The results showed that victims who received more negative social reactions assessed with the SRQ had more PTSD symptoms (than victims who received fewer negative reactions), controlling for other factors that might affect symptoms, such as demographics, assault characteristics, postassault perceptions of control, attributions of blame, coping, and positive social reactions (Ullman, Filipas, Townsend, & Starzynski, 2007). In a further test of a theoretical model using structural equation modeling of the relationship of social reactions to PTSD symptoms in this sample, degree of self-blame did not predict more symptoms, once social reactions were controlled statistically in the model. This suggests that negative social reactions may be more important to understanding PTSD symptoms than self-blame, which has been found in many studies to relate to worse symptoms (Ullman, Townsend, Filipas, & Starzynski, 2007).

LIMITATIONS OF THE RESEARCH ON THE IMPACT OF SOCIAL REACTIONS

Existing research shows that social reactions have various impacts on victims' recovery outcomes, but it is also important to recognize that much of the research on social reactions to victims of sexual assault is limited by nonrepresentative samples of victims, self-report methods, and cross-sectional research designs. In addition, most research has examined mental health consequences of social reactions. More work is needed to examine effects of social reactions on survivors' interpersonal relationships; patterns of help-seeking; health-risk behaviors, such as substance use and risky sexual behavior; physical health; and risk of revictimization.

Determining Directionality

Most studies documenting the impact of reactions on health outcomes have been cross-sectional in design. Sorting out the directionality of the relations between social reactions and symptoms is important so that we will know whether treatment or intervention should focus primarily on reducing negative social reactions or treating symptoms; that is, does receiving negative social reactions lead to poorer recovery, or does poorer recovery lead to receiving more negative social reactions? Longitudinal data are needed to try to determine the sequencing of social reactions and distress.

Zoellner, Foa, and Brigidi (1999) partially addressed this in their longitudinal study of sexual assault survivors. In that study, survivors' reports of interpersonal friction with others predicted their PTSD symptoms prospectively, whereas their earlier PTSD symptoms did not predict greater interpersonal friction with others over time. This study did not measure social reactions per se to victims' disclosures, but it does provide preliminary evidence that symptomatic victims are not simply eliciting more negative responses from others. A longitudinal study of recent violent crime victims, including sexual assault, also showed that initial negative support was related to greater PTSD symptoms at a 6-month follow-up, controlling for initial PTSD symptoms, again suggesting that social responses have powerful effects on survivors' symptomatology (Andrews et al., 2003).

A longitudinal study of victims of sexual assault (Ullman & Najdowski, 2009) revealed that there were no relationships between behavioral self-blame (i.e., blaming one's behavior for assault) and social reactions over 1 year, but negative reactions predicted more characterological self-blame (i.e., blaming one's character for the assault), and characterological self-blame predicted fewer positive reactions. PTSD did not have a direct effect on social reactions, only an indirect effect through revictimization. This implies that research trying to tease these relations out should also include measures of intervening revictimization experiences.

Negative Reporting Bias

Given that more symptomatic survivors may also be more likely to report more negative responses simply because of a negative reporting bias (i.e., a tendency of distressed individuals to respond negatively to all questions), it is important to obtain reports from those who respond to survivors' disclosures (i.e., disclosure recipients). The limitation of using survivor self-reported reactions from others was revealed in a study of 128 recent violent crime victims (two thirds of whom were victims of sexual assaults) and their significant others (R. C. Davis & Brickman, 1996). Reports of supportive and unsupportive behavior (using the Crime Impact Social Support Inventory, Davis et al., 1991) of the significant others were solicited independently in interviews with both victims and their significant others. Although victim and significant-other reports of supportive behavior were moderately correlated, their reports of unsupportive behavior were only weakly correlated. Both victims and significant others agreed, however, that victims of rape got more unsupportive behavior overall than victims of nonsexual assault.

In another study of formal support sources, interviews of both service providers and victims of sexual assault seeking emergency medical care after rape showed significant agreement between victims and medical and legal system personnel about what services were provided to victims and whether system personnel engaged in secondary victimization behaviors (Campbell, 2005). However, doctors and police underestimated the negative impact they were having on survivors. Victims reported much more postsystem contact distress than these service providers thought victims were experiencing.

These studies suggest that it is very important to study both the victim and those responding to her after assault. Both informal and formal support networks' responses need to be studied further to fully understand what happens following the assault, the meaning of postassault interactions, and their impact on survivors. Such information may be useful for designing interventions to assist survivors not only for professionals but also for informal support sources, on which survivors most frequently call for help.

RESPONSES THAT SURVIVORS WISH THEY HAD RECEIVED

In one study, participants were asked about what responses they wished someone had made (Filipas & Ullman, 2001). The results of this study are summarized in Table 4.3. Some participants said they wished the offender would apologize and/or admit that he had raped her. These types of responses may be particularly likely in cases of date or acquaintance rape, where the betrayal of trust is likely to be greater and the assault even more unexpected than in the case of a stranger rape:

- "I wish that my ex-boyfriend would have admitted to doing it." (White 18-year-old victim of intimate partner rape)
- "I wish my friends would have acknowledged it as rape instead of something bad that happened." (17-year-old White survivor of date rape)
- "I wish the [rapist] would have apologized or at least understood my side. What hurts most with this experience is that he didn't even acknowledge me as a person, just as a sexual object." (38-year-old Native American victim of acquaintance rape)

TABLE 4.3
Social Reactions That Survivors Wish They Had Received

Social reaction	Sample quotes from survivors
Offender admit rape	"I wished the guy who did this would have not done it to begin with and would stop making excuses about why it happened."
Offender apologize	"I wish he had apologized or at least admitted he had no right to do it."
Emotional support	"I wish my mom would have hugged me, kissed me, talked about it."
	"I wish my boyfriend would have comforted me and held me."
Belief/validation	"I wished someone would have confirmed my feelings that I had been raped and this was wrong, regardless of the fact that I knew the person and let him in my house."
	"I wish my mother had believed me."
Tangible aid	"I wish my mother had guided me to the police, a doctor and simply hugged me and asked me if I was okay."

CONCLUSION

Victims who disclose a sexual assault to others experience various negative and positive social reactions. These reactions are distinct from general measures of social support, and negative reactions probably emanate from social norms that blame victims for sexual assaults (Berkowitz, 2002, in press). Although negative responses to victims of rape, such as blame, have been long recognized in the field (Symonds, 1980), research assessing these reactions in studies of the aftermath of sexual assault has been more recent (Ullman, 2000). This growing body of research shows that social reactions may be important for survivors' recovery. Furthermore, social reactions may also be an important target of interventions aimed at social networks and formal support providers who are often important sources of help following assault.

Positive reactions of emotional support, tangible aid, and information support are helpful to survivors whether they come from formal or informal support providers. In contrast, negative reactions of blame, disbelief, and control are harmful from either source and may silence survivors and thwart help-seeking. Support sources must attempt to minimize their negative responses to victims and maximize positive responses to aid survivors' recovery.

There may be unique effects of specific reactions from different support sources. Circumstances under which specific reactions are perceived positively or negatively by different subgroups of survivors need to be studied further. Given how uniquely helpful some informal sources are, such as female friends, and the fact that most victims who disclose tell informal sources (two thirds), educating the general public about how to respond supportively to victims of rape is important. In addition, formal support providers (police, medical, and other providers) should be given advice about what is helpful and what is harmful when responding to victims. Although formal support providers may be unable to respond to rape optimally because of the demands of their jobs and organizations (Martin, 2005), they could still provide information to victims' informal network members when possible about how they can be of help, in addition to providing referrals to victim advocates and/or counseling.

Finally, much more research is needed to better understand racial/ethnic, culture, and social class differences in social reactions and their effects on recovery. Such information must be integrated into services and interventions in ways that address the unique needs of different survivor subpopulations.

5

ADVOCATES' AND CLINICIANS' EXPERIENCES HELPING SURVIVORS

Because social reactions to disclosure can have a significant effect on survivors of sexual assault, it is important to consider support providers' experiences hearing about and attempting to help them. It can be stressful for people to hear traumatic disclosures, and there is a ripple effect of trauma on persons surrounding the survivor (Figley, 1995). To help support providers better assist survivors, we must understand what the disclosure means to the support provider, how it makes him or her feel, and how support providers can be helped to deal with their own reactions.

Formal sources of support in particular can play key roles and should help survivors access resources; respond empathically; support survivors' seeking safety and reestablishment of control; and, it is hoped, mitigate the effects of trauma (Najavits, 2002). If a support person has a negative personal reaction to hearing about the assault, it will be difficult for her or him to provide emotional support, and he or she will probably be more likely to react to the survivor in negative ways. This problem entails not only purposeful negative reactions, such as judging the victim or overt victim-blaming statements, but also unintentional negative reactions and, to the extent that lack of positive reactions is perceived as a negative response, the inability to provide positive reactions. For example, if the support provider feels overwhelmed or frightened by what is said, he or she may not want to hear more about the assault. This may lead the support person to discourage and/or minimize the disclosure as a way of escaping her or his own feelings. However, support providers without training about sexual assault may also simply not know what constitutes an appropriate response, especially if they lack experience or training in dealing with this sensitive issue. Finally, support professionals may be thwarted in their attempts to help survivors when social systems intended to help victims gain access to services are unresponsive or revictimizing.

In this chapter, I first review the literature on the experiences of informal and formal support providers trying to help victims of sexual assault. This review focuses on the experience of secondary traumatic stress as well as its effect on providers' ability to be supportive to the victim. In the remaining sections of the chapter, I discuss a qualitative research study in which I interviewed 30 rape victim advocates from rape crisis centers and clinicians from rape crisis and other professional settings in the Chicago area. I use the words *clinician* and *mental health professional* interchangeably in this chapter, but some of the survivors whom I quote also used the term *therapist*. In-depth findings from the interviews, with extensive quotations from participants, are provided, covering topics such as the barriers the advocates face in helping victims of rape, strategies they use to cope with secondary traumatic stress, and rewards of helping victims of rape (see chap. 6, this volume, for a review of ethical considerations and precautions to avoid vicarious trauma and secondary traumatic stress in trauma research interviews).

SECONDARY TRAUMATIC STRESS, VICARIOUS TRAUMA, AND THEIR EFFECT ON SUPPORT PROVIDERS

Hearing about trauma may be distressing to the listener, especially if he or she is close to or similar to the victim. This may lead the listener to engage in cognitive strategies to minimize this threat (Taylor, 1983). For example, a female friend may feel threatened if her friend discloses a sexual assault due to her similarity to the victim and the realization that this could have happened to her. This may lead her to try to think about how she differs personally and behaviorally from her friend in order to maintain a belief that she would not have been assaulted. Supporters' assumptions about safety and the goodness of oneself, other people, and the world may be threatened when they hear about sexual assault, and this threat may lead to distress or symptoms of vicarious trauma or secondary traumatic stress (Janoff-Bulman, 1992).

Researchers recognize that there is some overlap between the concepts of *vicarious trauma* and *secondary traumatic stress* (Janoff-Bulman, 1992), but individuals who work with trauma victims typically experience both (Pearlman & Mac Ian, 1995). Vicarious trauma focuses on how cognitive schemas (e.g., basic beliefs) of trauma workers can be affected by exposure to other peoples' traumatic experiences. This occurs when empathic engagement with clients and exposure to traumatic material results in disruption of workers' basic beliefs about the self, others, and the world (McCann & Pearlman, 1990; Sabin-Farrell & Turpin, 2003). Secondary traumatic stress symptoms parallel some of the symptoms of posttraumatic stress disorder (PTSD) or acute stress disorder (e.g., reexperiencing, numbing, hyperarousal) listed in the *Diagnostic and Statistical Manual of Mental Disorders* (American Psychiatric Association, 1994), but they result from secondary exposure to another person's trauma, not one's primary trauma experience (Figley, 1995; McCann & Pearlman, 1990). Many studies have documented the prevalence of both vicarious trauma and secondary trauma among informal and formal support providers. In the following sections, I discuss these studies, along with the effects of vicarious and secondary trauma on providers' ability to support the victim.

Informal Support Providers

Early studies addressed the general supportiveness of informal social networks, including partners, in relationship to trauma of female victims of rape (Atkeson, Calhoun, Resick, & Ellis, 1982; Burgess & Holmstrom, 1978; Moss, Frank, & Anderson, 1990; Popiel & Susskind, 1985; Ruch & Chandler, 1983; Sales, Baum, & Shore, 1984). However, these studies were of small, selective samples (often rape crisis center clients) with limited assessments of social support, and they yielded mixed results (for a review, see Ullman, 1999).

In R. C. Davis, Taylor, and Bench's (1995) groundbreaking study of victims and their support networks, 138 significant others (e.g., romantic partners) of victims of sexual assault and victims of nonsexual assault were interviewed. Distress experienced by significant others did not vary according to victim distress or the type of assault. Female significant others experienced more fear of crime than male significant others. Fortunately, higher levels of significant-other distress did not interfere with their ability to engage in supportive actions. However, significant-other distress was also associated with higher levels of unsupportive behavior toward victims. For example, distress led helpers to engage in negative responses, such as judging the victim, acting uncomfortably around her, or distancing themselves from her. Despite this, they were still able to provide positive forms of support, such as information support or tangible aid after an assault. In addition, greater unsupportive behavior was more likely among significant others of victims of sexual assault than significant others of victims of nonsexual assault. Romantic partners also engaged in more unsupportive behavior than other family members or friends. Davis and colleagues interpreted this finding as being due to the greater psychological distress experienced by victims' romantic partners as compared with family members. Romantic partners may be less able to respond supportively because their own negative emotional reactions to their partners' victimization lead them to respond with negative reactions.

These results are important because they suggest that sexual assault not only affects significant others' mental health but also leads them to engage in more unsupportive behavior, such as egocentric responses, emotional withdrawal, and blaming the victim. The fact that distress did not interfere with significant others' supportive behavior toward victims is encouraging. These results are still troublesome, however, because other research on victims shows that negative social reactions survivors receive from others are related to worse psychological functioning, whereas positive reactions have nonsignificant effects (Andrews, Brewin, & Rose, 2003; R. C. Davis, Brickman, & Baker, 1991; Ullman, 1996a, 2000). This implies that reducing negative reactions may be more important than increasing positive ones to enhance survivors' recovery.

In another study, Dunn, Vail-Smith, and Knight (1999) asked college students about their experiences of hearing about an assault that victims of sexual assault had disclosed to them. In most cases, friends or romantic partners were the ones who disclosed sexual assault to the students. Disclosures occurred in a number of contexts, including within trusting, intimate relationships and during conversations, some of which were casual. Other in-depth disclosures occurred in the context of conversations about relationships, sex, rape, and other problems. Sometimes disclosures occurred while victims were drunk and recalling past experiences in social situations. They also occurred when victims sought support or demonstrated need; were trying to warn someone about or prevent someone from being victimized; or were responding to questions about their own behavior, such as emotional distress or unusual behavior. Students reported responding with supportive reactions to these disclosures overall.

In Ahrens and Campbell's (2000) study of 60 friends of college victims of rape, friends reported reacting positively to survivors' disclosures of rape, did not blame the victim, were not distressed, felt their helping efforts were effective, and believed their friendships grew closer. Despite these positive findings, Ahrens and Campbell found that specific factors were associated with how friends experienced the disclosures and with changes in their relationships with survivors. These factors were gender, the friend's own victimization history, and length of the friendship. Compared with women, men blamed the survivor more; felt more confused, more ineffective, and less empathic; and reported more negative and fewer positive changes in the friendship. Friends with their own past assault histories expected the assault to have a greater immediate impact on their friend, blamed the friend less, and reported more positive and fewer negative changes in the friendship than friends without assault histories.

Finally, friends who had been in the friendship with the victim for more than 5 years experienced more positive and fewer negative changes in the way they thought about the relationship and in how they interacted with the survivor.

Ahrens and Campbell (2000) also uncovered three distinct patterns of helping experiences: (a) *positive helping experiences* (i.e., feeling good about helping), which led to positive changes in the friendship; (b) *neutral helping experiences*, which led to no changes; and (c) *negative helping experiences*, which led to negative changes in the friendship. Positive helping experiences were more common for friends who felt more understanding about the impact of sexual assault, more empathy, and more validation and who reported less blaming of the victim, confusion, ineffectiveness, and fewer negative relationship changes. Neutral helping experiences (e.g., those that did not change the friendship and were appraised as moderately positive for the helper) were related to low levels of confusion, ineffectiveness, and distress and a moderate level of validating emotions for friends. Finally, negative helping experiences (e.g., when friends did not feel good about helping and negative changes occurred in the friendship) were related to friends' reports of strong emotions such as rage at the perpetrator, distress, and a sense of ineffectiveness at helping. In these cases, friends appeared to be caught up in their own emotional reactions to the assault and did not know how to respond or acted out negatively toward the survivor.

Another recent study of 1,241 undergraduates showed that 1 in 3 female students and 1 in 5 male students had been told by a friend they were a victim of an unwanted sexual experience (Banyard, Moynihan, Walsh, Cohn, & Ward, 2009). The authors found gender differences in students' responses to victims' disclosures: Compared with men who had been told about an assault, women reported more emotional distress in response to a friend's disclosure, greater positive responses to disclosure, and less perceived confusion and ineffectiveness about what to do.

Several recent qualitative studies have illuminated the impact of sexual assault on women's romantic partners and husbands. These studies also have examined the factors affecting their partners' responses to victims following assault and have yielded insights that may help advocates and clinicians better understand men's experiences of giving support and how their reactions to the rape affect their ability to support their partner. For example, Connop and Petrak (2004) conducted qualitative interviews with six men whose female partners had been sexually assaulted. They found that men who drew on rape myths to explain the assault were more likely to respond with anger and blame toward their partners. Men also reported feeling exhausted and burdened by their role of supporting their partner and putting her needs first. This study also showed that some of the psychosexual problems of male partners identified in past research (e.g., J. V. Becker, Skinner, Abel, Axelrod, & Cichon, 1984) might relate to the meaning of the assault for the man. Connop and Petrak found that in some cases men's views of sex changed after the assault because they felt discomfort with their own sexuality as they were forced to reconsider potentially coercive aspects of their sexual behavior with women. This study suggested the need to look at the impact of rape on both the victim and her partner to effectively address support and recovery of survivors, which often take place in the context of relationships. M. E. Smith (2005) interviewed 5 men whose female partners had been sexually assaulted and found effects on male partners in the areas of immediate painful thoughts and feelings, relationship with the victim, views about male attitudes, and long-term effects of trauma. Smith noted many effects of rape on male partners that were similar to those reported by victims of rape, such as depression, guilt, self-blame, loss of trust, withdrawal from others, sleep disturbances, and PTSD symptoms. One of the most serious effects of rape revealed in these studies is the dissolution of some relationships following rape because of the stress of the assault on one or both partners. An added problem was that men often did not feel able or willing to talk to their friends or seek help from rape crisis centers (Brookings, McEvoy, & Reed, 1994), which made it more difficult for them to deal with the impact of the assault on themselves and their partners (M. E. Smith, 2005).

In summary, studies of informal support providers show that they are often recipients of sexual assault disclosures (at least in college samples, which are the most often studied) and are helpful to survivors of sexual assault, especially if they are female and friends as opposed to male and significant others, respectively. This is perhaps due to the greater identification of women with victims of sexual assault, which may lead them to be more supportive, whereas men may be more likely to respond negatively, perhaps because of their greater rape myth acceptance. Also, women say they know more about how to respond to victim disclosures than do men, which may make them better helpers. However, female helpers experience greater secondary trauma than men in response to victims, perhaps because of their greater identification with victims, which is due to their shared greater vulnerability to sexual assault than is likely the case for men. Distress is particularly common among significant others of victims, and this distress can lead to negative social reactions, despite the fact that it does not preclude significant others from also responding with positive reactions to survivors. Thus, both female and male informal network members of victims may need information and emotional support of their own to effectively respond to survivors' disclosures and to take care of themselves and deal with their own reactions to the experience of providing help.

Formal Support Providers

Professional helpers' experiences working with victims of sexual assault have been studied more extensively than those of informal support sources.

Their relationships with survivors may be less intense because they are not in the close social network that has daily contact with victims. Still, the kinds of survivors with whom they come into contact may be harder to deal with, because more symptomatic victims may seek help from mental health professionals. In addition, victims who are in crisis soon after an assault are more likely to seek help from rape crisis centers. Thus, professional helpers, although more distanced in their relationships with survivors than family, partners, and friends, may face a more traumatized victim population overall.

Up to 50% of advocates and trauma clinicians report symptoms of anger and fear (Wasco & Campbell, 2002). In addition, secondary trauma affects clinicians and advocates who work with survivors (e.g., Baird & Jenkins, 2003; Schauben & Frazier, 1995) and may also emotionally affect nurses (Alexander et al., 1989; DiVasto et al., 1980) and other individuals who work with crime victims (for a review, see Salston & Figley, 2003). For example, Schauben and Frazier (1995) found that female mental health professionals who worked with survivors of sexual assault reported both vicarious trauma and secondary trauma symptoms (e.g., anxiety) from hearing violent details from their clients, continued client victimization over the course of therapy, and extreme client behaviors (e.g., emotional outbursts, trembling).

Salston and Figley (2003) recently reviewed studies on secondary traumatic stress in professionals who work with survivors of criminal victimization. They identified a personal history of trauma, trauma-specific training, and interpersonal resources of the worker as factors that mitigate the development of secondary traumatic stress, but evidence about the effect of personal trauma history was mixed. A number of studies have examined factors related to risk of negative impacts (e.g., secondary traumatic stress, vicarious trauma) on professionals' working with victims of sexual assault specifically.

Research shows that various factors affect the level of trauma symptoms among trauma workers, including age, tenure at work/training, victimization history, client caseload, and social support (Baird & Jenkins, 2003; Ghahramanlou & Brodbeck, 2000; Schauben & Frazier, 1995). Several newer studies suggest that less time working in the field and trauma history may be risk factors for developing secondary traumatic stress in professionals who work with survivors of sexual violence (K. B. Adams, Matto, & Harrington, 2001; Baird & Jenkins, 2003). Baird and Jenkins (2003) studied 99 sexual assault and domestic violence clinicians and found that those with trauma histories had more *compassion fatigue*: a gradual lessening of compassion over time; it is common among victims of trauma and individuals who work directly with victims of trauma. Sufferers can exhibit several symptoms, including hopelessness, a decrease in experiences of pleasure, constant stress and anxiety, and a pervasive negative attitude. This can have detrimental effects on individuals, both professionally and personally, including a decrease in productivity, the inability to focus, and the development of new feelings of incompetency and self-doubt (Beaton & Murphy, 1995). The trauma workers with trauma histories did not have more disrupted beliefs or burnout (e.g., long-term exhaustion and diminished interest), however, than those without trauma histories. K. B. Adams and colleagues (2001) studied 185 social workers and found that younger age, lower salary, lower support from friends, somatic symptoms, and burnout were related to more disrupted beliefs (e.g., beliefs that the world is not safe, that other people are untrustworthy); however, clinicians' personal histories of trauma did not relate to more disrupted beliefs.

It appears that working with trauma survivors has an impact on professionals, although the effects may not be present in all domains. This is an area in need of further research. The studies just discussed are useful in that they provide a quantitative assessment of vicarious trauma and secondary traumatic stress in relationship to various risk factors. However, qualitative data are also needed from these trauma workers to understand how their work with survivors is affected by the contexts of their work in their agencies and with other institutions. Qualitative interviews with eight advocates showed that fear and anger were common responses to rape crisis work (Wasco & Campbell, 2002) and that most of these reactions were attributed to extra-individual, system-level factors (e.g., institutions, societal issues), not individual factors (e.g., individual or characteristic of a person). This work suggests that more research is needed on how the context of rape crisis work and larger institutional and societal factors are related to both social reactions made to victims and vicarious trauma symptoms of workers. In the remaining sections of this chapter, I describe one such study in detail.

BARRIERS TO SUPPORT PROVIDERS

In this section, I discuss the barriers faced by rape crisis center advocates and clinicians who work with survivors in rape crisis centers and other settings, as revealed in interviews I conducted over a yearlong study (Ullman & Townsend, 2007, 2008). (For a detailed description of the Mental Health Provider Interview Study design, see the Introduction, this volume.)

Advocates and *clinicians* differ in their roles and training. A main function of advocates is to work on behalf of survivors to ensure that their rights are respected and that they receive all of the assistance to which they are entitled, including emotional, medical, and legal assistance. Advocates come from a variety of educational backgrounds and may or may not have psychological training in identifying and dealing with secondary traumatic stress and vicarious trauma; however, they typically do have specialized training in sexual assault issues and have chosen to work with this population specifically as their life's work.

Licensed mental health clinicians, in contrast, work with clients to help them with psychological problems and life stressors. Although some specialize in sexual assault/trauma issues, many do not. Despite this, most will encounter victims of sexual assault in various practice settings. Their experiences and training in this area may vary widely and affect how well they can deal with survivors. Unlike advocates, mental health professionals (except trauma specialists) typically do not have specialized training in sexual assault issues and have not necessarily chosen to work with this population specifically as their life's work. Unlike other professionals who may encounter victims of sexual assault, clinicians should help survivors deal with the impact of victimization. The clinicians in the interview study conducted counseling and therapy with survivors of rape in settings quite different from the settings in which advocates work. Because of the differences between advocates and clinicians, I discuss each perspective separately.

Advocates' Perspective

Secondary Victimization of Survivors

A major barrier mentioned by 72% of those interviewed was that survivors experience negative or revictimizing reactions, such as being blamed or disbelieved when telling other people about the assault or seeking formal services. In the advocate and clinician interview study, one advocate made the following statement:

> You (the victim of rape) have to deal with your friends not believing you, your family not believing you, your partner not believing you, institutions set up against you. You have to put yourself out there to get evidence taken from your body, from your pubic hair, from your anal area—it's just about being revictimized over and over. (27-year-old White medical advocate)

Hospitals were frequently cited as a common first contact for survivors and as a place where they may face unpredictable responses:

- "There are certain hospitals in this city that are wonderful. I mean I haven't dealt with very many yet, but I've heard the stories. I mean there are certain ERs that if I had a friend that was raped, I would probably send them to that ER first, even if it was 5 miles out of the way because their staff is compassionate, they're prepared to deal with this issue, they just take a good approach to it. And then you have other hospitals—it just depends on the luck of the draw. I mean if you've got a physician that's tired or cranky or doesn't want to deal with this or feels like this person has lied or the victim happens to be a prostitute." (26-year-old White advocate working in a rape crisis center)

- "Certainly one of the barriers is how people treat people who've been sexually assaulted and all the myths that they come to the table with. If the victim's first interaction with whomever they're disclosing to is negative, then that could sort of stop them from seeking other help. If their first contact is the hospital ER and a nurse or a doctor is rude or inappropriate or doesn't believe them, that could just end it right there. They're not gonna want to get help in any other way, they'll forget it, not want to tell anybody else feeling that no one will believe me. If it's the police who respond negatively initially, maybe they won't go on to get medical help. That's a huge barrier." (37-year-old mixed-race advocate working currently as an administrator)

- "When you do encourage survivors to get help, you're sort of sending them into the lion's den almost. I mean this is a scary thing to go to the hospital and it's kind of a gamble, whether or not the experience is going to go well. It's even worse to have your case taken into the legal system and frankly, I don't know. If I were raped right now, I don't know if I would go to the hospital. I certainly would not prosecute and there's no way I would go to court. So I was beginning to feel while I was [at the agency] even—how can I be doing this work, telling people what they should do with their case when I wouldn't do it myself?" (27-year-old White ex-advocate)

- "A lot of times [formal support sources] don't say things in front of the [victims]. But, out of the room, nurses and law enforcement would make comments to me that always are out of line, they say too much to me and that's when I get really frustrated. It happens a lot of times where nurses are revictimizing my clients, saying, 'Girl, what are you thinking? What were you doing like at 9 o'clock at night up there?'" (31-year-old Latina advocate)

These negative reactions to victims by the medical system make it difficult for advocates because they often are unable to protect survivors from further trauma following the rape. Because victims need these systems' services, and because advocates have less power than medical personnel, advocates are put in a bind if they try to confront personnel who are demonstrating negative reactions to victims. Advocates have to work with service providers on an ongoing basis, and although they may try to educate those service providers as best they can, they must walk a fine line in doing so or they might receive defensive reactions and hostility from these personnel. Even worse, providers' hostility may be taken out on survivors, who may subsequently be treated even more poorly. This problem clearly adds to advocates' burden, because they have to try to support survivors regarding not only the rape and its effects but also the revictimization they are experiencing from system personnel. Because of the problems of secondary victimization within the medical system, advocates also suggested that training of medical personnel was needed. However, pointing this out to those providers often led to anger or denial by personnel who did not appreciate advocates' viewpoints about system responses to survivors. One advocate made the following statement:

> I mean the hospital situation could also be equally frustrating with people, not really knowing how to do exams very well and doctors and nurses that just weren't really trained in how to do these things and didn't really have the bedside manner that we would have liked. We have contracts with various hospitals and we would try to go into hospitals and do trainings with folks in ERs and not only is it hard to do trainings, but when you get there, they're like, "We know how to do our job, we don't need you people having to tell us how to do our jobs." And we would say "Well, actually, we have all these cases where evidence was tampered with or a client is saying that this happened. That shouldn't have happened." So we knew that stuff was happening, and that was often frustrating too. (27-year-old White ex-advocate)

As a consequence of these attitudes, advocates are often unable to effectively ensure that victims' rights are fulfilled and that they get appropriate medical care and proper collection of forensic evidence in the rape kit (a set of items used by medical personnel for gathering and preserving physical evidence following a sexual assault). This inability to fulfill their goals as advocates, termed *mission failure* by Beaton and Murphy (1995), may be associated with greater risk of secondary traumatic stress; specifically, when advocates are blocked by institutional barriers of medical or other systems they may feel a sense of role stress induced when they are undermined in their efforts to carry out tasks for which they are trained.

The legal and criminal justice systems were also identified as sources of secondary victimization for survivors. Advocates have made the following statements:

- "I think another huge barrier is just the mythology that's out there and is so pervasive. Victim blame is, in my perception, the number one barrier to prosecution that victims face. If they're willing and want to prosecute, what law enforcement looks at primarily is how credible is this person and how credible is their story? Because if they're not credible, this isn't going to stand up in court and we don't want to take it. And there are 101 billion ways to discredit somebody and I've seen and heard them all.

What we know is that people are targeted [for rape] because of their vulnerability and their inability to be credible or tell the story in the way that law enforcement needs it to be told." (27-year-old White advocate)

- "I get very frustrated with felony review in the state's attorney's office in the sense that unless there is a statement from the offender, we can't charge this individual. The system doesn't like to give options. I've been in with state's attorneys who want the case to go a certain way and they don't give victims all their options and that is one of my jobs—to make sure they're aware of all their options. But, sometimes that doesn't sit well with the state's attorney's office." (46-year-old White legal advocate)

- "I promised her that she doesn't have to see [the offender]. She didn't want to press charges, she didn't want him in her life. They had already put him out of the house. He had snuck in. We go to the police station, there's a woman detective who I already knew, I had a history with her, and she was awful, awful. She questioned the [survivor] in the same room with the suspect handcuffed to a piece of wood on the wall. So we're at the other end of this conference table and he's right there the whole time. It was so unnecessarily abusive." (32-year-old Black ex-advocate)

- "The court system is really awful. If you get a good state's attorney, and there are some out there, that's fine. But most of the time and especially with sexual assault, they don't want to deal with it. We've been training people in the state's attorney's office, but they didn't even want to sit through the training." (41-year-old White advocate)

- "We still have a system where it's extremely tough for women to come out and allege a rape, let alone go through the process of a trial . . . I understand the profound expectations people have when they press charges and I know 9 times out of 10 it'll be plea-bargained out and you don't get your moment in court. If it does go to trial, you don't ever get to tell your story the way you want to, so I think expectations women have of what it means to go to court are derived from our popular cultural ideal of standing up in court, pointing at somebody and saying 'He raped me' and that of course does not happen. I've said, you know your job as a survivor now is to get stronger and here are all the different options you can use to get stronger. Don't let anybody tell you that the only way to get stronger is through the legal system, 'cause it will probably not be the result. So, I'm much more brutally honest with them and I think there's a lot of advocates who kind of feed into the mythology of what it means to press charges and that you have to press charges to get rapists off the streets. We're not getting them off the street! If we do get them off the street, it will be for 5 to 6 months and from what I've seen, chances are if a man rapes women, he is either going to participate as a rapist or be victimized by sexual assault in jail. When he gets back on the street, he's a much more dangerous rapist than he was before. I have no faith in the legal system to solve this issue." (31-year-old multiracial ex-advocate)

Secondary victimization from police and legal personnel makes it difficult for advocates to help survivors get any kind of real justice or accountability from the criminal justice system. Advocates can try to support survivors who choose to pursue a criminal case by helping to keep them informed about their case and going to court with them; however, they have little control over whether a case will be deemed credible and worthy of the prosecutor's time and effort in the first place. Police may also treat survivors poorly, violate their rights, and retraumatize them when they perceive that certain survivors are less valued by society, such as young women of color. This makes it extremely difficult for advocates, whose goal is to try to empower survivors within an inherently antivictim criminal justice system.

Secondary Traumatic Stress

In addition to feeling frustrated by medical and legal providers' insensitivity to victims of rape, advocates often experience secondary traumatic stress as a result of working with victims of rape. Drug-involved women were one example given of those who were distressing:

> I had a survivor that I was treating. I started treatment with her, she's living on an inpatient, rehabilitation drug unit, and I don't believe she was court-ordered to treatment. I started seeing her and her story was very traumatic, and very distressing to me personally with the transference and countertransference. (32-year-old White ex-advocate)

Although this advocate did not explain the details of how the survivor's story affected her, she clearly had strong emotional reactions to this drug-involved client. The client may have threatened some of her feelings of safety and/or control and caused her distress, which in turn made it hard for her to deal with her client. This may have led her to be less able to give support to the client because she was caught up in her own reactions. At worst, she may have responded in negative ways by pathologizing or patronizing the survivor.

Another advocate described a life-threatening ER call with a victim of aggravated rape whom she supported in the hospital shortly after her rape:

> When I first left the hospital, I had been up for a day and a half. I was on that case for 13.5 hours. And there was no one, I had to be completely on the ball at all times. She was in and out of consciousness, so I was up and talking to her the entire time running on adrenalin and when I left the hospital I don't have a lot of memory of driving home, cause I was in almost a state of shock by myself, and was shaking, and I had to take a day off to come down off all the adrenalin as well as the shock and the seriousness of the case, but it was well worth it and I would do it again in a heartbeat to know that I helped save somebody's life. Then to hear that she was doing well even 3 months later was incredible too. (27-year-old White advocate)

This case was psychologically and physically traumatizing for this advocate, who was a veteran in the field and was describing one of the most extreme cases she had encountered in her work.

Stress Related to the Social Service Agency

Although most of the advocates' frustration centered on the criminal justice and medical systems, the advocates also mentioned stressors related to the bureaucratic requirements of funders and treatment by their own agencies (e.g., lack of supervision, downtime). All of these factors were mentioned as leading to feelings of distress, burnout, and eventually leaving their agencies:

> I really think that the reason that the turnover rate is so high in social service organizations is actually because everybody who works there is doing everything that they can do and giving everything. But when it goes beyond you, it's really frustrating, because we can't do anything and it's frustrating to see a survivor have to deal with the system when they can't do anything about it and you can't do anything about it! (23-year-old Black legal advocate)

The lack of support for front-line service workers leads to less than ideal support for survivors:

> [Advocates] really need to be taken care of or they won't be able to do it in an effective way. In order to work with survivors in a way that's going to really help them, rape crisis workers need to feel really supported in their work or else it's not going to trickle down. (27-year-old White ex-advocate)

Difficult Survivors

One final barrier for advocates was dealing with isolated cases of difficult survivors (e.g., those who were on drugs, took out their anger on the advocates, or asked advocates to give them money or do illegal things for them). Such experiences were very hard for advocates emotionally and prevented them from giving survivors adequate support. One advocate provided her own explanation:

> I did have one person who I was working with who yelled. She didn't know how to communicate without yelling, and so she would call screaming at me. I would say, "You know, I'm sorry but I can't help you if you continue to yell at me. I know that you're angry, you should be angry, it's fine for you to be angry, but I just don't know how to help you unless we can talk about what your needs are." I would say that was very hard because the yelling never stopped, but I know that she was angry and frustrated, and so I don't hold that against her or anything. (27-year-old White advocate)

Societal Attitudes About Rape

Barriers to service provision exist within a larger societal context. At the macro level, it is important to consider how societal attitudes may be reflected in the responses that institutions make to survivors of rape. Some advocates (36%) spoke about attitudes toward rape manifested in system responses that interfered with advocacy. For example, one advocate discussed the larger barrier of societal denial of the problem of rape:

> We still haven't reached a point in our society where you can even acknowledge this problem for what it is and that's why people can't get over it. I don't care if [survivors are] sitting in an office an hour a week and somebody says "Yes you have a right to all these feelings," everything else in the world tells them that they don't. Until we acknowledge that, that's never going to happen! (32-year-old Black ex-advocate)

Societal Biases: Racism, Classism, and Other Biases

Race and class biases are also societal barriers reflected in organizations, including rape crisis centers and in institutions that respond to survivors' needs. These types of biases were noted by 56% of participants. Advocates have made the following statements:

- "So it's all based on the story that night. How credible is the witness? the victim? How credible is the perp? Well, you know racism plays into the account, classism plays into the account. I mean you name it, and it's there. Sexism plays a role, too." (27-year-old White advocate)
- "There's always this doubt. I've never heard a person who wasn't 'of color' told, 'Well, you can take it back if you want, you know if you tell me that you made it up, then we'll let you

go if you try to press charges.' They bully young people and particularly young people of color by saying, 'I'm giving you a chance to take this back.' Police say 'I'm giving you a chance to tell me the truth . . . You can take it back now, but if we go through with this and we try and prosecute and we find out that you're lying, then you're going to go to jail,' you know? It's like a script. I haven't heard an older person told that. I've never heard a person who wasn't of color asked those things. And when I say older, I mean people in their 40s or 50s, unless there was a situation where maybe they were mentally ill or they were a substance abuser. It's always people who are disenfranchised in some form or fashion who are completely silent and not believed." (26-year-old Black advocate)

This advocate went on to explain the ways survivors are treated differently on the basis of gender and sexual orientation:

It's even sexist because male survivors are treated horribly. [Service agencies] don't even take it seriously and act like they deserve it. The impression I've gotten is not as if [the agencies are] saying that it didn't happen, it was just that [the survivors] deserved it or they must have been doing something to condone it or they must be homosexual so it's because of their lifestyle. I've seen survivors who were not homosexual openly say, "Well you know, I'm not gay, but all the questioning was geared around that": "Did you know the guy, were you in a relationship with him?" Why does that matter so? People still have in their minds what the ideal rape victim looks like, behaves like, what type of lifestyle they have. It's amazing to me that we haven't gotten past that. I think it's partly the media and it's partly about just wanting to remain in your comfort zone.

Another advocate spoke of problems that survivors with disabilities and immigrants have in getting appropriate responses from service systems:

I think the hardest work that I've done is with people with any type of disability and with [elderly] people and not because they put up a barrier. It's hard also to work with people with mental illness because it's hard to work with them, and it's hard to make the system to understand them and respect them and their rights. It's also hard with immigrants for the same reason and because law enforcement doesn't cooperate with them and thinks what they're saying or what they think is because of their ethnicity. (31-year-old Latina advocate)

It is clear that these attitudes make it even more difficult for advocates to help survivors from marginalized groups who experience multiple sources of stigmatization and devaluation in the eyes of social institutions that deal with victims of rape. First, it is painful to witness unnecessary compounding of rape trauma in victims who face racist, heterosexist, or other biases in social systems such as criminal justice, medical, and mental health providers. Second, advocates may literally face a much tougher challenge in advocating for these victims, because they are viewed as less legitimate by society. Such victims may face a greater uphill battle in getting services they need from criminal justice and medical systems. Third, advocates who are also members of discriminated groups may experience secondary trauma in advocating for such victims when observing how poorly they are treated. Advocates may be more likely to identify with these survivors and feel that the secondary victimization of these victims is also an indirect assault on themselves. Negative social attitudes not only decrease advocates' likelihood of providing positive reactions but also increase advocates' likelihood of responding with negative reactions.

Racism in Rape Crisis Centers

Racism, in particular, is an issue that has been critically important in the contemporary women's movement in general and specifically in relation to the issue of rape and rape crisis centers (Campbell, Wasco, Ahrens, Sefl, & Barnes, 2001; Matthews, 1994; Scott, 1998). Racism is an issue that must be confronted not only in the broader society but also within rape crisis centers themselves. If left unaddressed, it undermines an agency's ability to provide quality services to survivors of color and replicates the dynamics of oppression related to the cultural causes of violence against women. Racism has an impact on survivors who may not seek services they perceive to be "White" or that they find unhelpful or insensitive to their needs. Racism may also affect sexual assault workers who have to cope with racist organizational practices, lack of trust, and perceived insensitive treatment in the workplace. Racism is part of the "rape culture" that spawns rape (Buchwald, Fletcher, & Roth, 1993). People's responses to rape are also colored by the racism in society at large and its institutions. Racism was spontaneously noted to be a problem in rape crisis organizations by 24% of advocates and ex-advocates in the interview study: "I think the whole rape crisis center thing is still a 'White feminist' women's movement thing and I think it's still painfully obvious. Especially at a center like X, which for the most part is White women" (27-year-old White ex-advocate). Another advocate stated that her organization tried to be nonracist by sponsoring events related to women of color; however, she felt that that action was not tantamount to doing a thorough critical self-examination and effort to be truly nonracist in everyday organizational practices: "We just had this event focused on women of color, which I think is good, but I think in some way it's almost like, we're not racist, we did that event!" (27-year-old White advocate). Another advocate discussed a systemic issue that she perceived affected workers in her satellite office. The workers all happened to be women of color and were treated with distrust by the manager at the main office of the organization, who was White:

> There was, in my mind, a ridiculous conflict with our manager, who had a basic lack of trust in people in our office, many of whom had had conflicts with her in the past. A lot of us perceived that this was related to the fact that everyone who worked in our office was a person of color. (27-year-old Asian ex-advocate)

Another, more structural manifestation of racism was the geographic distribution of services, which resulted in disproportionately poorer access to rape crisis services for women living in predominantly ethnic minority neighborhoods. This pattern of services was coupled with culturally insensitive, racist attitudes of White women staffing downtown and north side agencies:

> Downtown and the north side is [sic] where most services are! There are less on south side, yet huge populations reside there. There are not enough funds to publicize resources or to understand what people want or need. Many White feminists in the field who are college educated need to not "pooh-pooh" religion. We don't understand different cultural responses. (28-year-old White advocate)

A former advocate who was an administrator and worked for many years in the rape crisis movement explained the larger context of racism in rape crisis centers:

> The civil rights movement and the feminist movement really were on parallel but unconnected charts, whether it's the [National Association for the Advancement of Colored People] or the Urban League and the victims' organizations. Different institutions came out of the civil rights movement and civil rights history and then there's sexual assault and domestic violence that really came out of the feminist movement. So now you've got these organizations that are trying to go back and deal with some of these issues. Because they were segregationist in their thinking, which translated into a lot of segregation in their practices. They're trying to heal some of that, but a lot of Black women in their communities don't want to have anything to do with you, because they say: You have not been here for us when we needed you. (31-year-old multiracial ex-advocate and rape crisis center administrator)

The issue of racism was not mentioned by the majority of advocates in terms of how they were treated by rape crisis centers or as a barrier to their work with survivors; however, racism was mentioned as a problem by several women, both White and women of color. Specifically, they cited racist practices in the location of their services, in the racial/ethnic makeup of their leadership and staff, and in their allocation of resources to work against sexual assault. This occurred despite the fact that no questions in the interview focused on this specific topic. This suggests that issues of racism are likely a concern for many advocates working in rape crisis centers. Racism may alienate women of color who are advocates and cause them job stress working at their organizations. This stress may lead to burnout for these workers and indirectly negatively impact their ability to help survivors. In fact, more than one advocate suggested that frustration with apparent racist practices in their agencies led them to feel demoralized and even to drop out of doing the work. It is unclear how widespread this problem is, but it clearly exists (Campbell & Martin, 2001; Matthews, 1994).

In summary, advocates may be hurried or stressed in their interactions with survivors because of their frustration. Advocates who are actually burned out and numb to the trauma simply may no longer be able to empathically engage if they are depleted from their experiences of secondary trauma and/or exhaustion from the work. Some survivors suggest that being given information by a stressed advocate was harmful to them. Advocates who left their jobs alluded to an inability to care about or respond to victims as a reason why they felt it was time to leave the work. More research is needed to show how and when advocates react negatively to victims, including individual, survivor, agency, and institutional factors, all of which may play important roles.

Unfair Criminal Justice System

As mentioned previously, advocates in the interview study expressed frustration with the tendency of the criminal justice system to revictimize victims of rape by providing unsupportive responses (e.g., victim blaming, disbelief). Overall, advocates' accounts suggest that negative social reactions are common responses of formal system agents to victims of rape.

It is likely, however, that at least some of these reactions are attributable to conflicts between the organizational goals of these systems and the victims' needs following assault (see Martin, 2005). In another interview study, Regehr and Alaggia (2006) compared the goals of criminal justice personnel with those of rape victim advocates; specifically, their interview research on the processing of sexual assaults in Canada showed that although advocates and clinicians hoped that participation in the system would help victims gain some control and alleviate their pain, legal personnel saw this as unrealistic and based on misinformation. Legal personnel argued that victims get caught in this disjuncture and may expect to be heard and feel better. Unfortunately, the victims find out that they are not heard in the legal system and lose more control and experience reactivation of the pain associated with their assaults. Clinicians and advocates in this study felt that judges, lawyers, and police need more training to make the court become more sympathetic to victims. Conversely, legal system personnel saw the system as focused on protection of defendants' rights and not a place that can be therapeutic for victims. In their view, the goals of the justice system would have to change for victims' experiences to improve. Regehr and Alaggia argued that clinicians and advocates should be educated about the cold, hard facts of the legal system so they do not mislead victims they encounter about what to expect from engaging in the criminal justice process. In addition, it may help to prepare victims as realistically as possible for dealing with their cases in the criminal justice system.

Indeed, research supports legal personnel's claim that the goal of the current criminal justice system is not victim support. Victims are largely ancillary to the traditional criminal justice process, and they are typically needed only as witnesses for the state. They are judged and treated with skepticism in a system that seeks to adjudicate rape cases and protect defendants' rights (Alderden, 2008). Such a focus leads defense attorneys, prosecutors, police, and other justice system agents to question the credibility and character of victims in the course of investigating, founding, and trying cases of sexual assault in criminal courts. Extralegal factors were found to play a major role in the process of unfounding sexual assault cases in a recent study in Chicago, and victim credibility (e.g., consistency of her story) was a significant factor in most stages of the decision-making process that frequently led to the weeding out of rape cases from the criminal justice process (Alderden, 2008).

Clinicians' Perspective

Barriers in Traditional Health Care Services

Like the advocates in our study, clinicians described external barriers in the way traditional health care services are organized that increasingly do not suit the needs of trauma survivors, as well as a mental illness–oriented focus in the treatment of trauma, as opposed to a mental injury focus, which some clinicians feel is more appropriate for survivors of sexual assault:

> I've had a number of clients who had to be in the hospital, they had psychotic symptoms, were put on oodles of medication, and for these clients in crisis, their options are really limited. The partial hospitalization programs are closing, they have reimbursement and resolution problems. The ones who are there and have been there are not trauma specific and don't necessarily have trauma clinicians and even if one had a trauma clinician it would be moot. I was the only trauma clinician. They have a mental illness program and not a mental injury focus. And it's not a great fit. I had a survivor call me on the phone recently saying, "I really need something more, my symptoms are getting out of control, there's gotta be a program in the area that treats trauma." (Middle-aged White social worker working in a private counseling agency)

In addition, this clinician described how many mental health professionals pathologize survivors of sexual assault in a way that those who have other physical/bodily accidents are not:

It's important that you don't pathologize somebody who broke her leg, but somebody who is sexually assaulted, they get pathologized in many ways and I think that we don't, as a larger profession, adequately see traumatic responses as reasonable reactions to what happened. I think we're trying to get there and I do I think that means a lot of important thinking in the trauma field, but there's still, and especially in mainstream medical and mental health settings, a lot of pathologizing, and the term *borderline* gets thrown about all over the place in this really pathologizing kind of way of seeing people's relations to others. And [those clients are] hard, don't get me wrong, they're hard (laughs) to manage, but I think that's probably the barrier.

Another clinician described the problem of unhelpful mental health professionals who cannot help survivors of sexual assault. This can lead women to try one clinician after another before finding, if they are lucky, someone who can help them with trauma:

A number of [survivors of sexual assault] saw therapists in their childhood. So they're coming to me, very often as a last-ditch effort. You know they feel that [the mental health] profession sucks but [say] "I really need help." You know they don't say that, but that's sort of where they seem to be, sort of at the end of the line, feeling that their life just isn't making sense to them and they're really, they're almost past desperate. They were desperate maybe at the last therapist and just sort of gave up, so there's very often some learning that needs to go on that each therapy is a little different and that therapists aren't interchangeable and you know there's a difference! (54-year-old White clinical psychologist in private practice)

A couple of clinicians talked negatively about self-help groups their clients had attended and how that made it harder for them to conduct therapy with the clients. For example, the clinician quoted next tried to empower her clients in therapy but found that the ideology one client brought into the therapy from a support group conflicted with her approach:

There was one [client] I've been working with for over a year who has a pretty severe eating disorder and has a pretty significant history of sexual assault and it has been very difficult working with her. I mean she's a wonderful person to work with, but there's been so many blocks. And I just see this work that in so many ways, there's so many things that she's just beginning to talk about. One thing that stands out with the eating disorder is how it's really taken over her life. She's been in OA (Overeaters Anonymous). I think the language that I use in feminist therapy is really in conflict with the language she hears in OA, so it's been hard to kind of get through that [conflict] to get to the issue underneath. We've had one conversation in particular that has been difficult given that it's been a tug and pull between where she was at and the approach I'm trying to show a different side. I think with OA there's a lot of powerlessness language, and that's tricky when you're trying to empower, when you're working with someone who is very particular about language and words. So it's been a challenge. (30-year-old White social worker working in a community mental health center)

Secondary Traumatic Stress

Research has documented both secondary traumatic stress reactions (e.g., PTSD symptoms) and vicarious trauma (e.g., changes in cognitive schemas and core beliefs about self, others, and the world) occurring in clinicians who work with trauma survivors (McCann & Pearlman, 1990; Pearlman & Saakvitne, 1995; Sabin-Farrell & Turpin, 2003). Tenure in the field is clearly a factor for clinicians recalling their own negative experiences of vicarious trauma earlier in their careers, even among those who are now veterans:

I had a lot more trouble when I was first starting out. I tell the people I supervise now that one of the first kids I ever saw was 13, acting out huge behavior problems. It turned out her father had raped her when she was 7 years old to the point she almost died. The first images of stuff like that was really hard for me to think of—a 7-year-old who was so badly wounded in that part of her, that she almost died, she was bleeding so much. I remember, I had to run, so I ran, how I coped was I ran and ran and ran, until I started crying, because I couldn't access that level of feelings at first. I think a lot of times some of the newness of these horrific images when you're in an empathic mode is hard. You're never really coming to terms with how horrible the things are that human beings do to other humans, so it's really difficult. (37-year-old White clinician working in a rape crisis center)

Hearing gory details was also described as difficult. Listening to such stories brings up images that are hard to shake. A crisis worker who took a call on the rape hotline shared the following anecdote:

This guy on the phone was horrible, he was very dissociative and was telling me about an incident . . . where he said "My father was raping me in the garage and my mother came out and my father said 'Get back in the house, go away.' My mother said, 'I'm sorry,' and went back in the house. My mother came back out with a gun and pointed it in the air and said 'Get off of him' and which my father did to go after her. Then, I went out in the woods and hid and heard water dripping and thought that my mother would find me because of the water dripping. But then I realized it wasn't water it was blood, and it was coming from my anus and I had to have basically my whole insides reconstructed." So that was pretty bad because of the images that evokes. I mean that's a horrible image, think of a child sitting in a tree with blood dripping from their anus. I mean I'm like "God!" But I don't take that in anymore, just because you know, otherwise, I'd be insane. It's very intense, I mean it gets to you. The vicarious trauma is so hard and you really need to be taking care of yourself. (37-year-old White crisis hotline worker)

These examples suggest that certain clients' experiences may overwhelm a clinician, who may either discount them or be in shock. They may be caught up in their own reactions and unable to respond to survivors, or they may judge survivors negatively. This may occur if the helper projects onto the survivor the negative material with which she is being confronted in the form of blame, disbelief, horror, or even anger.

Numbing symptoms of PTSD or blocking out feelings/reactions to the trauma was another effect of doing this work that was cited as a warning sign that one was not up to the task and needed a break from the work:

Participant: Right when I felt that I was not affected at all by seeing and hearing horrible stories, that was the point where I needed to (laughs) step back and have a reality check again I guess for myself, because when it is just like a movie to you and you walk away unaffected, I feel like that was bad.

Interviewer: You can't be able to be there for them?

Participant: Right, right, well I didn't think I could be there as well as I needed to. (34-year-old White social worker in private practice)

Clinicians newer to the field who had less training related to working with trauma survivors described these effects most vividly. Although this could have been due to their younger age, it is also possible that they simply had less well-developed coping strategies. Because of these negative effects of the work, clinicians may find themselves unable to engage empathically with survivors and to provide acknowledgment and support of their experiences. They may make negative judgments about victims they encounter, which, when compounded by negative views of survivors from U.S. culture, may lead them to inadvertently express negative reactions to victims. Alternatively, they may simply be unable to process the traumatic material. This may lead their own reactions of anger, fear, and anxiety to come out in their responses to survivors whose stories they literally do not want to hear anymore. Fortunately, there are many helpful resources for dealing with vicarious trauma (Bell, Kulkarni, & Dalton, 2003; Figley, 1995; Stamm, 1995; Trippany, Kress, & Wilcoxon, 2004; Washington Coalition of Sexual Assault Programs, 2004), as well as research documenting these experiences in clinicians (S. A. Adams & Riggs, 2008; Pearlman & Mac Ian, 1995).

Transference and Countertransference

Clinicians often deal with a client's *transference reaction*, which is when the client transfers feelings she has about a person who victimized her in the past to the clinician (Figley, 1995). Clinicians in our study noted they had to deal with survivors' transference on an ongoing basis. One clinician who was newer to work with survivors had worked in a group private practice that was based on a feminist relational model of therapy. She described her most difficult case:

> This is the hardest case I've ever had as a therapist and it happened in the partial hospitalization center. I worked at [location name] for probably 2 years and she was a survivor of just horrific assault and among that the worst story I've ever heard of. And I respect that she has an enormous amount of trauma and her relational capacity had really been, she couldn't count on pretty much anybody in her life. But what happened in our interactions is that she would experience me, despite my good intentions and my earnest desire to help, be helpful, as a victimizer, as hurting her in some way, and that of course was heartbreaking to me. I was just very stuck in the sense that nothing I do is right here, and then she would get very suicidal or she'd hint at being suicidal and then shut down and refuse to talk with me about it. So I felt kind of stuck and trapped a lot, which I presume is exactly how she felt. (34-year-old White social worker in private practice)

This clinician then went on to explain why such behavior occurs in greater depth for some clients who have histories of trauma:

> People who have been really severely traumatized will tend to get into re-enactments, where the same scenario gets repeated and repeated and repeated. Not because they want to sign up for it, but because they're trying to solve something and they don't know how to do it differently and I think she was re-enacting something with me.

There is also a risk that clinicians will act in response to their own *countertransference reactions*, that is, reactions to a client that result from the clinician's personal life experiences (Figley, 1995); specifically, a worker may become too overwhelmed by her own emotional reactions, perhaps because a client's trauma is triggering her own unresolved experiences. If she cannot self-regulate them and work through these responses in a supportive environment, either in the context of clinical supervision or her own relationships in or outside of work, she may take out her anger, fear, and anxiety on her clients. Clinicians may verbally or nonverbally pass judgment on victims, fail to respond to them when they do not want to deal with disclosures, or subtly blame them for their experiences by asking questions or making remarks in an insensitive manner.

In particular, when clients evoke negative feelings or judgments it may be hard for clinicians to feel and behave supportively. These situations appear to be most common when clinicians feel that a client's anger toward them was unwarranted or when their own emotional reactions toward the client were strong:

> I have not been judgmental, but I know I may transfer some of these feelings. I know they may be there, but I talk about safety and I talk about, well, do you think you are safe, do you think your husband is a threat, or what could happen? Do you think you're really taking back power, this makes you feel powerful, how much power do you really have? There are cases where I have these mixed feelings and inner conflict and I cannot be that supportive of either the parents or the teenager who is the client, but still I have to be. So I really need to deal with my feelings in places like therapy or with my supervision or wherever I can to be able to be there for them, but it's stressful, it's tough. But, what am I going to do? (32-year-old Latina clinician rape crisis worker)

This clinician described trying to simply behave the way she felt she was supposed to with the clients, even though her own reactions and distress made it hard for her to be there for them and act in this manner. Clinicians described anniversaries of events related to clients that would remind them of what the person went through and what they went through in working with that client. In some way, they "carried" their clients with them even after they had long since had contact with them. For example, one clinician shared the following:

> I think I'm somewhere on the fence between the two, because while I don't think you take it home, I think it's kind of hard not to. I mean you think about your client, and a day might pass and you're like, "Oh, that's her birthday today, hey I remember that girl." You're gonna think about it. I think if you're getting traumatized when you go home, that's a bit much. (24-year-old Latina clinician working in a community mental health clinic)

The following quote is from an older clinician who ran her own agency and had years of experience working with survivors. It shows that the experience of having clients who trigger one's own psychological issues was not uncommon, even for seasoned professionals:

> A couple months ago, I had an elderly survivor who, oh my God, that lady reminded me so much of my mother. I don't know why but, after she left I cried and I thought "Oh my gosh." I called my supervisor and I told her "I need you to come over here, because I'm having a bad time right now." She was gonna help me through that. I was seeing this older woman client and she just reminded me so much of my mom, because my mom became a widow and then my mom started dating again. I'm just thinking, "Oh my God, you know, could this maybe be her also?" She was a

widow and started dating again and she was being sexually abused by one of her male friends. I don't know why this client just reminded me of my mom and made me realize that she could have been sexually abused and we don't even know because she never told us! (46-year-old Latina crisis clinician)

These reactions to dealing with survivors of sexual assault clearly affect mental health professionals' ability to respond empathically. The experiences preoccupy the clinicians to the extent that they may be unable to have the emotional space to process their reactions. Negative feelings and responses may come out toward survivors who are the sources of this stress, despite the clinician's knowledge that it is his or her role to listen and be supportive. To the extent that clinicians have not processed traumatic material presented by their clients, resolved it, or put it aside, they may be less effective in engaging, supporting, and connecting with them.

Somatic and Physical Health Symptoms

In addition to emotional experiences, there were physical signs of burnout and/or trauma that clinicians mentioned occasionally resulting from their work:

- "I think it's really important to know yourself, and to notice the cues in yourself. Like if you know that when you get stressed out and when you're starting to get burnt out you start feeling irritated or you start being sick all the time or something. You know that you need to take, as much as we preach self-care to our clients, we need to take care of ourselves as well!" (24-year-old Latina psychologist)
- "You have information and you know working with victims of sexual assault is not an easy thing to do. . . . My personal experience has been pretty good, regardless of the secondary effects, which you feel always, you know sometimes back pain—as you can see I contort my back a little." (46-year-old Latina clinical social worker)

During the end of the interview, this clinician said she was planning to leave her current job and look for other, less stressful work. This suggests that she may have been experiencing a high level of stress and burnout to the point of having physical health effects of a high client caseload of survivors of sexual assault. It is clear that the traumatic material may cause stress reactions that manifest in physical symptoms of fatigue and burnout. This may make clinicians irritable, tired, unsympathetic, or unresponsive to their distressed clients.

CLINICIANS' AND ADVOCATES' COPING STRATEGIES TO DEAL WITH TRAUMATIC MATERIAL

In the clinician and advocate interview study, both clinicians and advocates spoke of various ways they tried to manage their reactions to survivors and the traumatic material. One strategy discussed by workers was attempts to maintain therapeutic distance. Some described a conflict between wishing to engage on a personal level and needing to maintain a professional clinical stance:

> It is a very touchy subject and it's something that it's hard not to react to as a person, seeing it as a therapist, okay, well now I have better tools on how to deal with it, but still as a person, it's hard not to feel the emotions, the anger, a lot of the negative feelings that the clients are experiencing, I would say I'm still experiencing. (28-year-old Latina clinical psychologist working in a hospital)

This clinician also described attempts to soothe and calm herself, while at the same time expressing some distress at her self-perceived inability to react less to the client:

> I'd try to calm down, because sometimes I feel that my negative reaction maybe clouds the way I think about things. I guess I really need to, I don't know really, I don't know how to answer that. I think I would have to, I just feel as, I wish I wouldn't get as emotionally involved, I wish I wouldn't react as much.

Despite this clinician's wish to not react and not get emotionally involved, it is probably not possible to truly engage empathically with a survivor if one is not connected to the person, taking in what the survivor is saying, and responding to her on an emotional level. Therefore, to provide the genuine human emotional connection and response the trauma worker must be open to taking in the traumatic material and the survivor's emotional reaction to that material.

Another coping strategy mentioned was that of venting to let out the trauma with a supportive listener who knew and understood the work following a stressful visit with a client:

> The interesting part is that I've been trained at both locations and [agency X]. After I go to a hospital and spend 3 to 4 hours in an ER with a survivor, sometimes those calls are hard for us. So they've told us to call the rape crisis hotline and talk to someone who knows similar feelings. We tend to use each other to call and vent. (26-year-old White advocate)

Although this is clearly a useful strategy, a potential problem with it is that the hotline should be for the general public. Workers should have an outlet provided by their work organization for dealing with the need to vent emotions that result from the traumatic work. This clearly shows the need for greater peer support facilitated by built-in organizational support for rape crisis workers.

Although advocates and clinicians find ways to cope with secondary traumatic stress, greater training in self-care strategies is needed. In the interview study, one ex-advocate made the following statement:

> I think that the training for sexual assault is okay; it's adequate. But there's not enough about how to handle it when you get to the point of being really burned out and feeling really traumatized. What do you do when you start having nightmares about your clients and worrying about your clients? There wasn't enough on how to take care of yourself. There's enough information, but not enough on how workers should take care of themselves because it's a really hard population to work with. (27-year-old White ex-advocate)

A study conducted by Bober and Regehr (2005) of 259 clinicians revealed that few of them actually used coping strategies to ameliorate the effects of secondary traumatic stress, even though they knew about them and believed in their efficacy. Even those who did engage in adaptive forms of coping (e.g., leisure activities, self-care, supervision) were not functioning better as a result of using them. On the basis of these results, the authors questioned whether such individualist approaches will be enough to reduce symptoms of traumatic stress resulting from working with survivors of sexual assault, especially given that the sheer caseload of victims was the strongest predictor of trauma symptoms. They argued that individualizing the problem does not work and that limiting the number of such clients is necessary. Also, organizational solutions are needed to reduce the effects of working with victims and to protect workers from these negative sequelae.

Although workers' experiences helping survivors are not uniformly negative by any means, and such work can be rewarding, this is a difficult population to work with because of the effects that sexual assault trauma has on victims and their relationships. This problem is compounded by the fact that training for many professionals on this population is lacking and inadequate support systems exist for many trauma workers.

REWARDING ASPECTS OF WORKING WITH SURVIVORS

Despite the many negative experiences of advocates who work with victims of rape, there are a lot of positive aspects of doing this work, as noted in the interviews. In fact, when asked about rewarding aspects of working with survivors, all advocates and clinicians could think of rewarding aspects of their work with survivors of sexual assault, although they varied in how rewarding they found the work to be and how many different types of rewards they cited.

Advocates' Perspective

A few advocates said that they got few rewards from working with survivors. However, rewards are very important, because they provide motivation and reinforcement to advocates for their efforts to support and work with survivors. Such rewards may result from the positive outcomes of their work and reinforce the positive reactions they are providing directly to survivors and trying to facilitate in others around the survivor, including emotional, tangible, and information support, all of which can contribute positively to survivors' recovery.

Advocates noted several themes when asked about rewards of working with this population, including being appreciated by survivors (mentioned by almost everyone), feeling honored to work with survivors, realizing that healing is possible, appreciating the little things that made the work worthwhile, seeing stereotypes break down, seeing survivors become empowered, seeing that survivors are strong, and experiencing self-transformation.

Survivor Appreciation

Virtually all advocates mentioned that expressions of appreciation and thanks from victims and their families were very rewarding for them in their work with survivors:

- "At the end of the group, I can really see a change in some of the women. I mean even though they were in prison, there was something within them that had brightened up. Something in them that was set free. At the end of the groups they'd cry and tell me how much they appreciate me. They really thanked me for coming out there and for saying the things that I said to them. Nobody had ever said it and they felt that I really meant it when I said that. It was so amazing to me!" (23-year-old Black legal advocate who ran a support group for female survivors in prison)
- "It's truly rewarding. Not every single case turns out in a positive light, though, but more often than not, most people can say things like 'I couldn't have gone through this without you.' There was one woman who told me I was her guardian angel and I was helping keep her in consciousness because she'd lost so much blood. She held my hand and every time she would kind of come into consciousness, she'd be like, 'Oh, my angel is still here.' And that was incredible." (27-year-old White advocate)

Having an advocate who cared and was there for them clearly was instrumental in survivors' getting through the rape and its aftermath. Some advocates also received feedback from survivors with whom they had worked in the past.

Although survivor expressions of appreciation seemed more common in response to hospital and legal advocacy, sometimes callers to the rape hotline would call back to thank the hotline worker who helped them in a crisis later. One advocate stated the following:

> You have those very rare situations where a person will call back and say you really helped me through that. A person will write a letter to the organization and say "Your crisis line was invaluable to me." I mean that's very rare, so you can't really depend on that for the rewards, but of course that's a beautiful thing. (34-year-old Black advocate hotline coordinator)

Honor in Working With Survivors

Some advocates voiced the feeling that they were honored to work with survivors and to witness them surviving and coping with such a difficult traumatic experience:

- "I always felt kind of lucky that I was there to be with them during that time, because I think probably the lowest point in someone's life is to be in an emergency room after a sexual assault. I felt really honored to be there, and for the most part I felt really good about the work that was done in those in those rooms. It was really rewarding in a lot of ways. People would be really grateful to have somebody there and relieved that somebody could be with them, so that was really good." (27-year-old White ex-advocate)
- "I think for a lot of my victims and their families, when the victim did their victim impact statement at the very end of the impact statement, it says 'I want to thank [names of advocates] for all their support and their understanding and their caring' . . . For young people that go through the court system, they'll come up afterwards and say, 'You know, I don't think I could have done it without you.' And I know in my heart that they could have. This response may not seem like a lot [of reward,] but it is." (46-year-old White legal advocate)

Realizing That Healing Is Possible

Several advocates and rape crisis clinicians expressed that their reward came in witnessing the healing of the survivors. They watched the journey of survivors at a very traumatic time following assault and later on during their recovery and improvement:

- "Doing this work affirmed my belief that people can recover from this. I don't think that's the best word always. I don't think that the recovery kind of language is the best word but it's the best I have. I guess *healing* is maybe is a better word. There may still be effects, but they can move on in their lives. It's not as if it never happened, but they can be bigger in their life than the assault experience was." (32-year-old White ex-advocate)

- "Witnessing the resilience of the human spirit (laughs) is amazing. To see people bounce back and recover or even just have that hope of recovery when you're literally at your lowest point. That teaches me a very big lesson in life and it has also taught me a lot about myself since I've been doing this work." (26-year-old Black advocate)

It's the Little Things

Some advocates mentioned that it was the small things that were positive rewards of this work:

- "I think there were a lot of them. To me it was always the little things, partly because those happen more frequently than the big ones. So I think I drew more from those. It was just so wonderful to have someone, whether it was a support group or in one-on-one counseling, come in with that beaming look on their face and be able to say what they did. It could have been something that you'd been talking about for weeks, even something really little like that she didn't have a nightmare this week." (32-year-old White ex-advocate)
- "You know you can have the perfect case and it still somehow falls through the cracks. So, just having someone telling me 'Thank you' or being able to relate the positive information or good news to someone is definitely a positive. Even if it's something like that we were able to get you emergency contraception because you went to a Catholic hospital and they're not gonna provide you with emergency contraception. So we found a way to get you emergency contraception, which is positive information I can tell the client." (26-year-old Black advocate)

This theme suggests that it is the small victories on which advocates can draw to get some rewards from this doing difficult work, which may be essential given that few big, positive things happen in rape crisis work.

Seeing Stereotypes Break Down

Some advocates said doing this work led to changes in themselves and other people. They expressed that doing the work helped them to avoid stereotyping people and to get to know them without making judgments. This suggests that doing this work may help advocates to overcome their own assumptions and preexisting beliefs about survivors of sexual assault:

- "You always hear, never judge a book by its cover. Always get to know people. But I really learned [at the rape crisis center] that you have to get to know somebody before you can make a judgment about them and before you can decide that I'll form this relationship or I won't. There were some really great people there, but they just had the wrong circumstances all of their lives." (23-year-old Black legal advocate)
- "There is this stereotype that Latinas won't follow up for treatment, but I've been surprised because it's totally the opposite, and I don't have any less attendance, people not coming or dropping out than the rest of my coworkers. We find if you offer the services, promote them, and talk clearly about them, people will come for help." (32-year-old Latina clinician working from a suburban rape crisis center)

Seeing Survivors Become Empowered

A number of advocates described the reward of seeing survivors become empowered as a positive aspect of doing their work, and they spoke of these experiences quite eloquently. Their examples show how the survivors' empowerment seems to be rewarding and perhaps even empowering for advocates on both a professional and personal level:

- "I encouraged the survivor, saying that you have every right to feel whatever it is you're feeling. Don't feel like you're being hostile or mean. [The survivor] was totally taking her power and speaking up for herself. So I felt there's nothing I can do for her that she can't do for herself. But, the fact that she asked for me, and after I had quit that job, and that later I saw her family walking down the street and they told me how big of a help I was so that was comforting for my own selfish reasons, to know that I made a difference." (26-year-old Black advocate)
- "[Advocates] don't back down from much of anything, but sometimes it's hard to be that type of person. When I see survivors who aren't normally that way, that's really important. With the teenage girls, when their level of self-esteem changes and it clicks in their head that they're worth something, it is amazing." (41-year-old White advocate)

- "I am working with someone now who is really awesome. I'm making a zine (a nonprofessional publication produced by adherents of a particular cultural phenomenon) about confrontation. It's basically a way for people, like the average person, to write something up and get other people to write stuff up and just kind of put it out there. I've been trying to come up with ways that I can work with survivors that don't have to do with the legal system that could be empowering for them. I think one thing that's really empowering is to find different ways to share stories. I think that whenever I work with survivors and they hear other people's stories, it always helps them in some way. The zine is going to be about confrontation. It's about confronting perpetrators or confronting institutional people, or confronting people who didn't believe you or didn't protect you, or it can be other people confronting those people. . . . I'm working with a survivor who directly confronted the perpetrator. She said that she is so glad she did it and has helped her to feel okay. She feels like she was able to address it and say what she thought about it, namely that it wasn't okay and that was really empowering." (25-year-old White advocate)
- "I find survivors whose family members, like maybe a sister or their mom or someone, was also a victim. They will come in and talk to the survivor and they'll sound like an advocate, saying it's not your fault, you didn't do anything wrong, you know people are gonna try to blame you and don't let anybody tell you that you did anything wrong. It's because they're coming from that experience of either knowing someone or having been a survivor themselves. They've gotten to that point where they are so empowered and so changed and influenced by that experience that they literally sound like they've been trained as an advocate. This made me realize okay, my work here is done." (26-year-old Black advocate)
- "I had a couple positive experiences. Survivors finish the counseling sessions, and then they've gone to the Latina leadership group. That's helped them with their self-esteem, they have some community work, or can just get a job in the community, and that helps them also grow." (46-year-old Latina advocate)

Seeing That Survivors Are Strong

An important theme was realizing the strength that survivors have within themselves to become empowered and recover from the assault. Although this theme is related to empowerment, it seemed to reflect an insight of some advocates regarding an inherent quality of victims of sexual assault. This quality impressed advocates, perhaps because being a victim is typically associated with being weak, not strong. Seeing this strength contradicted their expectations and was all the more impressive to witness in survivors with whom they worked:

> I saw clients in a group I ran as being like butterflies who emerge from a shell in a growth process, where each woman could see herself as a wonderful person. I felt this process was the most powerful thing. The client was fabulous and she came to it herself, seeing the rape as his fault not hers. Watching the process of seeing her stop seeing herself as the bad one, but the hurt one, she saw her strength, turned into a positive—I was in awe of the client. Looking back, I feel that watching self-blame is hard, but seeing it "click" is rewarding. I would work with guilt, which comes up with most clients. How it's dealt with is different for each client, some tell others stories, write, etc. They discuss different parts of themselves. One part always is the child/vulnerable part—core—and other layers—[and we] to try to understand all of those parts. (24-year-old Latina advocate)

Advocates described seeing survivors in a multidimensional way and witnessing their recovery. The reality is that weakness and strength can coexist for survivors. Many women may struggle with practical problems and psychological trauma symptoms and simultaneously cultivate positive emotions, faith, social support, and inner strengths to make positive life changes.

Experiencing Self-Transformation, Self-Efficacy, and Empowerment

Advocates also spoke of working with survivors in terms of rewards for themselves, including their own growth, feelings of self-efficacy, and even empowerment. Some of this may be the vicarious experience of empowerment they have in working with survivors and/or advocates' ability to achieve some of their own empowerment through the process of working with survivors. It is commonly known that helping others can be beneficial to people and make one feel better about oneself (Winerman, 2006). This seems to be part of what advocates are expressing, and it involves survivors' development of assertiveness, advocates' successes in advocating for cases in the system, and advocates' ability to see how their work makes a difference in the lives of survivors:

- "I've seen other advocates who started after me and I see the transformation in people who do this work, positive and negative, in all of our personalities. I think it makes you more assertive, because I've never been the type of person who would necessarily speak up for myself or say anything that would lead to conflict, because I don't like confrontation. So, I can kind of say how I feel about something, but I'm not gonna argue with you about it. When people find out what I do, there's always a rape joke that follows it or something. I have come to understand that that is due to their discomfort level and ignorance. Trying to actually sit down and have a dialogue with them about why they feel like that's appropriate to say is important." (26-year-old Black advocate)

- "Well, I know I impacted the type of evidence that was collected, just by pointing something out that was being done incorrectly. I was trying to keep the procedure from going the wrong way before it was too late, so evidence would be collected. I'm sure that has some impact. Just being thanked afterwards for being there is a rewarding feeling—someone telling you "I appreciate you being there" and [saying] that it was helpful to them." (37-year-old White advocate)

- "I have had great experiences where I feel like I'm actually helping someone in need. They're looking for someone to help support them through a very difficult time. I feel that being there and helping them probably rewards me just as much as it helps them, because I feel like I'm making a difference." (26-year-old White advocate)

Clinicians' Perspective

Clinicians had a slightly different perspective and way of talking about some of the same themes the advocates discussed. In particular, clinicians who did not work in rape crisis centers had less to say about rewarding aspects of working with survivors. This may be because they tended to be older and perhaps less passionate about their work in this area. Many of them did not specialize in working with this population or even have specialized training related to rape, which all of the advocates had. Despite these differences, the two major rewards they mentioned—seeing clients empowered and watching survivors heal—overlapped with advocates' responses.

Seeing Clients Empowered to Make Changes in Their Lives

Clinicians also noted examples of survivors who were empowered to make positive changes in their lives, to free themselves of violence, and to achieve their goals:

> She had a very extensive sexual abuse history and had been in therapy before, but I don't think she'd ever really worked with anybody who could really sit and listen and really stay with her. She came in describing a lot of depression, but when we really looked at what the depression was, it was dissociation, long periods of dissociative experience, so with her a lot of

education about trauma problems helped. She got herself out of a bad relationship and into a much more supportive one, she made some career choices, and got to where she was able to build a safe place in her life, do her artwork, which was very important to her, and create some real stability in her life. This is not to say that a lot of times she doesn't get all upset again, but now she can regroup and figure it out. The periods of upset are shorter and the periods of stability and feeling ok in the world are longer. (47-year-old clinical psychologist in private practice)

Witnessing Survivors Heal

A reward mentioned by a number of clinicians was the ability to see their clients change and grow following sexual assault or other forms of victimization:

- "I suppose what feels the most rewarding [is that] I've had some clients where I got to see, not the whole process, but a lot of the process, and that person had found healing. I could see that the work we did played a big role in this. I saw them come out the other side, and that was such a joyous thing. That is what keeps me going." (34-year-old White social worker)
- "I think that I felt really rewarded with her growth. She was a particularly insightful woman with a personality where she just wanted to dig in and didn't want to be burdened with these lost memories and didn't want it to ruin her life. So she was probably one of the more satisfying clients, because she was very insightful, had the ability to talk about things, even if they were painful, and wanted very much to be able to come and talk about them. I think she grew and she was eager to be in a satisfying relationship and now she has one child." (63-year-old White social worker)

CONCLUSION

Because of the negative effects that can occur, support providers are sometimes called *secondary victims*. This is an important newer area of study, because *indirect* or secondary victims are also likely to be psychologically affected by sexual assault, albeit to a lesser degree than the victims. The emotional impact of sexual assault on the individuals around the survivor is a concern in its own right, but also because emotional distress of support providers may cause further distress to the survivor and could reduce support given to survivors. Such outcomes may be more likely if helpers are preoccupied with their own reaction or have expectations for how survivors should deal with the assault.

Sexual assault has significant negative effects on the informal and formal support sources in the victims' networks. Although these effects may not impair their ability to provide positive support to victims, there is evidence that distress at the victim's plight leads to more negative social reactions. Sexual assault clearly affects relationships with romantic partners, who often report significant psychological symptoms when their partners are assaulted. Given that friends have greater social distance, at least some of them may be better able to provide positive support without making negative social reactions. However, friends report that they vary in their responses to victims, from helpful to neutral to negative in their appraisals. Friends' ability to help appears to be clearly related to their knowledge and ability to handle their friends' sexual assault. Informal network members need to be targeted in treatment for survivors, because they face mental health symptoms as secondary victims and may be more likely to respond negatively to victims because of these effects. Family, friends, and partners may all benefit from education about sexual assault, its effects, and ways of taking care of themselves and supporting victims.

One theme that emerges from the accounts of advocates and clinicians regarding their work with survivors is how difficult and how rewarding it is to work with survivors of sexual assault. Advocates and clinicians commonly experience vicarious trauma and secondary traumatic stress as a result of working with victims of rape, which makes it more difficult to provide optimum support to victims. However, they also appear to gain intrinsic rewards from helping and providing support to survivors. When they see and facilitate positive change in survivors they may also experience parallel changes in themselves. These rewards may be positively reinforcing and make clinicians more supportive toward clients. Appreciative clients may make them feel efficacious and rewarded for being empathic and helpful, leading them to be more positive toward their clients. Seeing survivors grow and heal may inspire clinicians to provide greater emotional support, engage and listen closely to their clients, and even facilitate their own healing from trauma in their own personal lives. Clinicians' own growth may come from seeing the impact they have had in empowering survivors and feeling good about themselves, which they may then project onto their clients in therapy. These findings suggest that more support is needed for advocates and clinicians who work with survivors of sexual assault in the form of mutual support; clinical and/or peer supervision; self-help resources on how to manage and cope with secondary traumatic stress; and information on how to use the rewarding aspects of their work to buffer them against the difficult aspects of helping survivors, especially those who have had negative encounters with their social networks and social systems.

6

CONDUCTING INTERVIEWS WITH SURVIVORS OF SEXUAL ASSAULT

This chapter builds on the previous chapter's theme of presenting and analyzing experiences of advocates and clinicians working with and listening to sexual assault survivors. In this chapter, I provide a first-person account of my own experience interviewing sexual assault survivors about their experiences of help-seeking following assault. I also discuss the ways I reacted to this experience and coped with it and the positive and negative aspects of interviewing survivors. I highlight ethical issues in interviewing survivors and giving back to survivors in the context of such research. This account is intended to provide an example of how listening to survivors and hearing their stories can affect researchers in this area of work. By describing the process of coping with this experience and seeking support to process the interviews I hope to provide ideas about how to take care of oneself and cope with hearing about sexual assaults. This information may also be informative to clinicians, other professionals, and informal social network members who hear survivors' stories and wish to provide support to female victims.

I decided to write about my experience interviewing survivors in part to help myself cope with the stressful nature of this task but also to respond to

Campbell's (2002) challenge to sexual assault researchers to become more emotionally engaged in their research. She argued that we should become emotionally engaged in all stages of rape research. This includes our design and evaluation of research, interviewing victims, caring for oneself and one's research team, and dissemination of results. Part of her call involves demystifying the process of researching sensitive topics by writing about the nature of doing that work. In that spirit, I think that reflecting on my personal experience of conducting qualitative interviews after coming from a background of conducting quantitative survey research may be helpful to others navigating this transition. This task is important because our reactions as researchers can impact the reactions we give to survivors in the research context, including in interviews, the ways we construct our surveys, the debriefing/support material we provide, how we answer participants' questions, and what we say in our recruitment materials. Our reactions can also impact how we interpret the data (e.g., do we focus on individual-level analyses as a way of making ourselves feel safer?). When survivors participate in our research we are asking them to disclose their experiences. We need to recognize that the research experience itself is a social reaction to those disclosures and that, although we are not doing therapy or advocacy, we have a big responsibility to be not only ethical but also supportive in the design and conduct of our work and in our interactions and responses to survivors.

I began work in the area of sexual assault by using archival and quantitative survey-based research methods. In an earlier article (Ullman, 2005), I described my experience of moving from my training in quantitative, logical positivist survey research methods in psychology to conducting qualitative semistructured interviews. I began with interviews of advocates and clinicians about their experiences working with sexual assault survivors (see chap. 5, this volume) prior to interviewing survivors. Thus, I already had experience conducting interviews related to this topic (see Introduction, this volume, for a description of the Mental Health Provider Interview Study).

In this chapter, I begin by discussing an empowerment model that guided my work interviewing the survivors. Next, I describe my experience of conducting the Women's Life Experiences Interview Project, which involved interviewing female sexual assault survivors about their experiences talking with others about their assaults, including both informal and formal social support providers (see Introduction, this volume, for a detailed description of the study design). I then discuss some ethical considerations involved with the research, primarily the need to protect myself and my graduate student researchers from vicarious trauma and secondary traumatic stress. Finally, I reflect on my experience overall in the hope that this will be helpful for other researchers.

EMPOWERMENT MODEL

In general, I believe that an *empowerment model* is the appropriate approach to working with survivors. This approach is common among rape victim advocates and feminists working against sexual assault and with survivors (Ullman & Townsend, 2008). There is a delicate balance in conducting interviews between allowing the survivor to define her own experiences, trying to do psychoeducation, and trying to provide emotional support to counter women's experiences of self-blame and secondary victimization. It is important at some point in interviewing survivors to attempt to communicate that we believe women, support them, and, of course, do not blame them for their experiences. It is also essential to attempt to reinforce their strengths and help them to explore their experiences as they talk about them so that we can contribute to their recovery. Although this may sound like it verges on therapy or taking an active stance in interviewing, there is a distinction between the two. In the clinical session, clinicians not only listen to survivors but also apply specific treatment/therapy approaches aimed at ameliorating the psychosocial consequences of sexual victimization. On the other hand, while conducting an interview, researchers, including myself, cannot and should not do therapy. This may be somewhat different in the case of clinical treatment research in which therapeutic and research aims are combined (Disch, 2001; Mason & Clemans, 2008). Of course, providing referral information is important and a responsibility for researchers working with survivors, so participants can seek mental health help if they wish to do so. In rare occurrences, researchers should also be prepared to give immediate crisis referrals and to help survivors get help quickly if they are in a state of emergency. Apart from this, though, we can all work to be supportive and serve as interested, active listeners for survivors trying to better understand themselves and work through their experiences by being heard and responded to in an interview. In fact, this is an important aspect of research, for several reasons. When participants are asked, before they discuss their disclosure experiences why they wished to be interviewed, most survivors interviewed in our study as well as in others' research on sexual assault (Campbell & Adams, 2009) mentioned that they did so for three reasons: (a) as part of their recovery; (b) because they perceived that this would be a safe, supportive space in which to have their personal experiences heard; and (c) to be able to use their experiences to help other women survivors of sexual assault.

I strongly endorse Campbell's (2002) suggestions for research teams who plan to interview survivors of sexual assault. These include preparation for the interviews, plans for talking about the interviews afterward by phone or in person, and sometimes follow-up contacts with survivors if they wished for this (see also Campbell, Adams, Wasco, Ahrens, & Sefl, 2009, for recommendations for training sexual assault interviewers). Specific things we did for survivors to be sure we treated them ethically and were responsive to their needs included responding to survivor requests, such as referrals to services in other cities, a copy of their interview tape, and/or additional reading material.

I had never thought of research as therapeutic or personally transformative, beyond just trying to learn new information, but this research felt that way both for me and for the survivors I interviewed. I often wished I could harness all of the energy of these individual women together to help to fight sexual assault in the larger sociopolitical context, and I felt sad that all these women were suffering the same problem, and often the same struggle, in relative isolation. On the other hand, in contemporary society, at least there was a more supportive climate to talk about sexual assault, whereas many women who had been assaulted years ago told me that they could not say anything then and that that has now changed. Demystifying the social context of rape has become a major part of my agenda, because I believe the rape culture that exists in U.S. society is both what spawns rape and what revictimizes survivors who try to talk about it or take action against their attackers.

THE INTERVIEWING EXPERIENCE

Preparation for Interviews

I sought the advice of colleagues in developing the interview instrument in collaboration with my research team and came up with a semistructured protocol that asked about adult female sexual assault survivors' experiences talking with others, including who they first told, their most helpful and least helpful disclosures, reasons for telling or not telling mental health professionals, and reactions from each person they told about their assaults. Again, with input and advice from colleagues, we prepared a comprehensive packet for the women, consisting of community resources, a reading list, and follow-up contact information, as well as $30 payment. We followed Campbell's (2002) suggestions for our interview preparations, and she visited with our research group to tell us about her research team's experience of conducting interviews with survivors. Campbell gave us advice about how to introduce the interview such that we connected it back to our mail survey the women had already completed in the previous year, which worked well. This strategy emphasized that we had an ongoing connection with the survivors and probably led them to feel greater trust and likely increased our rapport during interviews. In addition, because we had already obtained a lot of information from survivors about themselves, their assault experiences, and their responses to the assault, we would not need to ask for that information during the interview. The interview would be focused on areas we did not assess in the survey in great detail, such as their reasons for and experiences of disclosing assault, responses from each support source, and their appraisal of these responses.

Campbell (2002) suggested that we initially give women the opportunity to talk more about the assault at the beginning of the interview in case they wanted to talk about it and/or were nervous about talking about it. We would also make it clear that it was fine if they preferred not to do so. Campbell's advice on this matter was excellent, because survivors would vary from not wishing to talk about the assault at all, to vaguely referencing it/talking about it briefly, to describing it in great detail. Right from the start, this approach would give survivors control over whether and how to talk about it. Campbell also suggested we offer them breaks if needed and check to see how they were feeling at various points during the interview, which we would do. She also suggested that we be flexible with our interview protocol to let participants talk about what they wished as they preferred, which we would do and, in fact, is common practice in semistructured interviews. If survivors raised follow-up questions, we would answer them, and if survivors wanted to shape the interview so they could tell their story as they wished, we would accommodate this, although we would also try to fit in all of our questions when possible.

I had learned about crisis intervention and peer counseling from reading and speaking with trauma therapists, but I had hoped I would not need such techniques. I also had referrals available, so that if a woman got too upset to continue, we could access professional help for her as soon as possible. In such interviews, I believe that flexibility is important to give survivors some control over the process of disclosure and the interview itself. This is essential for it to be an empowering, positive experience for survivors. Traditional research interviews can reflect a power dynamic in which the researcher, who has more power, controls the agenda by asking the questions and the interviewee responds. Although some may see more flexibility as less rigorous, with this kind of semistructured interview it seemed important to let survivors have some control and for the interview to be a more collaborative process. Campbell (2002) also suggested that we ask how they felt after the interview and whether they had questions of us. We would follow this advice, which seemed helpful and like a natural way to wrap up interviews on a sensitive subject and give survivors a chance to question us about whatever they wished.

We believe our interview protocol fulfilled several of Campbell's criteria intended to meet the overarching goal of having an ethic of caring infused into the research. She argues that caring is reflected in emotionally engaged research. In interviewing, this involves providing a supportive setting for catharsis, a medium for self-acknowledgment, a sense of purpose, a chance to develop one's self-awareness, a reflection and discussion of experiences that may be therapeutic, and a voice for the disenfranchised (Campbell, 2002). I believe our interview protocol accomplished some of these goals for several reasons. Many women told us that they did the interviews for one or more of several reasons: as a part of their recovery process, because it was a "safe space" to talk about assault, it was a way for them to help other women, and because they wanted to contribute to research and improved treatment for survivors. Given the lack of a defined community for survivors of rape, research studies can and should be one space in which survivors feel safe to discuss their experiences (Campbell, Sefl, Wasco, & Ahrens, 2004).

Beginning to Interview Participants

To initiate the interviews, I called women on the phone, reminded them about the study, and asked whether they would be interested in being interviewed. If they said yes, I set up the interview. I offered a reminder call to survivors who wanted one before the interview and gave all survivors my number to call if they had any questions or concerns. I answered any questions they had about the research and discussed any concerns they expressed. Most did not have concerns, although some had specific requests and needs about how the interview should be conducted (e.g., seating arrangements). Some would sit close to me and to the tape recorder, whereas others would sit farther away from me and/or the tape recorder. Others had specific needs they told me about on the phone, such as that I dress in clothes washed in bleach because of their allergies or, in one case, to sit on their bed, because there was no other room in the house to sit.

I found from the start that, in general, in terms of distress level, the way women sounded on the phone was often well correlated with the way they presented in person; that is, if they sounded depressed on the phone, they were so in person, whereas if they were upbeat and cheery on the phone they tended to be so in person as well. The women had often thought about what they wanted to tell the interviewer before the interviews. Some referred to this specifically and to this interview being part of their recovery and a safe place to talk about it, which was unavailable elsewhere. To my surprise, we even had women participating in the study who had never told anyone about their assault, often because they feared receiving negative reactions from others. Some said this was not a concern in doing a research study with us because we were not part of their lives or social networks. Some women were nervous about the interview.

The interviews ranged from 45 minutes to 2.5 hours in length and were done at a time and place convenient for women, usually the women's homes. I first invited survivors to talk about their assault as much or as little as they wanted. The women, who had already written about their experiences on the survey, tended to recount their assault experiences fairly quickly and only to provide the context for understanding their disclosures and the reactions they received from others, which was the interview's focus. I did not feel very distressed when they talked about their assault histories, which tended to be somewhat detailed but not a major focus of the interviews. The women appreciated not having to talk about the assaults, although many did do so, either briefly or intermittently throughout the interview but rarely in one long narrative segment.

The women varied in how distressed they were, and interviews with more distressed women were more stressful for me because I worried whether they would be okay. I would ask them during the interview if they were okay periodically and assured them they could stop at any time. I always took notes during the interview on what the women said and did, which survivors seemed to expect, as well as tape-recorded the interviews with their consent. However, I was careful to vary the amount of attention paid to note taking on the basis of how the survivor seemed to be doing. If she was more distressed, I paid more attention to her and less on taking notes. I did not have anyone "break down" or be unable to finish the interview. After the interview, I asked how they were feeling about what we had talked about, to which women all said "Fine" or "Good." I felt that, although it was painful, the women seemed to say that talking about it helped and that it (i.e., talking about the victimization experiences) was worth it to try to cope with it and to help other women (which women have always cited as a motivation to participate in my past surveys, not just these interviews).

Initial Impact of Interviewing

Before beginning the interviews, I had been nervous about talking to survivors and about what my reaction would be to doing the interviews, likely a common concern for anyone not having done this before. I had wondered whether I would be able to handle it, but I felt I had enough experience and emotional resilience to manage this task, whereas in earlier years I preferred not to challenge myself in this way. I believe this change was due to several factors, including my own personal growth and feeling of being ready to engage with survivors more personally in my work; having a manageable level of stress, space, and good support in my personal and professional life to handle doing such interviews; and being more established as a researcher with confidence in my ability to do a good job in interviewing survivors.

As it turned out, I had little problem in doing the interviews and felt quite comfortable with the method because I had just finished interviewing 40 service providers in my other project (Ullman, 2005). This helped me to feel more relaxed about doing interviews and to be comfortable with the interviewer role; that is, I was not using a new method that I had not used in my previous work and interviewing a potentially difficult population (e.g., women about their victimization experiences) for the first time without prior experience.

Having the interview process and type of interviews be familiar to me before I interviewed survivors seemed important. In fact, in my discussions with Campbell, she specifically told me that interviewing survivors would be much easier after my experience conducting interviews with advocates and counselors. This made me feel confident and more able to focus on the task of interviewing survivors about their experiences. This was a more sensitive interview (e.g., focused on women's own victimization experiences) and population (e.g., victims) than the professionals I had interviewed about their experiences working with survivors. I think it would have been much harder to interview this population without prior interviewing experience with a less stressed population.

I was relieved when I quickly found I could do about one interview a week, which I found to be a comfortable pace. This was not based on any advice I received, just on what felt optimal for me to be able to give my maximum attention and support to each survivor and to myself afterward in processing each interview once completed. I assume this is something that differs among individuals, with researchers likely varying in the pace and number of interviews they feel comfortable doing. I think it is very important to teach our graduate students that we all differ in our preferences and abilities to deal with trauma and that sometimes it is hard to know this without experimenting to see what is optimal.

Of course, I had some reactions of anger and sadness at the women's stories, but I was able to process them in a day or so by talking about them in confidence with my research team. This was a strategy that Campbell strongly suggested and is also recommended by trauma therapists in general. I also wrote about the interviews in case summaries following each interview as well as in my research log. These practices were suggested to me by several of my qualitative research mentors, who provided guidance throughout this process. Some of the entries in my research log were as follows:

- I didn't find the interview stressful really, though somewhat uncomfortable. This interview made me sad and made me wonder if there is anything our society has to offer to help this woman. I realized her life is so complex and has many levels of disadvantage, of which rape is just one part. (After interviewing a survivor going through heroin withdrawal living in poverty)
- I was not stressed because [the survivor] was fine while we talked. I found her experience distressing though and the neg-

ative responses she has gotten from others. I felt anger also at what she had been through. (After interviewing a survivor who received negative reactions from family and authorities)

- I interviewed a young Latina woman who seemed different from me (in her demographics), yet her conflict, self-blame, and inability to call her assaults "rape" reminded me of some of my own past experiences and lack of resolution of them. (After interviewing a survivor with whom I ended up identifying strongly)

- I so enjoy interviewing survivors, but I think it's having a slow cumulative effect that is not always obvious to me. On one level, I'm fine and I handle it, but on another level, it is disturbing to me, I think on a more subconscious level, because only when certain stimuli later distress me do I realize the stuff is there bothering me, even though I am not aware of it on a conscious level. (Right before taking a 2-week break from interviewing to process the initial effects women's stories were having on me)

I was pleased to be able to do the interviews with seemingly little impact besides mild reactions I had read about that researchers and clinicians have had in working with survivors. My reactions included some psychological distress at hearing their stories, feeling sorry for what they had experienced, anger at the way they had been treated by others, and a sense of resignation about many stories of negative interactions with informal and formal sources that I felt should have been better. I found that my reactions mirrored the survivors' emotional responses, although I did not express these responses to them during interviews. I tried to put myself in the role of a calm, positive listener connecting to and absorbing what they told me. I showed some reaction of acknowledgment, empathy, and general mirroring of their emotions, but I also tried to show that I could be someone who would fully engage and hear them during the interview, whom they could trust not to react with distress or in any way give them something else they had to cope with.

Survivors' descriptions of assaults did not distress me particularly, perhaps because that was not the focus of these interviews except to provide context regarding the aftermath of their disclosures. In contrast, however, the responses of others to them and the impact that those negative responses had on them were at times quite upsetting to me. Of course, hearing about and witnessing the substantial trauma histories of some of the women were also difficult. I tried to nonverbally and verbally communicate that I was safe, nonjudgmental, empathic, and responsive to them when appropriate, but not overly reactive, and always focused on them.

The fact that these women had come through these experiences and were sitting with me, able to talk about them, said to me that they were strong survivors who had been able to cope at least somewhat effectively and that surely I was going to be able to hear them and be able to take in whatever they told me. In fact, I saw this as part of what I had to offer in return for them being willing to participate in the research and talk to me (a stranger) and trust me with painful details of their traumatic experiences.

The experience of listening to women talk about their sexual assault was not completely new. I had previously had similar reactions in my personal life when women I knew who had been assaulted or abused told me about their assaults, and with women who have contacted me because of my work in this area to tell me their stories, request information about research or community resources, or offer help with my research. As an aside, I believe this is also an important ongoing part of conducting rape research, not only for research participants but also for survivors who contact us informally and need help to find support sources, research information, or referrals to services. Over the years, I have had many women contact me, both related and unrelated to specific research project participation, to ask for information, share their stories, and ask how they can help respond to rape. This has given me a sense of camaraderie with these women, which makes me feel that despite our feelings of being alone in this work and in dealing with rape in our lives, we are not really alone in that we know how endemic rape is in women's lives and can connect about our mutual interest in fighting this form of victimization.

Later Impact of the Interviews

Not surprisingly, the impact of interviewing survivors became apparent to me when triggered by specific interviewees. For me, this occurred when I did my sixth interview, which hit me harder, surprised me, and led me to take a break from interviewing for 2 weeks. I thought that I would be able to predict when I would get distressed and assumed it would be when a woman was very upset or symptomatic, but I had encountered a couple of women like that already. The woman I talked with who upset me instead seemed quite resilient. Although she had experienced a lot of assaults, she was not that different or in any way "worse" than the other women I had talked to in terms of her assault history or current functioning. I enjoyed this interview and did fine, like the others, and felt okay afterward and thought that it was a positive experience for us both. However, after talking with my therapist in detail and the research team more generally, I realized my stronger reaction of upset and feelings of vulnerability after this interview were due to my greater identification with this survivor. It was not about her sexual assaults specifically, but instead about her childhood and the ways she had been treated by family and professionals as well as her current functioning. Some of these aspects were parallel to my own life, even though they were not directly or obviously so to me at the time. I had to talk about and work through these feelings of my own and did not want to schedule another interview after this one, which I had always wanted to do before, which again made me realize I needed a break.

It was not that I "could not" go do another interview, but I realized I should not do so until I had resolved this one. I also realized I had made some errors and that maybe six interviews was a good, reasonable number after which to take a break. The errors were things I had read about but did not think about, because one often does not notice the effects of factors triggering these emotional reactions until afterward. I had watched too much disturbing television and had watched a movie after this interview that had a rape scene that I did not anticipate would be in it, so I had already consumed more traumatic material before and after this interview than normal, plus the interview was more personally disturbing to me, which all together perhaps was harder for me and induced a stronger reaction.

Initially, I did not want to take a break, but after my therapist and research team seemed to validate taking a break, I decided it was the right thing and did so. I started to feel relieved that I did not have to do an interview for awhile. Still, I worried about how long it would take to feel better and whether I had reached some point of no return or threshold and would now be distressed or less able to deal with the interviews. Assured by my reading that processing and coping with these feelings would restore my equilibrium and allow me to continue, I tried to let go of these worries. I tried to stop judging myself, which my team thankfully challenged me to do, and not to feel I was not tough enough, because I had read about therapists who fall into this trap and then end up with secondary traumatic stress. I read Saakvitne and Pearlman's (1996) *Transforming the Pain: A Workbook on Vicarious Traumatization*, which addresses coping with the effects of working with survivors, and found it extremely helpful and validating. This book was helpful because it was quite accessible; it described all of the symptoms and reactions that came up in work with survivors of trauma and offered specific coping strategies for dealing with those effects. Thus, this book was practically useful while I was undertaking this work. In fact, I ordered a number of copies so that my research assistants could have it in addition to our other reading material on interviewing female survivors of violence and trauma.

The impact of interviewing survivors had been only theoretical to me prior to this experience, and although I knew it could have this effect on me, it seemed remote and unreal until it did. I was glad to be informed and to be catching these effects early and not just going on without really dealing with the impact on myself. I also felt this would help me to help my research assistants once they started interviewing so they would not be at risk of being harmed in this process either. I started being very good to myself in giving myself time off of interviewing and letting myself work more slowly on other work I had to do. Part of my work tasks at the time involved coding my previously conducted service provider interviews. This task actually proved to be great timing, because I would read about how these service providers coped with working with survivors at the same time that I personally needed to reread/hear this advice because of my own interviews with survivors. I also tried to do what I felt like in terms of fun and relaxing activities and to not let work pressure dominate. I focused on exercise; my relationships; and other nurturing, restorative activities that studies show help trauma workers cope with vicarious trauma.

In addition to these things, writing in my research log anytime I felt like it about my reactions and beginning to write this chapter helped me to cope and feel stronger, which I needed, because these feelings make one feel alone, vulnerable, and out of control, similar to reactions of survivors.

Processing During the Interviewing Break

As mentioned earlier, I took a 2-week break, which was important because although I was able to talk about and write about the immediate feelings and thoughts I had, I initially recognized and started to process only the obvious things, such as similarities and differences of the survivor to myself and disturbing aspects of her assault history and the reactions she got from others. Only after a week had passed since this disturbing interview did I realize the deeper issues that hearing the survivor's story evoked in me. I was out running exactly 1 week since I had interviewed her when I realized suddenly that this woman's story upset me because of some of her childhood/adolescent experiences that related to my own unresolved childhood issues; that is, the more long-standing unresolved issues that she evoked in me came into my awareness without warning.

In her case, she had had a mother who did not protect her from several abusers in the extended family, and this reminded me of my mother, who allowed my father to administer physical corporal punishment and did not protect me. The trauma of having to acknowledge that both of my parents did not protect me, not just the overtly abusive one, was difficult because it forced me to face that there was no safe, protective parent in childhood and as an adult there is no absolute safe place/person either. Even though I had been aware previously of these parental issues prior to doing this study, they were still emotionally powerful and triggered by doing the interviews. This experience seemed to me to be an example of having one's basic beliefs in the benevolence of others and safety in the world be threatened, as described by Janoff-Bulman (1992) and others who study psychological trauma (McCann & Pearlman, 1990).

I also realized that because it took a week for me to recognize and deal with this deeper material, it was important that I had not done another interview in a week as I had been doing, because that would have likely taken my energy, attention, and focus and perhaps precluded my ability to process this experience and the reactions I had to it. Not knowing how long this processing would take, or when I could get back to interviewing was hard, but having the issues come up and dealing with them made me feel I could have faith that I was doing what I should be doing to care for myself and be in good shape when I again began interviewing.

Getting Back to Interviewing

Two weeks later, I did an interview and was greatly relieved to find that I felt much better and did not experience the same emotional reaction as I had to the previous one. Although I was not back to where I started before I began interviewing survivors (which maybe I never would be), my equilibrium seemed to be restored, and I felt my reactions were more proportional. I was less agitated in general in my life, and my feelings were on a more even keel. I was also able to engage with the woman I interviewed, was glad to be doing the interview, and felt it went well and that I was fully present for her. I began to realize that this experience was a learning process that would unfold over time, and I also became aware of the positive attributes that doing these interviews was bringing out in me. I felt I was able to empathize and be supportive and validating of the positive steps survivors told me they were taking in their lives. I was also able to have the interviews be a positive disclosure experience and a collaborative process whereby together we could do something by talking about survivors' experiences to help women (which, as mentioned earlier, almost all mentioned this as a reason they agreed to do an interview).

In contrast to the negative feelings of fear, anger, sadness, and threat to my assumptions about others and my own safety that hearing about women's assaults brought up, I was now able to feel and recognize that I was also manifesting positive attributes and feelings such as warmth, supportiveness, empathy, and wonder/awe at the strength of the women. Although this process was an individual one in terms of talking to each survivor in individual interviews, I felt that we could learn from each other and take away helpful lessons and even empower each other, even though the focus was on them and their experiences in the interview. I hoped they would gain something from talking to me and having me reflect back support and affirmation to them. I also felt that I was indirectly learning from them, often feeling that they were telling me in very eloquent ways things I needed to know about recovery from sexual assault for my research as well as for me personally. Sometimes women would say something about their recovery that would echo the very issue that I felt I was thinking about as if they could read my mind or knew me better. I felt a sense of kinship and that in doing this work they were on this journey with me as partners trying to address this issue in their individual lives as well as for women collectively.

Self-Transformation

After conducting 12 interviews, I decided to read my research log, in which I described my interviews and reactions to survivors. I realized that the way I cope with the survivors and hearing about their assault experiences parallels the way I have coped with my own past stressful life experiences. I perceived that I coped in general by attuning myself to the survivors and what they told me during the interviews, taking in what they said, and trying to connect with them and support them. Later, however, I tried to move past it by processing the interview, absorbing the impact, and then, I hoped, putting it aside. Much of my own coping with past emotional and physical abuse as a child and adult sexual assault has involved minimizing its impact, acknowledging it, and trying to move past it. Anger can be a useful emotion that I experienced because of my own past experiences and that I re-experience in hearing survivors' stories. Harnessing this anger has energized me to continue working against sexual violence with others dedicated to this task and has helped me to feel less alone in this world where so many women share these experiences.

Sometimes survivors said wise and insightful things that I feel I needed to hear even though they were talking about their own reactions and recovery—often, they had lessons to teach me. I think I see how much easier it is to understand survivors' assaults for what they are and to have compassion for them, which I realize is what I need to have for myself. At one point, I remember feeling that doing these interviews could make me a better person—a more caring, patient, understanding listener with more to give to others in my life. I wondered if bearing witness to survivors' stories could soften my often-harsh views of people and the world and make me less defensive and more open to the good and bad in life. Despite occasional vicarious trauma symptoms and the general stress of interviewing survivors, there is also the positive side of connecting with women, supporting them, and validating their experiences. I can be helpful/empowering to the women and also learn and broaden my experience by talking to them. There are lessons I learn from each survivor, which I hope to use in my research as well as in my personal life. Witnessing their strength and resilience despite adversity gives me hope and makes me see how everyone has to work individually to recover and collectively to end rape.

To be able to do our best work in interviewing survivors, it is important that the rest of one's life be in the best order possible, in terms of having a support network in both one's personal and professional life. This is important so that one will have others to talk to about the impact of doing this work and to enjoy life with and escape from the ever-present issue of sexual assault. Therapy is also important in that one can always have a trained clinician to help in debriefing from traumatic interviews, if needed, and in processing one's own reactions when particular survivors' stories resonate with one's own experiences. Other self-care routines identified by other researchers to take care of one's health and general well-being are also important. One can be there for survivors only to the extent to which one is there for oneself and functioning optimally. For me, this meant that it was important to cut back or take a break from interviewing sometimes during more stressful work periods. All crisis workers know the importance of self-care and support in avoiding vicarious trauma and burnout that can occur in working with trauma survivors.

ETHICAL CONSIDERATIONS

There are ethical concerns to consider when conducting interviews with survivors of sexual assault, both with regard to survivors who are studied and researchers undertaking the work. Others have written about how to carefully train oneself and one's research team and how to take care of interviewers and survivors during research projects involving interviewing trauma survivors (Brzuzy, Ault, & Segal, 1997; Campbell, 2002; Hlavka, Kruttschnitt, & Carbone-Lopez, 2007). Here, I discuss the precautions I took to ensure the safety and protection of my research team, myself, and the survivors.

Protecting Graduate Student Researchers From Vicarious Trauma and Secondary Traumatic Stress

Researchers who interview trauma victims are not immune from the experience of secondary trauma, especially student researchers, who have less experience and training than licensed mental health professionals. As the leader of a research team consisting of graduate-level psychology and criminology students, it was my ethical obligation to protect the student researchers from potential secondary trauma reactions (e.g., anger, sadness, anxiety) resulting from interviewing survivors.

I began conducting interviews myself before other members of our research team did, which seemed best because I wanted to be sure I understood what this would be like and how I handled it personally before asking my research assistants whether they also wished to do interviews. We were fortunate to have a 2-year period during which to conduct 60 interviews in our study. This was very important in that it allowed us time to do the interviews at a pace that was comfortable for each us and that fit with our other work responsibilities.

I felt it was important that we all be in a situation in which we were not overly stressed by other work or personal demands so that we could devote our full attention and energy to survivors during the interviews. This sometimes meant checking in with each other to be sure we were each feeling comfortable about interviewing. I found that if I felt tired or stressed or was experiencing vicarious trauma symptoms, like after the difficult interview I described, it was critical to be able to step back and give myself time away from interviewing. This type of research is not the kind that one should try to "push through" and continue to interview even if one can get by and manage to do it. This is because burnout and worsened stress reactions may result, given the cumulative nature of vicarious trauma exposure (McCann & Pearlman, 1990), and this, in turn, affects survivors. Because we may not be able to see when we are too stressed or not in a good place to be in contact with survivors, we need to rely on each other to tell each other if we think a member of the research team is not up to interviewing. Of course, this has to be done in a sensitive manner and in a way that brings this issue up as one's perception. This can, it is hoped, engender a discussion that leads the person to conclude on his or her own that he or she wants to wait to interview until he or she is in a better life situation. It is an ethical responsibility to proceed in this manner, for both taking care of ourselves and taking care of survivors. This is probably a key reason why clinicians who do this work talk about limiting the number of clients with victimization histories that they see as a way to cope with vicarious trauma (Schauben & Frazier, 1995; Ullman, 2005).

Just as I conducted most of the interviews with survivors before anyone else on the research team did interviews, I modeled talking about my interviews in the group before students did this. We applied the same model to transcription of the interviews, which can also yield reactions that need to be processed and/or any issues related to conducting rape research or sexual assault in general that any of us wanted to raise, such as media portrayals of rape cases or other issues surrounding rape that came up. We all spoke to others after we did an interview and when we felt we wanted to do so, sometimes at research group meetings, as Campbell (2002) suggested, but other times to each other individually, as sometimes students or I preferred.

I realized that my role as professor/supervisor with more power on the team made it risky for them to talk about sensitive issues, especially their own reactions to interviews. Thus, I also acknowledged that my graduate students should make their own decisions about whether and how much to talk about their interviews in the group context and/or to me, depending on what was comfortable for them. Sometimes they did discuss sensitive issues, which made me feel glad that there was the trust to do that and that my graduate students and I could provide support to each other in the group context. However, although I emphasized the confidentiality of these discussions I did not expect or mandate that students discuss anything unless they wished to do so, and I believe there were times when they sought support from each other or from persons outside the research context in their social networks. I also told them I was available by telephone if they wanted to talk to me privately. I believe it was important to provide a safe space for discussing the interviews in terms of the research process and how they were proceeding as well as in terms of the effects on us of conducting the interviews. Sometimes the feedback graduate students and/or I would give each other was very validating and/or helped us to get perspective and simply feel supported. I think this is essential in this work and can model what we collectively and individually were trying to provide to survivors in the research project.

I tried to protect my research team in several specific ways, including providing information, such as articles on interviewing trauma survivors; developing plans for conducting the interviews and talking about them afterward; providing students with support individually and on the research team in weekly group meetings where they were given time to discuss their reactions to conducting interviews and/or transcribing them; and giving students copies of Saakvitne and Pearlman's (1996) self-help book *Transforming the Pain*. In addition, the students had access to all of the community and clinical resources provided to survivors in the study as well as to the university counseling center. Also, the graduate students on my research team who chose to do interviews (and it was a voluntary choice, not a requirement, which I made very clear) all had prior training and experience about how to deal with victims of sexual assault and domestic violence from their previous work in rape crisis centers as advocates and/or on crisis hotlines. Thus, they also had access to those community resources and collegial sources of support from their work in those contexts.

In my view, the nature of what is needed to train interviewers to do such research will partially depend on their background and past experience working with survivors of sexual assault. Various researchers have provided some helpful guidelines to the research community on how to conduct interviewer training for research on sexual violence that suggest various approaches that may be effective (Campbell, Adams, Wasco, Ahrens, & Sefl, 2009, in press; Jansen, Watts, Ellsberg, Heise, & Garcia-Moreno, 2004). All of these writers, including myself, seem to agree that specific training on and/or background in issues related to violence against women is needed as well as support for interviewers during the interview process.

Protecting Myself From Vicarious Trauma and Secondary Traumatic Stress

I discussed my experiences with my research team periodically when they would bring up stories in the news or experiences they had had doing advocacy or other work regarding rape that we discussed in what I believe was a supportive research group context. However, because I was the professor/supervisor in this context, I provided only a general summary of interviews with my team and would let them know about my decision-making processes with regard to conducting the interviews. In terms of the emotional impact of doing the interviews, I sought support when needed from my own therapist and did not expect to get such support from my students. I was careful not to lean on them for emotional support; however, when I spoke about the interviews, my students did express support and asked questions, sometimes giving me their perspectives and advice, which was quite helpful.

Self-Disclosure to Survivors

An important experience of self-awareness occurred when I was planning to interview a woman who had given me her narrative of her sexual assault experience and whom I had talked with on the phone. She had asked me on the phone prior to the interview if I was a survivor, and I said yes. I did not talk in detail about my assaults because I did not want the interviews to focus on my experiences, but I was willing to at least briefly answer the question if a survivor asked. Although there are no standard guidelines about self-disclosure in trauma interviews, and social science methods vary widely on this issue, my view is that these interviews are for the participant and should be focused on them with minimal self-disclosure and that only if asked a direct question would I answer, and even then only briefly. Campbell et al. (in press) echoed similar views about how to handle researcher self-disclosure, reporting recently that it was quite rare in their interview study of survivors of sexual assault that interviewees asked interviewers about their own sexual assault histories.

I realized, though, when this woman asked me about my survivor status, that I really had not talked that much about my own experiences of victimization with others. I then was somewhat worried about whether that mattered, especially if she wanted to ask me more about the issue during or after the interview. I realized that this woman had a lot in common with me in terms of her survey experiences and her demographic background. I worried about what would happen if I somehow responded to her on the basis of my own reactions and similar assault experience. I ended up talking to a senior member of my research team about this concern before the interview, and I told her briefly about my experiences after she suggested that maybe I should talk about them. She was, of course, supportive, and I had no problem telling her what happened to me and about my concern about my similarities to this other woman I planned to interview. I felt fine about my disclosures to her and that my experiences were resolved as much as possible. Talking about my experiences helped me clarify them and my responses to them for myself and enabled me to receive a supportive response from my team member. I believe that it was important for me to disclose my own experiences and receive supportive responses before I interviewed someone similar to me who might ask me about them. I also found it ironic that I was studying a topic that was personally relevant and that I was having the women talk about their assaults but had not really talked about my own experiences more than minimally in the past!

POSTINTERVIEWING REFLECTIONS

Growth as a Researcher: Shift to a More Interpretive Stance

Interviewing survivors showed me the limits of survey approaches I had been using to study recovery from sexual assault. Although theoretical models may best be tested with quantitative survey–based methods, the nuances and multiplicity of both women's assaults and their constructions of themselves and their experiences are best captured with qualitative interview data.

As a social psychologist, I was trained in research methods based on the logical positivist philosophical tradition (for a review of philosophies of science, see Singleton & Straits, 2005). This approach assumes that a reality exists that can be studied and observed, such that objective known empirical facts can be uncovered and confirmed by others. However, challenges to the notion of an empirically verifiable reality have come from phenomenological/ interpretive traditions. These philosophies suggest that science and scientists are subjective and that both the subjects studied and researchers' views may affect the phenomenon being examined. Furthermore, these subjectivities should be acknowledged and studied to understand their influence on social phenomena. Such approaches include critical theory, historicism, discourse theory, and postmodernism (see Singleton & Straits, 2005). These critiques suggest that one must acknowledge the biases of researchers and participants in social science research; however, some scholars argue that although these perspectives have contributed to development of social science theory and method, they have not undermined the scientific approach (R. Collins, 1989).

Feminist theory is an example of such a critique. According to feminist theory, no method is without bias, multiple methods are needed in research, power relations between the researcher and persons studied should be reduced to facilitate trust and disclosure, female participants should be allowed to connect with each other in research where appropriate, and we need to recognize emotionality of women's lives as well as the emotional responses of the researchers (Campbell & Wasco, 2000). Campbell and Wasco (2000) discussed various feminist approaches that recognize gender and other factors as structuring our understanding of reality. I agree with both the empiricist perspective that argues we can uncover social realities by studying them and the feminist perspective that suggests we need to understand rape as a "gendered" phenomenon. Taking a feminist standpoint is also important in order to acknowledge the variety of truths and experiences survivors have based on race, class, gender, sexual orientation, and other identities.

Overall, doing this research clarified for me that studying survivors' experiences from their own perspectives is essential. They can contribute vital knowledge about their experiences in narrative forms and tell us how they feel informal and formal support providers can be helpful. The lack of survivor-informed scholarship is a problem that has been noted by many in the field of sexual assault (Gilfus, 1999; Wasco, 2003). Qualitative research can be just as theoretically driven and rigorous as quantitative data, but it yields a richer and more complex set of data that go beyond quantitative research that limits women to the few response options that researchers think of to offer respondents. Thus, such methods can help us to understand phenomena that are not captured with other methods, such as surveys. This is important because it leads to novel insights about what psychological mechanisms are affecting women's decisions about disclosure and how responses to disclosure impact their recovery.

Mistaken Assumptions

Many of my own assumptions of how decisions about whether to disclose and the timing and sequencing of disclosures were brought into question by these interviews. For instance, our interviews showed that there are numerous patterns of disclosure and nondisclosure to informal and formal support sources and that no simple linear model explains the multiple patterns of talking about assault evidenced among survivors of sexual assault. I assumed that negative disclosure experiences would lead survivors to stop telling others, which in some cases was true. In other cases, however, survivors saw rape as an important thing to tell others, whose responses would affect whether they wished to continue a relationship or friendship with that person. In other words, they wanted to be sure that people in their lives were really those whom they could trust. Telling them about sexual assault was a way to find this out, even if it carried the cost of negative social reactions, which it often did.

Another mistaken assumption of mine was that telling informal support sources would always precede telling formal sources about assault, because most women tell informal sources of friends or family, and few typically tell formal support sources only. Although this pattern was true of some women, in other cases (e.g., child, adolescent assault), assault circumstances and other events outside of survivors' control led formal sources to find out about assaults. This led me to realize that I would need to consider women's lifetime history of victimization to really understand women's disclosure and help-seeking regarding sexual assault. Experiences earlier in life clearly were often linked to later victimization experiences. For example, disclosure and reactions to child sexual abuse often played a role in decisions about whether to talk with others about sexual assault in adulthood. This is not completely surprising, because other research shows that having a history of sexual assault in both childhood and adulthood is associated with worse psychological consequences and greater rates of mental health–service-seeking (Follette, Polusny, Bechtle, & Naugle, 1996; Ullman & Brecklin, 2002). This type of information was helpful given how little we know about why and how women seek help following sexual assault, and it can help to inform future research to better understand this issue from the perspective of support providers and survivors. It is unlikely that this information could have been uncovered with quantitative methods; in fact, subsequent qualitative research suggests we cannot fully understand complex patterns of recovery among individual survivors without using both qualitative and quantitative data (see also Ahrens, 2006; Ahrens, Campbell, Temier-Thames, Wasco, & Sefl, 2007).

Survivors' Appraisal of Sexual Assault

A striking thing I have noticed in interviewing women about their experiences and then talking about my experiences is how different one's own appraisal of sexual assault is from those of others. In general, individual women, including myself, are harder on themselves than are supportive others. Because the interview provides a safe, supportive place to disclose sexual assault, women who participate are not afraid of getting the negative reactions they fear getting, or have often gotten, from others they told (Ullman, 1999). This is critically important, because most trauma experts feel that validating responses to trauma disclosure are therapeutic (Wortman, 2004). It is amazing to realize how easy it is to make judgments and have harsh attitudes about one's own assault, while at the same time being able to see how other women are not to blame for their assaults, even when they cannot see it (see also Phillips, 2000). The ability to self-reflect and be sympathetic and supportive toward other woman disclosing sexual assault and to oneself probably constitutes the most positive transformative possibility of interviewing survivors of sexual assault.

Giving Back to Survivors

As much as we can gain from talking to women about their experiences, it is also important to give back in multiple ways to survivor participants in our research. We did this by paying women; going to interview them when and where convenient for them; giving them comprehensive community resource packets should they wish to seek further help, as advised by other researchers (Campbell, 2002); and talking with women as needed by telephone and after the interview should they wish to connect with us.

Although as researchers we see women as helping us to understand sexual assault by telling us their stories, women also frequently told us they wanted to help us and other survivors in working against sexual assault. Although responding to such offers is not often part of formal research protocols, and certainly not often taught in formal research methods courses, we believe that we must respond to the offers sensitively and with humanity. Examples from our study include responding to survivors' requests of us and offers of help to us when and where possible. For instance, I connected a survivor with resources in a new city where she planned to move soon, because our local resource packet would shortly be of little use to her. I also accepted, when appropriate, offers of help from survivors, such as offers of written material, including books they had access to and wanted to share with us regarding sexual assault and offers to advertise our study in their own local community publications/newsletters. I considered this part of an effort to empower survivors and to collaborate with them in both of our efforts to respond to the problem of sexual violence in society and in our own lives as women.

CONCLUSION

Writing about the process of interviewing survivors was one of the ways I chose to cope with the task. Despite the professional and personal risks involved in exposing parts of my own life in this piece, I think that without doing so we may not fully understand the impact on ourselves and perhaps on others in our field of doing this type of work. Graduate students and faculty need access to information about how others embark on interviewing survivors in an ethical manner and how they deal with it in their lives. That type of account is sorely needed and particularly lacking in the field of psychology, which is based on objective, non–self-disclosing, logical positivist methods. Therefore, inspired by Campbell's (2002) entreaty to researchers to acknowledge the emotional engagement involved in studying sexual assault and to discuss this aspect of our work, I decided to share my own experience. Some time after completing these interviews, I also wrote an account of my own experiences, which I shared with my therapist and have reflected on from time to time. It is unclear whether this has had any impact for me, but it seemed like a logical step and one that is fairly safe in comparison to talking in detail about one's assault experiences with other people. Such narratives are common in certain areas of qualitative research (see Denzin & Lincoln, 2000), such as autoethnography and in the field of sociology in general as well as in accounts of research written by feminists. Researchers have argued that by examining our own role in the research process, the impact of those we research on us, and the impact of ourselves on those we research (Hertz, 1997; Reinharz & Chase, 2002; Stanko, 1997), we may come to a fuller understanding of the phenomena we seek to explain.

7

CHALLENGING THE RAPE CULTURE: RECOMMENDATIONS FOR CHANGE

As discussed earlier in this volume, we must move from a trauma disclosure focus, which is grounded in the mental health field, to a more activist focus of talking about and/or refusing/resisting sexual assault in order to repoliticize women's disclosures of sexual assault and link them to activist efforts to collectively stop rape. I recommend using Gavey's (2007) concept of a *refusal paradigm* to bridge the trauma disclosure focus of much current work on sexual assault disclosure with the need to speak out against rape and the rape culture. Gavey advocated adopting a paradigm of refusal of sexual assault to combat sexual violence against women and establish a more activist and action-oriented agenda in resisting and attacking rape as a social problem. When women refuse rape, they then refuse to be blamed for or ashamed of being raped, refuse to minimize the seriousness of rape, refuse to accept rape-supportive social norms, and refuse to keep quiet about the problem of rape. In light of this goal, I offer the following recommendations for future research, treatment, and interventions.

RESEARCH RECOMMENDATIONS

Researchers Should Study the Social Context of Rape

To inform treatment and prevention efforts for survivors of sexual assault, we need more research on the real contexts of women's lives. How can current psychological treatments focused on reducing psychological symptoms of posttraumatic stress disorder (PTSD), depression, and anxiety, and changing women's thoughts about their assaults (Foa & Rothbaum, 1998; Follette & Ruzek, 2006) be adapted to take into account contextual factors, such as social support, that may influence their efficacy (e.g., social cognitive behavior therapy; Tarrier & Humphreys, 2003)? In particular, the following questions should be addressed:

- How do social reactions to sexual assaults differ according to type of perpetrators (e.g., romantic partners, acquaintances, dates, family, strangers), victim abuse history, and whether assaults involved alcohol? Such data may help service providers better respond with appropriate treatment and prevention for women assaulted in different contexts and with different assault histories.
- How do victims come to acknowledge/self-label as victims, and how do disclosure and reactions affect that process? This is critically important for learning how to encourage disclosure and reporting of sexual assault, the rates of which remain very low.
- Are improved responses to victims of sexual assault helpful to survivors and to the individuals trying to help them and their cases?
- What mechanisms connect the rape-supportive social climate and associated attitudes justifying violence to offenders' actual behavior?
- What are the specific social contexts of intimate partner rape?
- What are the experiences of mental health professionals who encounter and treat survivors who do not disclose assault? This group is mixed in supportiveness to victims, according to studies of survivors (Campbell, Raja, & Grining, 1999; Golding, Siegel, Sorenson, Burnam, & Stein, 1989; Ullman, 1996b, 2000), and research is needed to understand why this is the case. One variable to examine may be amount of training for clinicians regarding sexual assault, because research shows that a significant proportion of clinicians receive no special training in this area (Campbell, Raja, & Grining, 1999).

- How does rape—and rape disclosure—affect survivors' support networks and relationships with others? This may enhance our understanding of the impact of victimization on survivors' relationships and the risk of disruption of significant relationships known to occur for some victims.

Studies Should Include Diverse Populations

Longitudinal studies of large, representative samples of diverse victims are important to help researchers better understand the role of social reactions along with other factors in survivors' recovery process, including physical health, mental health, and social adjustment. This kind of work is important for identifying how various modifiable social and psychological factors interrelate to explain recovery for all survivors. Such research is clearly needed because of the dearth of available data on experiences of sexual assault in women of varying racial/ethnic subgroups of the population (see Abbey, Jacques-Tiura, & Parkhill, in press).

Studies of Attitudes Toward and Treatment of Victims of Rape Need to Use Multiple Methodologies, Including Experimental, Survey, Interview, and Other Methods

This is important for ascertaining whether and when the results of experimental studies actually generalize to how victims and their cases are treated in society. Field studies of actual victims and professionals responding to victims and/or handling their cases in social systems are particularly important for addressing the social desirability bias inherent to research based on self-report methods. In addition, both quantitative and qualitative studies are needed to better understand the nature of survivors' experiences; how we can best help them following assault; and the experiences of professionals working with survivors, who have a substantial influence on survivors' recovery process and the handling of their cases.

Studies Examining Factors Related to Recovery in Survivors of Sexual Assault Should Incorporate Objective Measures of Secondary Victimization

Instruments such as the Social Reactions Questionnaire (Ullman, 2000) can objectively measure negative reactions of blame, control, stigma, distraction, and egocentrism, which can all contribute to worse PTSD symptoms directly, and possibly indirectly, through survivors' use of avoidance coping and increased attributions of self-blame.

Research on the Role of Social Support/Reactions Should Incorporate Both Quantitative and Qualitative Data Sources

In this way, the richness and complexity of survivors' experiences will be better understood.

Researchers Should Develop and Evaluate the Efficacy of Support Network Interventions for Survivors and Their Informal Network Members of Friends, Family Members, and Romantic Partners

Such interventions are needed to improve support and reduce negative reactions to victims and associated psychological symptoms as well as risk of revictimization, especially given that positive reactions are related to reduced risk of revictimization (Ullman & Najdowski, 2009).

TREATMENT RECOMMENDATIONS

Treatment Providers Such as Clinicians and Medical/Health Practitioners Should Screen Women for Sexual Abuse and Assault

Service providers need to screen for multiple forms of violence when an individual or family presents to a social service agency so that all of the problems can be addressed, because multiple forms of violence are common among women (Campbell, Greeson, Bybee, & Raja, 2008). They should also assess whom survivors have told and what reactions survivors have received for use in devising treatment plans.

Clinicians should be trained to be culturally competent in general and should learn how to apply that training to working with survivors of sexual assault specifically. This is important so that they will be able to consider different cultural experiences of rape that exist in diverse populations of women (Bryant-Davis, Chung, & Tillman, in press) and respond in a supportive way that is tailored to specific subgroups of women in the community (Briere & Scott, 2006; L. Brown, 2008).

Providers Should Refer Victims of Rape to a Safe Space in Therapy or Support Groups That Are Professionally Facilitated by Persons Trained in This Area of Work

This is important because silence, shame, stigma, and self-blame are all common among female victims, and a caring professional can be invaluable by simply asking about this type of victimization; listening and providing a sympathetic response as needed; and referring victims to relevant services, such as support groups or rape crisis services.

Survivor Therapy Groups Should Be Feminist

Social work researchers have presented useful recommendations for conducting feminist therapy groups with survivors of sexual assault (Clemans, 2005; Wood & Roche, 2001; Yassen & Glass, 1984). Such groups may be particularly empowering for women in helping them to understand the larger context of their individual experiences and to take actions in their lives (see also Mason & Clemans, 2008, on use of a participatory research model for rape survivor groups). Professionals who work with survivors in therapy may be able to acknowledge this trauma, validate and empower survivors, and help them to take actions in their lives that enhance their recovery.

Therapy Should Address the Social Context of Rape

Clinicians may be able to help victims reestablish feelings of safety, control, and positive assumptions about themselves, the world, and other people often shattered by victimization by enhancing their support networks and helping them to process any negative reactions they have received from others. In general, treatment that integrates the social worlds of survivors, including their support networks and social ties, probably has a better chance of facilitating recovery than those that do not (Goodman & Epstein, 2008; Najavits, 2002). This may simply be because if one treats symptoms in a vacuum and then sends the survivor back to a victim-blaming environment, the symptoms are likely to reemerge if the person or persons blaming the survivor do not change their responses toward her.

Informal Support Network Members Should Be Incorporated Into Treatment When Possible, and They Should Be Taught to Avoid Negative Reactions and to Provide Positive Responses to Victims

Tarrier, Sommerfield, and Pilgrim (1999) showed that inappropriate support behaviors from close relatives of victims assessed at the start of therapy affect the efficacy of cognitive behavior therapy (CBT) for PTSD. Some preliminary clinical research has integrated social support into traditional CBT and shows promise for social CBT treatment based on a single-case study design (e.g., Billete, Guay, & Marchand, 2008; Tarrier & Humphreys, 2003).

Couples and Family Therapy Should Be Available

The essential social networks to which victims most often turn for help must be able to assist survivors and not revictimize them. Such treatment might involve therapy or support groups for women and/or for their partners/couples.

Family Therapy Should Be Feminist and Safe

It is unfortunate that many of the traditional forms of family therapy (e.g., the family systems approach) do not take gendered relations of power into account (Yllo, 2005). Such gendered relations may disadvantage women in their less powerful roles in traditional nuclear families. Interventions in families should ensure that the safety of women and children is the first priority. Treatment or intervention based on a family approach does not mitigate the fact that rape and other physical forms of family violence are products of a patriarchal family structure, at least in cases in which men are involved as fathers and husbands.

Although feminist models of family therapy may be the best suited to addressing these issues regarding gender (McGoldrick, Walsh, & Anderson, 1989), there may be cases in which families are too dysfunctional and/or violent for healing to occur in a group context. In such cases, family members may need to be separated and have their own individual support and therapy away from those who are causing violence in the home. Although disagreement remains in the field over whether family unity should be preserved, protecting women and children is paramount (Gelles, 2005). Situations in which perpetrators are willing to confront their violent behavior and are motivated to stop assaulting their wives may be treatable, but they must be carefully assessed.

INTERVENTION RECOMMENDATIONS

The Social Context of Rape Should Be Addressed

The social climate that contributes to gender inequality and men's rape of women and girls is partially responsible for creating harmful beliefs (e.g., rape myths) and negative social reactions (e.g., blame) toward victims of sexual assault and abuse. Without larger societal change in social norms and institutional and organizational practices, U.S. society will remain an unsafe place for women, who continue to face risk of sexual assault and confront negative responses from others if they choose to talk about their experiences or the isolation of silence that is still far too common for too many women. By taking an ecological approach to issues of disclosure and social reactions to victims in treatment, prevention, and activism against rape and secondary victimization of survivors, we can empower women and men to speak out and work collectively to stop rape in our society.

Informal Support Sources Should Be Taught How to Respond to Disclosure

Informal support sources can help victims engage in targeted, safe disclosures that take place in a context in which survivors feel comfortable initiating talking about rape. Rape takes away control and power, at least in the moment, and unless talking about it is voluntary and occurs when the victim is ready and wanting to do so in a safe, comfortable context the result may be a form of secondary victimization. For survivors who are comfortable writing or talking about rape either privately or publicly, this should be encouraged, because it appears to be helpful to many survivors (Ream, 2004). However, if people are not appropriately prepared to respond to those disclosures the survivor is more likely to receive negative reactions. Therefore, more must be done to prepare informal support providers to respond positively to victims.

This intervention can take place in a variety of contexts. The news and entertainment media can be harnessed to educate the general public about how to respond supportively to victims of sexual assault and how to avoid negative social reactions when encountering a survivor. This also can be done in secondary schools and universities, where a great deal of rape education occurs already. Most existing school-based discussions of rape, unfortunately, focus on facts about rape and risk reduction, with little practical information about how to resist and fight rape and how to respond to survivors and avoid negative reactions.

Programs that teach informal support sources to provide positive responses should focus on conveying positive social norms:

> Men think that other men are more sexually active than themselves, are more comfortable behaving in stereotypically masculine ways, are less uncomfortable with the objectification of women and violence, are more homophobic and heterosexist, and are more likely to endorse rape myths. Because of the powerful influence that men have on each other, correcting these misperceptions can free men to act in ways that are healthier and more aligned with personal values. (Berkowitz, 2004, p. 4)

It is important to show real victims' experiences and depictions or examples of how informal support sources can respond positively to a victim's disclosure. The public can learn several things from such an approach. First, this approach can endorse active listening, which is the most important thing to do and may be all that is needed by some survivors. By listening, people can learn what support the survivor needs and perhaps provide referral source information. Second, the public can learn about positive and negative social reactions to disclosures and be given a list of things to say or do as well as things to avoid, based on current research. Third, the public can learn about services provided by rape crisis centers and other community agencies that are available to assist victims of sexual assault. Rape hotline numbers and other quickly digestible pieces of information can be given to the public, similar to public education initiatives about depression, domestic violence, suicide, smoking, drunk driving, and other social/health problems. Fourth, the public can learn how they can help victims and fight sexual assault, for example, by volunteering to help at a rape crisis center or participating in community events such as speak-outs to raise awareness about sexual assault.

Potential Bystanders Should Be Taught to Intervene

In the bystander approach, both men and women are trained to intervene in potential assaults to stop their occurrence as well as situations in which sexist comments are made that promote the rape culture. These programs also teach people how to support a friend or any person who discloses a sexual assault. With this dual focus, bystander programs can help to accomplish goals of stopping rapes and reducing victim blame in society (e.g., Banyard, Moynihan, & Plante, 2007; Schewe, 2006). One recent social marketing campaign utilized rape prevention posters with a bystander focus. The campaign was evaluated with a pre- and posttest experimental design used in several college dormitories as well as a community-wide Internet survey, and positive effects were seen both in attitudes toward and knowledge about how to intervene as a prosocial bystander to stop assault (Potter, Moynihan, Stapleton, & Banyard, 2009; Potter, Stapleton, & Moynihan, 2008). This poster campaign was designed to complement messages being promoted by rape prevention programs in the same community and exemplified an integrated approach that might prove to be successful for reducing sexual assault over time.

Specific Groups of People Should Be Targeted at Various Ages

Specific groups—for example, students, parents, teachers, and professionals—can be targeted in schools, parent–teacher association meetings, teachers' meetings, and professional association meetings, respectively. All of these groups and organizations should be provided with information about sexual assault, preferably by the most credible sources, such as leaders in those settings in which people are already embedded. Depending on the specific group and setting, time should be spent not only discussing the problem of rape, rape myths, and reactions to victims but also enlisting people as helpers who can make a difference for victims. Because many people, even helpers, may also need help dealing with their own past experiences and reactions to this topic, referral service information should be made available for helpers on how to deal with their own reactions to sexual victimization personally as well as reactions from those around them.

Formal Service Providers Should Be Trained in Sexual Assault Issues

Many professionals do not get adequate training about sexual assault, and education about social reactions to victims of rape, rape stereotypes, and rape myths is needed. This material should be covered in the regular curricula and continuing education training for health care professionals, mental health professionals, social service agency professionals, and legal/criminal justice personnel. These groups all encounter survivors of sexual assault and should be knowledgeable about how to avoid revictimizing survivors, how to respond supportively, and how to get appropriate referrals for them. Rape issues should be part of required educational training, not just options in continuing education for those who seek them out.

Criminal justice personnel, including police, are in particular need of training on how to respond. Such training may need to be facilitated and/or reinforced by leaders in the state's attorneys' offices, judges, and police superintendents, who should assert that responding sensitively to victims is important and may even make performing their jobs easier. Leaders' involvement is likely important, because early experimental evaluation data did not show sustained improvement in police responsiveness to victims in general following training (Rosenbaum, 1987). In addition, because the legal system was not designed to promote healing, criminal justice personnel should be trained to inform victims of how traumatic the process of police reporting and pursuing a criminal case can be and how rare it is to successfully prosecute and imprison rapists. Victims should not be discouraged from seeking justice, but they do need to be aware of the realities of what they are likely to face in the criminal justice system.

Getting involved is not easy to do, as advocates have indicated; however, if criminal justice officials—including prosecutors, defense attorneys, judges, and others—treated victims better it could improve victim participation in the criminal justice process and result in more just case outcomes (Erez & Roberts, 2007). Accomplishing this goal should involve getting key leaders to change the culture and behavioral expectations in police and legal organizations (e.g., departments, courtrooms).

Safe Disclosure Should Be Encouraged and Facilitated

Collective disclosure may be a particularly potent form of refusal and resistance (Gavey, 2007) when rape is widespread within an institution.

Examples include the recent disclosures of sexual abuse by many survivors that were perpetrated by priests in the Roman Catholic Church (Finkelhor, 2003), rape speakouts, take-back-the-night marches, Internet forums, zines, and women's support groups. These avenues provide powerful ways for women to communicate about and express their experiences. Revitalization of activism is critical, whether in online groups/forums or in-person marches. Safe spaces are needed so collective disclosures are positive experiences for victims and their voices can be heard and validated.

Speaking should always be voluntary, and both public and private spaces are needed so survivors can have confidentiality if they do not wish to speak publicly. We now live in a culture where the "good victim" (i.e., victim of a stereotypical rape) speaks out, yet survivors of nonstereotypical rape also need to be heard and to get services. Although in some ways there are more avenues for victims to speak out about their experiences, especially with the advent of the Internet, safety concerns may be greater given the risks of online participation (see Boudreau, 2008, for a report of a teenage victim of rape who posted a video of herself sharing her story of sexual assault and plea for help). Public Web sites and chat forums must be moderated, and safeguards are needed to monitor and enhance confidentiality and safety for survivors of sexual assault (e.g., see the Web site of the Rape, Abuse, and Incest National Network, http://www.rainn.org, for the new National Sexual Assault Online hotline). Service agencies need to limit or remove rules and policies that discourage help-seeking, such as excluding certain women (e.g., those with drug problems, prostitutes). Although support groups and opportunities to talk to mental health professionals or advocates should be available, they should not be required for victims to get help.

Survivors Should Be Empowered to Be Activists

Many survivors in research studies have said they participated to help themselves and other women (Campbell & Adams, 2009; Ullman, Townsend, Filipas, & Starzynski, 2007). Expanding on potential available avenues for survivors may empower them to cope with and respond to sexual assault individually and collectively in ways most comfortable for them. A range of alternatives is needed because collective action may be more easily expanded in online forums and groups in addition to the traditional in-person events sponsored by rape crisis centers and other organizations in the community. Collective disclosures of rape and the resulting empowerment of women can be enhanced by facilitating survivors' ability to connect with each other, take action, and create positive change. Rape crisis centers and other groups fighting violence against women can help to provide resources and support to women who wish to spearhead such strategies. One strategy to help girls and women creatively resist and survive sexual assault, which was mentioned by one advocate interviewed in Chicago, may be to try to facilitate the creation of zines (Ullman & Townsend, 2007).

Although some people may respond that the purpose of crisis centers and mental health agencies is to provide services, for many survivors the goals of healing and activism are compatible and overlapping. Part of healing and recovering from assault may go beyond seeking individual therapy or talking to one's own social network. Many survivors may find healing in taking action against violence against women, especially by joining other women organizing for social change in groups such as INCITE!, the Voices and Faces Project; Promoting Awareness, Victim Empowerment; and others. These are some of the many online forums, such as the Voices and Faces Project (Ream, 2004) described earlier, and other grassroots antirape and antiviolence groups, such as Promoting Awareness, Victim Empowerment, founded by rape survivor Angela Rose in Chicago, and INCITE! Women of Color Against Violence (http://www.incite-national.org), a global network/organization of activist women working to combat violence against women. Founded in 2000 by activists around the United States, INCITE! is the largest multiracial, grassroots, feminist organization in the country, with chapters in many U.S. cities, and has published an anthology of writings by activists that focuses on movement building and resistance to violence strategies used by women worldwide (INCITE! Women of Color Against Violence, 2006). These are just a few examples of organizations with which survivors of rape and their significant others can connect to help others and get support about their violence experiences (see also Survivor Matters, http://www.survivormatters.btik.com). These resources are important and remind us that recovery/treatment of survivors does not need to be completely separate from prevention and efforts to stop rape. Taking action individually and collectively to stop rape is likely to attract many survivors who are trying to help themselves and other women who have been victimized by rape.

Self-Defense Training Should Be Available

Another approach may be to provide access to risk reduction and self-defense training not only through rape crisis centers but also in schools, given that this is one of the few strategies known to reduce women's risk of being sexually assaulted and having a completed rape outcome (Brecklin, 2008; Gidycz, Rich, Orchowski, King, & Miller, 2006; Orchowski, Gidycz, & Raffle, 2008; Ullman, 2007a). For at least some women, strategies to facilitate prevention and healing may include self-defense. Self-defense training is important to provide to women and girls, because research shows that it is another way to empower women to resist rape and their socialization to be passive and/or not to stand up for their rights. Although this does not stop rapists and may only displace attacks to weaker targets, it is still a form of refusal and individual response that can help women avert attacks and improve their confidence and self-worth (Brecklin, 2008; McCaughey, 1997). Research also suggests that self-defense training may enhance recovery from sexual assault, not just avoidance/resistance to future attacks (Brecklin, 2008; David, Simpson, & Cotton, 2006).

Specific Interventions Should Target Victims of Intimate Partner Rape

Multiple forms of violence are likely to coexist. For example, rape or incest in the family context may occur in isolation, but they may also occur in the context of other violence, such as domestic violence between adults and/or other forms of child abuse (Rossman & Rosenberg, 1998). Rape between spouses or romantic partners cannot be divorced from other forms of emotional and physical abuse in which power and control are likely to be motives of perpetrators (Stark, 2007). Thus, rape in this intimate-partner context is much different from rape in other relationships. Because we know that at least one third of domestic violence includes sexual assaults, we need to identify and target those victims separately, given the added risk of psychological and physical health impacts for women and children in these situations (Bergen, 1996; Russell, 1982; L. Walker, 1979).

The Media Should Help the Public Identify and Counter Aspects of Rape-Supportive Culture

Several examples of this exist already. Ms. magazine has had readers send in pictures of advertisements promoting violence against women for many years for their "No Comment" section and encourages readers to complain to advertisers and challenge them to remove such ads. A media campaign offered by Strength Mediaworks called "Men of Strength" was devised by the community group Men Can Stop Rape (1987) to counter popular media presentations supportive of violence against women (http://www. mencanstoprape.org/info-url2698/info-url.htm). The campaign is widely recognized as the nation's best designed and most effective public service advertising sexual assault prevention outreach to young men and is organized around the theme line "My Strength Is Not for Hurting." Strength Mediaworks's initiative targets young men with provocative, inspiring images and messages highlighting how men can be strong and empowered without overpowering others or resorting to violence in relationships. Strength Mediaworks's materials have been distributed across all 50 states and in 20 foreign countries. Initial evaluation data from focus groups and surveys of young men participating in the My Strength Is Not for Hurting campaign have shown positive results in terms of knowledge, beliefs, and behaviors related to sexual assault (Hawkins, 2005). Most media-facilitated programs for rape prevention (e.g., the My Strength campaign, Red Flag campaign, White Ribbon campaign) have not been evaluated, because evaluation methods for media interventions are complex and difficult to implement, although such evaluations are needed.

Media Outlets, Formal Service Providers, and Institutions Should Be Held Accountable for Any Rape-Supportive Actions

Interventions are needed to demand accountability from the media, service providers, public officials, and professionals in many contexts (e.g., schools, medical settings, churches, community organizations, the legal system) to challenge harmful social reactions to victims that revictimize individuals and support the rape-supportive culture. In particular, the mass media must be called to account when they use biased portrayals of rape cases to increase ratings. Social change organizations are needed to create alternatives to violence, and messages and depictions of violence perpetrated by the media, corporations, and advertisers supporting the rape-supportive culture need to be challenged.

Violence against women has saturated U.S. culture and become increasingly mainstream and normalized in recent years. For example, much of women's victimization is now portrayed as their "choice," or at least something other than violence. This has been partly facilitated by the infiltration of pornography into the mainstream of society and the rise and proliferation of violence against women, both real and depicted, on the Internet. Citizens need to be directly engaged by antiviolence and antirape organizations to join efforts to challenge the corporate marketing of violence in advertisements, television, movies, music, and videos. We need to convince and/or pressure those who promote violence against women to promote prosocial messages instead. Public shaming of officials and CEOs through op-ed pieces in newspapers, Internet blogs, and demonstrations organized by citizens are needed, in addition to positive appeals to these same sources to make it part of their public platform that violence against women is not acceptable.

Rape Crisis Centers Should Receive More Funding to Conduct Public Education Work

Rape crisis centers are already doing much of the social norm intervention work. Despite the fact that some centers reach thousands of people a year, the scale of what they do is inadequate because of their limited funding and the well-financed, profitable mass media portrayals of violence and rape on television and movies as well as widely available violent pornography. The scale of rape crisis center prevention education efforts must be increased substantially, and both public and private funding sources are needed to promote antirape messages and to stop the rape-supportive messages that are endemic to U.S. media culture. Rape crisis centers are not sufficient by themselves to fully address rape and responses to it in terms of treatment, prevention, and justice. Therefore, we also need other institutions—including those related to families, churches, education, health, social welfare, criminal justice, the military, and the media—to take on issues of violence against women and sexual assault to educate against rape, respond to victims supportively, and directly address the rape-supportive climate endemic to many organizations and institutions.

Victim Advocates Should Be Available in Formal Medical and Legal Settings

Victim advocates are important providers of support and information to victims who prosecute their cases and have been shown to lead to better outcomes for victims of rape compared with victims who do not have advocates (Campbell, 2006), especially in a retributive criminal justice system that continues to prioritize needs of offenders over those of victims. In a quasi-experimental study, Campbell (2006) compared victims' medical examination experiences in two urban hospitals. One hospital used rape crisis medical advocates, and the other did not. Victims who had help from an advocate were more likely to receive comprehensive medical care and less likely to experience secondary victimization. This suggests that victims may benefit from some advocates' help in hospital ERs. This is likely to be true in the courtroom as well, although evaluation studies of the impact of victim advocacy in this area are lacking.

One excellent example of victim advocates embedded in the hospital setting is the Sexual Assault Nurse Examiner (SANE) program. SANE nurses can be helpful to victims and can educate other hospital workers about rape and how to respond sensitively to victims. SANE programs were created by nurses in 1970s and grew during the 1990s (Ledray, 1999; Little, 2001; U.S. Department of Justice, 2004) to circumvent many of the problems of traditional hospital ER care by having specially trained nurses provide 24-hour medical and mental health care to victims in the ER or community clinics. These programs work to improve consistency of medical services to victims and decrease victims' trauma by treating them with dignity and respect (e.g., explaining the process, letting them stop the examination to give them control), and they have been positively appraised by victims (Campbell, Patterson, Adams, Diegel, & Coats, 2008; Ericksen et al., 2002). National surveys of SANE programs have found service provision rates of 90% or higher for HIV testing and pregnancy prophylaxis care (Campbell et al., 2006; Ciancone, Wilson, Collette, & Gerson, 2000; Crandall & Helitzer, 2003), suggesting that victims who have access to such programs do in fact receive superior care.

SANE programs may also improve legal prosecution for reported cases because of higher quality forensic evidence collection (Campbell, Patterson, & Lichty, 2005), which leads to plea bargains (Little, 2001), and the SANE's expert testimony, which may help obtain convictions (Ledray, 1999). Further evidence suggests that police referral and prosecution rates have increased significantly after the implementation of SANE programs (Campbell, Patterson, & Bybee, 2007; Crandall & Helitzer, 2003) and that the coordination of legal and medical services may reduce secondary victimization and increase victims' participation in the prosecution process (Campbell et al., 2007; Crandall & Helitzer, 2003).

Victim Service Agencies Should Collaborate With Victims and Other Service Organizations

Different organizations could collaborate to increase and facilitate online networks and forums for survivors who cannot or will not come in person to seek services. Also, rape crisis centers could work with other community organizations focused on issues of poor women of color to address health, social justice, and crime issues. Accomplishing this goal will not be an easy task, but it is clear that improved coalitions are needed among organizations working on behalf of women's issues and those working on issues related to racial and economic justice. Zweig and Burt (2007) compared communities with coordinated responses to sexual assault and reported that the response to victims in such communities was better than in those without coordinated services. Such innovative practices may reduce secondary victimization and improve recovery outcomes of survivors seeking services.

Sexual Assault Response Teams Should Be Considered

One example of effective community response coordination is *sexual assault response teams* (SARTs; see http://www.stopvaw.org/), which are designed to ensure that victims are provided with a broad range of necessary care and services (e.g., legal, medical, social services) and to increase the likelihood that assaults can be successfully prosecuted. Often, the teams comprise a forensic examiner, a sexual assault advocate, a prosecutor, and a law enforcement officer. All responding actors follow specific protocols that outline their responsibilities for treating and providing services to victims of sexual assault. The response of the SART can be activated at any stage during which the survivor interacts with the system—for example, when the survivor reports to the police station, seeks medical services at an ER, or calls a sexual assault program's crisis line. A SART has the potential to provide a greater continuum of care for survivors of sexual assault, increased quality of care for survivors, and a reduction of the secondary trauma survivors often experience (in part through a reduction in the number of times they must tell their story) as they move through the medical and judicial/law enforcement systems (Michigan Sexual Assault Systems Response Team Task Force, 2001).

The four goals of SARTs generally include (a) meet the immediate needs of the victim with crisis intervention and support services; (b) provide a joint, effective, sensitive approach to victims of sexual assault; (c) conduct an investigation of the crime; and (d) document and preserve forensic evidence for prosecuting the perpetrator of the crime. The roles of three members of a SART—the advocate, the law enforcement officer, and the health care professional (often a SANE)—are clearly delineated:

> Advocates provide support to the victim, answer any questions the victim may have, and inform the victim of the process for the interview and examination. The advocate does not participate in the gathering of evidence, fact-finding, or the investigation of the assault. Rather, their focus is placed on ensuring that the victim is supported throughout the process. As advocates often provide individual and group support for months and sometimes years to come, the initial bond that develops between advocate and victim is critical. Advocates do not provide an opinion on the merits of the case or participate in conducting the interview, nor do they generally testify in court. Law enforcement's role is to investigate and report the facts of the case. Law enforcement will be responsible for the immediate safety needs of the victim; interviewing the victim; investigation of the crime; identifying, arresting, and/or referring charges on the suspect; arranging for forensic examination of the suspect when necessary, writing a report, participating in court proceedings; and all other duties normally associated with investigative and law enforcement functions. The health care professional's role is to provide the health care component of the SART. He or she performs the physical assessment of the sexual assault victim; collects, documents, and preserves forensic evidence; provides information and referral to the victim on health care matters; documents the examination in the medical record; and presents expert testimony in court. Although a law enforcement officer may become involved in the case through the SART, the decision about whether an assault is "reported" to the police and whether, once the assault is reported, a complaint is made that would lead to a prosecution, should ideally remain with the victim. The victim should always be encouraged to see a doctor to address any health concerns; in addition, the victim

might be informed about the option of having a forensic examination that would aid in a prosecution, should she decide to proceed with a complaint. This would leave the options open for the victim, and she would not be required to decide immediately what course of action is best for her to pursue. (Michigan Sexual Assault Systems Response Team Task Force, 2001)

In another example, the Minnesota Coalition for Sexual Assault's (MCASA) training manual describes the legal system in Minnesota, which allows victims a range of choices in deciding whether to report an assault. The MCASA manual emphasizes that a victim should never be pressured to report the assault. It is the advocate's role to provide information about options. Only the victim herself can make the decision about whether to report. MCASA's training manual also provides additional information about the role of the advocate during medical examinations.

The SART model has taken different forms in different communities. As Ledray (1999) explained, some SARTs are composed of a team of individuals who respond together to jointly interview the victim at the time of the sexual assault examination. Other SARTs are composed of individuals who "work independently on a day-to-day basis but communicate with each other regularly (possibly daily, and meet weekly or monthly) to discuss mutual cases and solve mutual problems[,] thus making the system function more smoothly" (Ledray, 1999, p. 13). The Rape Treatment Center in San Francisco, a nonprofit organization, is another comprehensive rape crisis unit. The center provides 24-hour emergency medical care, evidence collection, crisis intervention, advocacy, court accompaniment, legal assistance, and psychotherapy services. It also conducts outreach and public education campaigns; trains police, members of the media, mental health professionals, and prosecutors; and consults with the government.

Whatever model is chosen, all actors within the community should ensure that they are working for the same goal. Before implementing a coordinated response, "sexual assault programs and the systems and individuals in their community should work together to define the roles, duties, and responsibilities of the criminal justice system, the medical system, victim advocates, and other professionals in responding to sexual assault" (Michigan Sexual Assault Systems Response Team Task Force, 2001, p. 30). It can be helpful to put in writing the agreements reached about each actor's role, duties, and responsibilities. A coordinated and victim-centered response not only results in more effective service provision and evidence collection but also helps increase the likelihood that survivors will proceed with a complaint.

Although many benefits accompany the coordinated response of a SART, there are also disadvantages, in particular in terms of the protocols regarding interviewing and reporting. For example, a victim who is uncertain about whether to report an assault to the police may feel pressured to report when protocol requires law enforcement personnel to interview the victim before the SANE becomes involved. The advocate will support the victim in whatever decision she makes, even if the decision is not to prosecute. If the victim decides not to report, however, she should still be able to access health care for STD and pregnancy risk evaluation and prevention, but in reality this varies depending on laws in the state where she resides.

Although repetition of the account of the sexual assault is certainly an unpleasant experience that most victims want to avoid, the notion that they will be better off if they do not have to do so is only a presumption. Research on treatment efficacy has in fact shown that repetition of the account of the assault in detail has a beneficial, desensitizing, healing effect (Ledray, 1999), although this is likely to be the case only if there is a supportive response and milieu for disclosure.

The Culture of Victim Blaming in the Legal System Should Be Changed

Researchers, practitioners, and community members must come together to convince police chiefs, state's attorneys, and judges that fair treatment of victims is possible and in everyone's interest. Research shows that victims of crime in general are more satisfied if they feel they are treated justly and fairly (Tyler & Huo, 2002), although examination of victims of sexual assault specifically is needed. Police may have already changed more than other legal agents (e.g., judges) in their responsiveness to violence against women (e.g., making arrests) because of activist pressure following negligent responses to female victims of domestic violence, although data are needed to document this. Because changes to date are still not enough, community policing and initiatives that involve the community working with the police may improve accountability and responses to victims (Skogan, 2006).

Improved response in the legal system will happen only if key leaders/ stakeholders, such as leaders in the criminal justice system, from judges to police chiefs to attorneys, take on this challenge as part of their agenda to treat survivors more sensitively and communicate these victim-sensitive and -supportive social norms to their departments and courtrooms on a daily basis. Insensitive judges and/or legal processes should be identified publicly to force change in the criminal justice system. Legal action may also be important for improving accountability of police and the criminal justice system.

Men Should Join the Effort to Stop Rape

Bringing men into rape prevention and efforts to challenge the rape-supportive social climate as well as their own socialization is also important in making responsibility for rape everyone's problem. This has been done in some rape prevention programs, but it is still too limited (Berkowitz, 2002; Foubert, 2000). Men can be involved by supporting women's organizations and efforts to fight violence against women both financially and by taking action in support of women's initiatives. Also, of course, men should learn to respond supportively to rape disclosure. They need to offer care and support but not try to rescue or take over in responding to survivors individually or in their work in the antirape movement (Funk, 1993). It is important to avoid replicating traditional gender dynamics in interactions with survivors and in organizations (Funk, 1993). This may take a lot of work on the part of both men (who have been socialized to have women defer to them) and women (who have been socialized to defer to men).

Bringing men into this work is challenging but important to do by showing men how rape is a problem for both women and men. Appeals to men may involve describing how rape may negatively affect women they care about and how it may harm their relationships with women because of women's fear of men's violence, which may reduce women's willingness to have relationships with men. It may also be helpful in rape prevention programs with men to show the impact of rape on a male victim, which may increase men's ability to relate to rape and its impact on women (Schewe, 2006). Also, men may feel empowered to confront the victimization they experience growing up male, including the oppressiveness of having to repress their emotions and be tough. This socialization process denies men full humanity and the ability to respond to male violence that gets targeted against them in the form of bullying and adolescent and adult violence, which is overwhelmingly male against male. In other words, connecting different forms of male violence to violence against women specifically may help men to see how it is in their own self-interest to work to stop male violence.

Men may be able to best get support in groups with other men doing antirape work, such as Madison, Wisconsin's Men Stopping Rape. Men can work both in women's organizations in appropriate roles and in collaboration with women. They can have their own organizations that work against sexual violence by educating men to help stop rape; support survivors; and challenge sexist and violent beliefs, including rape myths (see also Schwartz & DeKeseredy, 1997). This may help them to create a space where they can challenge their own ingrained socialization to male privilege, get support from other men, and learn by role modeling how to reformulate their ways of interacting with other men and women. A limited body of evidence suggests that some prevention programs might reduce men's actual sexual aggression (Foshee et al., 2004; Foubert, Newberry, & Tatum, 2007), although more research is needed to document sustained behavioral change in men.

Restorative Justice Approaches Should Be Considered

Restorative justice approaches are another tool to empower victims to get some form of justice when pursuing a criminal case is impossible and/or not what the victim needs or wants (Koss, 2000). Restorative justice programs offer a way to try to make whole or "restore" survivors (Koss, 2006) by creating an alternative process that focuses on victims' need to talk about the assault, be heard, and recognized. This is typically not possible in the traditional adversarial criminal justice system, despite frequent misleading mass media portrayals of victims having a voice in court settings. Unlike traditional criminal justice, in the restorative process offenders are held accountable for their actions and must make amends to their victims. Survivors have reported wanting the offenders to acknowledge, apologize, and/or make amends, which can be done without a stressful, time-consuming court process (Koss & Achilles, 2008). Restorative programs for survivors of sexual assault have yet to be rigorously evaluated, but they offer a promising alternative to the traditional criminal justice process.

Racism, Classism, and Other Social Biases Should Be Combated

In general, it is critical to fight against inequalities based on race, class, gender, sexual orientation, and disability, factors that leave the most vulnerable victims trapped in violent situations and relationships. For women in violent relationships or those dealing with chronic stressors of poverty, drug use, and community violence, rape may be a fact of life with which they have little time, space, or energy to cope in comparison to other stressors (Fine, 1983). Increased attention to communities of color, women of lower social classes, women who are immigrants, women with substance abuse problems, and women who are homeless is warranted. These subgroups of women may face greater risk of violence and negative consequences for speaking out about their experiences in a racist, classist society that still privileges experiences of violence against White, middle-class women (A. Y. Davis, 1978/1981; Donovan & Williams, 2002).

CONCLUSION

In this book, I have argued that the social context, in particular societal responses to victims of sexual assault, is critical for treatment and prevention of this crime. U.S. society has a long way to go in reducing harmful beliefs and attitudes that support violence against women and perpetuate victim-blaming responses commonly experienced by women after assault. Harmful responses from informal and formal support providers not only reduce survivors' ability to disclose, seek help, and recover but also perpetuate the rape culture in which we live and provide a foundation upon which perpetrators can continue to offend with relative impunity, in particular against women they know. Survivors, their partners and families, advocates, professionals (including mental health, medical, and criminal justice personnel), and concerned citizens all need to come together in challenging the rape culture, holding perpetrators accountable, supporting survivors, and working to create a society that is free of sexual assault.

FURTHER READING

Gavey, N. (2007). *Rape, recognition, and refusal*. Distinguished publication award address delivered to the Association for Women in Psychology, San Francisco.

Gavey (2007) discusses the increasing problem of "psychologizing" and individualizing the problem of rape and calls for a collective refusal of rape. Refusal may entail women resisting rape behaviorally, speaking out about it individually and collectively; working for social changes in laws and policies that revictimize survivors; and demanding that offenders and men generally share in the burden of speaking out against rape, stopping rape, and supporting survivors. She rightly states that we have lost the context of gender analysis and a focus on the collective; instead, we have focused on rape at the psychological and individual levels instead of on dismantling rape in society. Gavey states, as have other writers (Hollander, 2002), that although recognition of the harm of rape can lead to a focus on women's vulnerability, we need to see agency in victimization (see Lamb, 1999, for similar arguments). She argues that to address this problem we must reconnect recognition and refusal, by focusing on the social context, something Heberle (1996) also argued. Like Gilfus (1999), Gavey encourages questioning of the trauma model that keeps women defined as vulnerable (see also Maracek, 1999). As in the early feminist movement that emphasized speak-outs, take-back-the-night marches, self-defense training, and rape patrols, it is vital to emphasize women's strength and defiance instead of vulnerability and harm. Refusal of rape positions women as active agents who can defy fear and restrictions, resist assaults, take action to survive, and refuse to be blamed or ashamed or to have the harm of rape be minimized. Gavey asserts that both individual and collective refusal are needed; specifically, resistance to rape is needed at an individual level with collective support for women's self-protection and self-defense in the community. Also, refusal of the stigmatization and social rejection that happens to rape victims following rape is needed on the part of society.

Gavey (2007) sees refusal as encompassing resistance during rape; action after rape, such as attempts to recover; and women's collective action to stop rape. She also believes that public intellectuals must take a stand and examine and acknowledge resistance to rape or mental control as a form of political resistance, not just behavioral resistance (see also Rozee & Koss, 2001). Gavey also argues that society needs an expanded, complex notion of resistance: Refusal is necessary, even if one cannot always avoid completed rape.

Refusal entails not only speaking out about rape and resistance to rape at an individual level but also a collective effort to fight the cultural backdrop that supports rape in society. Gavey (2005) wrote earlier that we must challenge heterosexuality because it supports rape, a thesis she develops and supports with extensive research in her 2007 book. She echoes earlier radical feminists who coined the term *compulsory heterosexuality* (A. Rich, 1980) and who claimed that sex in a context of unequal power between men and women is tantamount to rape (MacKinnon, 1987). Gavey (2007) argues that heterosexuality is the scaffolding on which rape and societal support for rape rests. By this she means that, in a societal context where heterosexuality is the dominant model of sexual relations, much of what passes for "just sex" may in fact legally be rape. This argument reflects a radical feminist perspective.

According to Gavey (2007), activism is tantamount to a collective refusal of rape, and survival of rape should be turned into a political strategy. However, it is hard for victims to stand up to the rape culture, because victims are viewed negatively because they have been raped, when in fact those who come forward should be seen as heroes. They must also fight their own expectations about others' reactions and judgments. Gavey also claims that we fail to recognize private forms of resistance and must view women as powerful, not allowing information about the trauma of rape to reinforce women's helplessness and vulnerability or societal perceptions of women as weak.

The question of how to apply the refusal paradigm effectively to rape in relationships is more challenging, because it is much harder for women to refuse/resist rape in an intimate partner relationship (Bergen, 1996; Ullman

& Siegel, 1993). Furthermore, rape crisis centers are now more institutionalized and professionalized and must meet state funders' requirements, which makes it hard to address rape in intimate partner relationships. This occurs because funding for domestic violence and sexual assault is typically separate, yet these forms of violence against women sometimes overlap. Gavey (2007) asserts that academics must speak out, and I maintain that all those concerned about this issue need to do so, including health-care workers, advocates, therapists, and concerned citizens in general.

Gavey's (2007) arguments are powerful calls to action to provide public forums wherever possible where people can speak about rape, respond with collective action against rape, and organize to condemn and fight against a social climate that is harmful to girls and women. This includes the rape-supportive climate that is fueled by sexualization of girls in the media (American Psychological Association, 2007), the proliferation of pornography (Dines, Russo, & Jensen, 1998), an epidemic of prostitution (Paul, 2005), and sex trafficking in women and girls (Barry, 1979; Farley, 2003).

Russo, A., & Spatz, M. (2007). *Communities engaged in resisting violence.* **Chicago: Women and Girls Collective Action Network.**

Russo and Spatz (2007) review a number of ideas emanating from grassroots community-based projects to resist violence that can be applied to sexual assault, in addition to changes to existing systems and innovative services. The groups that sponsor these projects argue that multiple approaches are needed and that they must address multiple sources of inequality, not just gender, such as sexual orientation and disability. Russo and Spatz provide examples of organizations that question existing structures that may be oppressive to victims. They argue that projects are needed that are outside of established antiviolence agencies and free of funders' constraints. With regard to survivors' ability to disclose and get support from others, their recommendations for creating a safe space for survivors, especially for marginalized women, include town hall meetings, healing circles, and participatory action research. Other recommendations include a need to create self-sustaining support systems and self-care for antiviolence workers and survivors and to reject the helper–helped dynamic common in existing service systems/organizations. Survivors have much to offer and can be active participants in their own recovery and in social change initiatives (to the extent to which they are able and willing to do so). Survivors may gain strength by helping others and have important knowledge and experience that needs to be considered by researchers, policymakers, activists, and service providers. No one group can solve this problem, so all of these constituencies must find more forums in which to come together so multiple voices/perspectives can be represented and connections can be made.

Funk, R. E. (1993). *Stopping rape: A challenge for men.* Philadelphia: New Society.

Funk (1993) gives invaluable advice to men on how to support a victim in terms of helping her find safety and encouraging her to seek help from hospital and rape crisis centers and/or the police if she wishes to do so. He tells men to remind survivors of their strength and courage and to reinforce to survivors that they are not to blame for the attack. He gives a lot of information about listening well by recognizing a survivor's strength in disclosing rape, not inquiring about details, letting her set the pace of disclosure, and meeting the victim where she is. He also tells men to both be aware of and deal with their own feelings about the attack and the survivor and, if they feel overwhelmed, to acknowledge that and be honest and prepared to consult someone with training in dealing with rape victims and their support providers. He suggests that men remind survivors that they survived the attack and that they can take their time in talking about it and dealing with it. He recommends letting the survivor indicate what support she needs. Recognizing that survivors' needs come first is paramount, according to Funk, and may force men to challenge their own gendered socialization whereby they have become used to women taking care of them and their feelings instead of the reverse. Avoiding taking revenge against the perpetrator, or engaging in other actions to solve the problem without regard to what the survivor wants or needs, is critical because it takes more control away from victims. He also gives specific advice to men whose partners have been assaulted, telling them to also acknowledge and take care of their own reactions to their partner's assault on their own so that they can best support their partner in dealing with the assault. He advises men on how to seek support from others to deal with the impact on themselves of helping survivors, and he describes how to cope with the trauma of dealing with a survivor in general with self-care strategies. He carefully explains how men have to challenge their own traditional gender role socialization because it often does not include seeking support for themselves or talking about their own emotions.

Orton, R. S. (1993). Outside in: A man in the movement. In E. Buchwald, P. Fletcher, & M. Roth (Eds.), *Transforming a rape culture* (pp. 237–246). Minneapolis, MN: Milkweed Press.

Orton, who wrote about his experience working in the late 1970s in a rape crisis center in Austin, Texas, offers an example of men's transformation and change. He argues that it is men's job to wake other men up and involve them in social change to stop violence against women. He describes his experiences of being the only man in this movement and the only one to attend the first National Coalition Against Sexual Assault conference. He realizes that the antirape movement is not about him or other men and explains that

that is what many men find frightening and threatening. He also describes how he became aware of his own belief in masculine entitlement and hidden male privilege as well as how he was able to transform old gender habits and confront the part of himself that has caused pain in the world. He discusses realizing what women experience after rape after he went to an ER to advocate for a rape victim and how this experience forced him to confront the vulnerability that women experience as women, something that men are able to deny and avoid dealing with. He argues that men must confront their own vulnerability to the violence of other men and take ownership with other men of their role in confronting sexism and rape, which men have created and maintained collectively (see also Stoltenberg, 1999).

Schewe, P. A. (2006). Interventions to prevent sexual violence. In L. Doll, S. Bonzo, J. Mercy, & D. Sleet (Eds.), *Handbook of injury and violence prevention* (pp. 223–240). New York: Springer.

In this review of interventions to prevent sexual violence, Schewe notes several intervention foci that have the most empirical support, including bystander interventions, rape myths, self-defense skills, communication training, assertiveness training, and limit-setting. Possible intervention practices with mixed evidence of efficacy he notes include victim empathy, avoidance of high-risk situations, negative consequences for perpetrators, and changing social norms. He states that unsupported practices include knowledge/rape awareness programs and education without actual training in self-defense (see also Lonsway et al., 2009, for a critical review of rape prevention programs with implications for practitioners).

REFERENCES

Abbey, A., Jacques-Tiura, A. J., & Parkhill, M. (in press). Sexual assault among diverse populations of women: Common ground, distinctive features, and unanswered questions. In H. Landrine & N. Russo (Eds.), *Bringing diversity to feminist psychology* (2nd ed.). New York: Springer.

Acock, A. C., & Ireland, N. K. (1983). Attribution of blame in rape cases: The impact of norm violation, gender, and sex-role attitude. *Sex Roles, 9,* 179–193.

Adams, K. B., Matto, H. C., & Harrington, D. (2001). The Traumatic Stress Institute Belief Scale as a measure of vicarious trauma in a national sample of clinical social workers. *Families in Society, 82,* 363–371.

Adams, S. A., & Riggs, S. A. (2008). An exploratory study of vicarious trauma among therapist trainees. *Training and Education in Professional Psychology, 2,* 26–34.

Ahrens, C. A. (2006). Being silenced: The impact of negative social reactions on the disclosure of rape. *American Journal of Community Psychology, 38,* 263–274.

Ahrens, C. A., & Campbell, R. M. (2000). Assisting rape victims as they recover from rape: The impact on friends. *Journal of Interpersonal Violence, 15,* 959–986.

Ahrens, C. A., Campbell, R. M., Temier-Thames, N. K., Wasco, S. M., & Sefl, T. (2007). Deciding whom to tell: Expectations and outcomes of rape survivors' first disclosures. *Psychology of Women Quarterly, 31,* 38–49.

Alderden, M. (2008). *Processing of sexual assault cases through the criminal justice system.* Unpublished doctoral dissertation, University of Illinois at Chicago.

Alexander, J. G., de Chesnay, M., Marshall, E., Campbell, A. R., Johnson, S., & Wright, R. (1989). Research note: Parallel reactions in rape victims and rape researchers. *Violence and Victims, 4,* 57–62.

Allen, M., Emmers, T., Gebhardt, L., & Giery, M. (2006). Exposure to pornography and acceptance of rape myths. *Journal of Communication, 45,* 5–26.

American Psychiatric Association. (1980). *Diagnostic and statistical manual of mental disorders* (3rd ed.). Washington, DC: Author.

American Psychiatric Association. (1994). *Diagnostic and statistical manual of mental disorders* (4th ed.). Washington, DC: Author.

American Psychological Association. (2007). *Report of the APA Task Force on the Sexualization of Girls.* Washington, DC: Author.

Anderson, I., & Quinn, A. (2009). Gender differences in medical students' attitudes towards male and female rape victims. *Psychology, Health & Medicine, 14,* 105–110.

Anderson, J., Martin, J., Mullen, P., Romans, S., & Herbison, P. (1993). Prevalence of child sexual abuse experiences in a community sample of women. *Journal of the American Academy of Child & Adolescent Psychiatry, 32,* 911–919.

Anderson, K., Cooper, H., & Okamura, L. (1997). Individual differences and attitudes towards rape: A meta-analytic review. *Personality and Social Psychology Bulletin, 23,* 295–315.

Andrews, B., Brewin, C. R., & Rose, S. (2003). Gender, social support, and PTSD in victims of violent crime. *Journal of Traumatic Stress, 16*, 421–427.

Antal, H. M., & Range, L. M. (2005). Psychological impact of writing about abuse or positive experiences. *Violence and Victims, 20*, 717–728.

Arata, C. M. (1998). To tell or not to tell: Current functioning of child sexual abuse survivors who disclosed their victimization. *Child Maltreatment, 3*, 63–71.

Atkeson, B. M., Calhoun, K. S., Resick, P. A., & Ellis, E. M. (1982). Victims of rape: Repeated assessment of depressive symptoms. *Journal of Consulting and Clinical Psychology, 50*, 96–102.

Bachar, K. J., & Koss, M. P. (2001). From prevalence to prevention: Closing the gap between what we know about rape and what we do. In C. M. Renzetti, R. K. Bergen, & J. L. Edleson (Eds.), *Sourcebook on violence against women* (pp. 117–142). Thousand Oaks, CA: Sage.

Bachman, R. (1993). Predicting the reporting of rape victimizations: Have rape reforms made a difference? *Criminal Justice and Behavior, 20*, 254–270.

Bachman, R. (1998). The factors related to rape reporting behavior and arrest: New evidence from the National Crime Victimization Survey. *Criminal Justice and Behavior, 25*, 8–29.

Baird, S., & Jenkins, S. R. (2003). Vicarious traumatization, secondary traumatic stress, and burnout in sexual assault and domestic violence agency staff. *Violence and Victims, 18*, 71–86.

Ballou, M., & West, C. (2002). Feminist therapy approaches. In M. Biaggio & M. Hersen (Eds.), *Issues in the psychology of women* (pp. 273–297). New York: Springer.

Banyard, V. L., Moynihan, M. M., & Plante, E. G. (2007). Sexual violence prevention through bystander education: An experimental evaluation. *Journal of Community Psychology, 35*, 463–481.

Banyard, V. L., Moynihan, M. M., Walsh, W. A., Cohn, E. S., & Ward, S. (2009). Friends of survivors: The community impact of unwanted sexual experiences. *Journal of Interpersonal Violence.* Advance online publication. doi: 10.1177/0886260509334407

Baron, L., & Straus, M. (1989). *Four theories of rape in American society.* New Haven, CT: Yale University Press.

Barry, K. (1979). *Female sexual slavery.* New York: New York University Press.

Batten, S., Follette, V., Hall, M., & Palm, K. (2002). Physical and psychological effects of written disclosure among sexual abuse survivors. *Behavior Therapy, 33*, 107–122.

Baumgardner, J., & Richards, A. (2000). *Manifesta: Young women, feminism, and the future.* New York: Farrar, Straus, & Giroux.

Beaton, R. D., & Murphy, S. A. (1995). Working with people in crisis: Research implications. In C. R. Figley (Ed.), *Compassion fatigue: Coping with secondary traumatic stress disorder in those who treat and the traumatized* (pp. 51–81). New York: Brunner-Routledge.

Becker, D. (2005). *The myth of empowerment: Women and the therapeutic culture in America.* New York: New York University Press.

Becker, G. S. (1968). Crime and punishment: An economic approach. *Journal of Political Economy, 76,* 169–217.

Becker, J. V., Skinner, L. G., Abel, G. G., Axelrod, R., & Cichon, J. (1984). Sexual problems of sexual assault survivors. *Women & Health, 9,* 5–20.

Bell, H., Kulkarni, S., & Dalton, L. (2003). Organizational prevention of vicarious trauma. *Families in Society, 84,* 463–470.

Bergen, R. K. (1996). *Wife rape: Understanding the response of survivors and service provides.* Thousand Oaks, CA: Sage.

Berkowitz, A. D. (2002). Fostering men's responsibility for preventing sexual assault. In P. A. Schewe (Ed.), *Preventing violence in relationships: Interventions across the life span* (3rd ed., pp. 163–196). Washington, DC: American Psychological Association.

Berkowitz, A. D. (2004). Working with men to prevent violence against women: Program modalities and formats (Part Two). Retrieved May 1, 2008, from http://www.vawnet.org/Category/Main_Doc.php?docid=414

Berkowitz, A. D. (in press). Fostering healthy norms to prevent violence and abuse: The social norms approach. In K. Kaufman (Ed.), *Preventing sexual violence and exploitation: A sourcebook.* Oklahoma City, OK: Wood & Barnes.

Best, C. L., Dansky, B., & Kilpatrick, D. (1992). Medical students' attitudes about rape victims. *Journal of Interpersonal Violence, 7,* 175–188.

Billette, V., Guay, S., & Marchand, A. (2008). Posttraumatic stress disorder and social support in female victims of sexual assault: The impact of spousal involvement on the efficacy of cognitive–behavioral therapy. *Behavior Modification, 32,* 876–896.

Blake, P. J., Heesacker, M., & Marks, L. I. (1993). Judgments regarding rape: A comparison of rape counselors, police, hospital staff, and citizens. *Journal of Social and Clinical Psychology, 12,* 248–261.

Bletzer, K. V., & Koss, M. P. (2006). After-rape among three populations in the Southwest: A time of mourning, a time for recovery. *Violence Against Women, 12,* 5–29.

Block, R. (1974). Why notify the police? The victim's decision to notify the police of an assault. *Criminology, 11,* 535–569.

Bober, T., & Regehr, C. (2005). Strategies for reducing secondary or vicarious trauma: Do they work? *Brief Treatment and Crisis Intervention, 6,* 1–9.

Bohner, G., Jarvis, C., Eyssel, F., & Siebler, F. (2005). The causal impact of rape myth acceptance on men's rape proclivity: Comparing sexually coercive and non-coercive men. *European Journal of Social Psychology, 35,* 819–828.

Borja, S. E., Callahan, J. L., & Long, P. J. (2006). Positive and negative adjustment and social support of sexual assault survivors. *Journal of Traumatic Stress, 19,* 905–914.

Bottoms, B. L., Rudnicki, A. G., & Epstein, M. E. (2007). A retrospective study of factors affecting the disclosure of childhood sexual and physical abuse. In M.-E. Pipe,

M. Lamb, Y. Orbach, & A.-C. Cedarborg (Eds.), *Child sexual abuse: Disclosure, delay, and denial* (pp. 175–194). Mahwah, NJ: Erlbaum.

Boudreau, A. (2008, May 15). *Rape victims go on YouTube for help.* Retrieved May 16, 2008, from http://ac360.blogs.cnn.com/2008/05/15/teen%e2%80%99s-plea-for-help-heard-on-youtube/

Boudreaux, E., Kilpatrick, D., Resnick, H., Best, C., & Saunders, B. (1998). Criminal victimization, PTSD, and comorbid psychopathology among a community sample of women. *Journal of Traumatic Stress, 11,* 665–678.

Bourque, L. B. (1989). *Defining rape.* Durham, NC: Duke University Press.

Brecklin, L. R. (2008). Evaluation outcomes of self-defense training for women: A review. *Aggression and Violent Behavior, 13,* 60–76.

Breitenbecher, K. H. (2000). Sexual assault on college campuses: Is an ounce of prevention enough? *Applied and Preventive Psychology, 9,* 23–52.

Brener, N. D., McMahon, P. M., Warren, C. W., & Douglas, K. A. (1999). Forced sexual intercourse and associated health risk behaviors among female college students in the United States. *Journal of Consulting and Clinical Psychology, 67,* 252–259.

Brewin, C. R., Andrews, B., & Valentine, J. D. (2000). Meta-analysis of risk factors for PTSD in trauma-exposed adults. *Journal of Consulting and Clinical Psychology, 68,* 748–766.

Briere, J., & Scott, C. (2006). *Principles of trauma therapy: A guide to symptoms, evaluation, and treatment.* Thousand Oaks, CA: Sage.

Brison, S. J. (2002). *Aftermath: Violence and re-making of a self.* Princeton, NJ: Princeton University Press.

Broman, C. L. (1996). Coping with personal problems. In H. W. Neighbors & J. S. Jackson (Eds.), *Mental health in Black America* (pp. 117–129). Thousand Oaks, CA: Sage.

Brookings, J. B., McEvoy, A. W., & Reed, M. (1994). Sexual assault recovery and male significant others. *Families in Society, 75,* 295–299.

Brown, E. J., & Heimberg, R. G. (2001). Effects of writing about rape: Evaluating Pennebaker's paradigm of a severe trauma. *Journal of Traumatic Stress, 14,* 781–790.

Brown, L. (2008). *Cultural competence in trauma therapy: Beyond the flashback.* Washington, DC: American Psychological Association.

Brown, W. (1995). *States of injury: Power and freedom in late modernity.* Princeton, NJ: Princeton University Press.

Brownmiller, S. (1975). *Against our will: Men, women, and rape.* New York: Simon & Schuster.

Bryant-Davis, T., Chung, H., & Tillman, S. (in press). From the margins to the center: Ethnic minority women and the mental health effects of sexual assault. *Trauma, Violence, & Abuse.*

Brzuzy, S., Ault, A., & Segal, E. A. (1997). Conducting qualitative interviews with women survivors of trauma. *Affilia, 12,* 76–83.

Buchwald, E., Fletcher, P., & Roth, M. (1993). *Transforming a rape culture*. Minneapolis, MN: Milkweed Press.

Bureau of Justice Statistics. (1984). *The National Crime Survey: Methodological studies*. Washington, DC: U.S. Department of Justice.

Bureau of Justice Statistics. (2003). *Criminal victimization in the United States, 1999*. Washington, DC: U.S. Department of Justice.

Burgess, A. W., & Holmstrom, L. L. (1974). Rape trauma syndrome. *American Journal of Psychiatry, 131*, 981–986.

Burgess, A. W., & Holmstrom, L. L. (1978). Recovery from rape and prior life stress. *Research in Nursing & Health, 1*, 165–174.

Bursik, R., & Grasmick, H. (1993). *Neighborhoods and crime*. New York: Lexington Books.

Burt, M. R. (1980). Cultural myths and supports for rape. *Journal of Personality and Social Psychology, 38*, 217–230.

Burt, M. R., & Albin, R. S. (1981). Rape myths, rape definitions, and the probability of conviction. *Journal of Applied Social Psychology, 11*, 212–230.

Campbell, R. M. (1998). The community response to rape: Victims' experiences with legal, medical, and mental health systems. *American Journal of Community Psychology, 26*, 355–379.

Campbell, R. M. (2002). *Emotionally involved: The impact of researching rape*. New York: Routledge.

Campbell, R. M. (2005). What really happened? A validation study of rape survivors' help-seeking experiences with the legal and medical systems. *Violence and Victims, 20*, 55–68.

Campbell, R. M. (2006). Rape survivors' experiences with the legal and medical systems: Do rape victim advocates make a difference? *Violence Against Women, 12*, 1–16.

Campbell, R. M., & Adams, A. E. (2009). Why do rape victims volunteer for face-to-face interviews: A meta-study of victims' reasons for participating in research. *Journal of Interpersonal Violence, 24*, 395–405.

Campbell, R. M., Adams, A. E., Wasco, S. M., Ahrens, C. E., & Sefl, T. (2009). Training interviewers for research on sexual violence: A qualitative study of rape survivors: Recommendations for interview practice. *Journal of Interpersonal Violence, 15*, 595–617.

Campbell, R. M., Adams, A. E., Wasco, S. M., Ahrens, C. A., & Sefl, T. (in press). "What has it been like for you to talk with me today?" The impact of participating in interview research on rape survivors. *Violence Against Women*.

Campbell, R., Ahrens, C. E., Sefl, T., Wasco, S. M., & Barnes, H. E. (2001). Social reactions to rape victims: Healing and hurtful effects on psychological and physical health outcomes. *Violence and Victims, 16*, 287–302.

Campbell, R. M., Greeson, M. R., Bybee, D., & Raja, S. (2008). The co-occurrence of childhood sexual abuse, adult sexual assault, intimate partner violence, and sexual harassment: A mediational model of PTSD and physical health outcomes. *Journal of Consulting and Clinical Psychology, 76,* 194–207.

Campbell, R. M., & Martin, P. Y. (2001). Services for sexual assault survivors: The role of rape crisis centers. In C. Renzetti, J. Edleson, & R. Bergen (Eds.), *Sourcebook on violence against women* (pp. 227–241). Thousand Oaks, CA: Sage.

Campbell, R. M., Patterson, D., Adams, A. E., Diegel, R., & Coats, S. (2008). A participatory evaluation project to measure SANE nursing practice and adult sexual assault patients' psychological well-being. *Journal of Forensic Nursing, 4,* 19–28.

Campbell, R. M., Patterson, D., & Bybee, D. (2007, October). *Prosecution rates for adult sexual assault cases: A ten-year analysis before and after the implementation of a SANE program.* Paper presented at the International Forensic Nursing Scientific Assembly, Salt Lake City, UT.

Campbell, R. M., Patterson, D., & Lichty, L. F. (2005). The effectiveness of sexual assault nurse examiner (SANE) program: A review of psychological, medical, legal, and community outcomes. *Trauma, Violence, & Abuse, 6,* 313–329.

Campbell, R. M., & Raja, S. (1999). Secondary victimization of rape victims: Insights from mental health professionals who treat survivors of violence. *Violence and Victims, 14,* 261–275.

Campbell, R. M., & Raja, S. (2005). The sexual assault and secondary victimization of female veterans: Help seeking experiences with military and civilian social systems. *Psychology of Women Quarterly, 29,* 97–106.

Campbell, R. M., Raja, S., & Grining, P. L. (1999). Training mental health professionals on violence against women. *Journal of Interpersonal Violence, 14,* 1003–1013.

Campbell, R. M., Sefl, T., Barnes, H. E., Ahrens, C. E., Wasco, S. M., & Zaragoza-Diesfeld, Y. (1999). Community services for rape survivors: Enhancing psychological well-being or increasing trauma? *Journal of Consulting and Clinical Psychology, 67,* 847–858.

Campbell, R. M., Sefl, T., Wasco, S., & Ahrens, C. (2004). Doing community research without a community: Creating safe space for rape survivors. *American Journal of Community Psychology, 33,* 253–261.

Campbell, R. M., Townsend, S., Long, S., Kinnison, K., Pulley, E., Adames, S., et al. (2006). Responding to sexual assault victims' medical and emotional needs: A national study of the services provided by SANE programs. *Research in Nursing & Health, 29,* 284–398.

Campbell, R. M., & Wasco, S. M. (2000). Feminist approaches to social science: Epistemological and methodological tenets. *American Journal of Community Psychology, 28,* 773–791.

Campbell, R. M., Wasco, S. M., Ahrens, C. A., Sefl, T., & Barnes, H. (2001). Preventing the "second rape"? Rape survivors' experiences with community service providers. *Journal of Interpersonal Violence, 16,* 1239–1259.

Cauce, A. M., Domenech-Rodriguez, M., Paradise, M., Cochran, B. N., Shea, J. M., Srebnik, D., et al. (2002). Cultural and contextual influences in mental health seeking: A focus on ethnic minority youth. *Journal of Consulting and Clinical Psychology, 70*, 44–55.

Centers for Disease Control and Prevention. (2004). *Sexual violence prevention: Beginning the dialogue*. Atlanta, GA: Author.

Charuvastra, A., & Cloitre, M. (2008). Social bonds and PTSD. *Annual Review of Psychology, 59*, 301–328.

Check, J., & Malamuth, N. (1985). An empirical assessment of some feminist hypotheses about rape. *International Journal of Women's Studies, 8*, 414–423.

Chen, Y., & Ullman, S. E. (in press). Women's reporting of sexual and physical assaults to police in the National Violence Against Women survey. *Violence Against Women*.

Cheng, D., Leong, F. T., & Geist, R. (1993). Cultural differences in psychological distress between Asian and Caucasian American college students. *Journal of Multicultural Counseling and Development, 21*, 182–190.

Cheung, F. K., & Snowden, L. R. (1990). Community mental health and ethnic minority populations. *Community Mental Health Journal, 26*, 277–291.

Ciancone, A., Wilson, C., Collette, R., & Gerson, L. W. (2000). Sexual Assault Nurse Examiner programs in the United States. *Annals of Emergency Medicine, 35*, 353–357.

Clay-Warner, J., & Burt, C. H. (2005). Rape reporting after reforms: Have times really changed? *Violence Against Women, 11*, 150–176.

Clemans, S. E. (2005). A feminist group for women rape survivors. *Social Work With Groups, 28*, 59–75.

Coffey, P., Leitenberg, H., Henning, K., Turner, T., & Bennett, R. T. (1996). The relationship between methods of coping during adulthood with a history of child sexual abuse and current psychological adjustment. *Journal of Consulting and Clinical Psychology, 64*, 1090–1093.

Collins, K. S., Schoen, C., Joseph, S., Duchon, L., Simantov, E., & Yellowitz, M. (1999). *Health concerns across a woman's life span: 1998 survey of women's health*. New York: The Commonwealth Fund.

Collins, P. H. (2004). *Black sexual politics: African Americans, gender, and the new racism*. New York: Routledge.

Collins, R. (1989). Sociology: Proscience or antiscience? *American Sociological Review, 54*, 124–139.

Connop, V., & Petrak, J. (2004). The impact of sexual assault on heterosexual couples. *Sexual and Relationship Therapy, 19*, 29–38.

Conte, J. R. (2002). *Critical issues in child sexual abuse: Historical, legal, and psychological perspectives*. Thousand Oaks, CA: Sage.

Crandall, C., & Helitzer, D. (2003). *Impact evaluation of a Sexual Assault Nurse Examiner (SANE) program* (Document No. 203276). Washington, DC: National Institute of Justice.

Crawford, M., Edwards, K., Calhoun, K., Gidycz, C., Mondillo, K., & Desai, A. (2008, August). *The applicability of Pennebaker's writing paradigm to survivors of sexual trauma.* Paper presented at the 116th Annual Convention of the American Psychological Association, Boston.

David, W. S., Simpson, T. L., & Cotton, A. J. (2006). Taking charge: A pilot curriculum of self-defense and personal safety training for female veterans with PTSD because of military sexual trauma. *Journal of Interpersonal Violence, 21,* 555–565.

Davis, A. Y. (1981, November–December). Rape, racism, and the capitalist setting. *The Black Scholar,* 39–45. (Original work published 1978)

Davis, A. Y. (1984). *Women, culture, politics.* New York: Vintage Books.

Davis, R. C. (1987). Studying the effects of services for victims in crisis. *Crime & Delinquency, 33,* 520–531.

Davis, R. C. (2007). The key contributions of family, friends, and neighbors. In R. C. Davis, A. J. Lurigio, & S. Herman (Eds.), *Victims of crime* (3rd ed., pp. 267–276). Thousand Oaks, CA: Sage.

Davis, R. C., & Brickman, E. (1996). Supportive and unsupportive aspects of the behavior of others toward victims of sexual and nonsexual assault. *Journal of Interpersonal Violence, 11,* 250–262.

Davis, R. C., Brickman, E. R., & Baker, T. (1991). Supportive and unsupportive responses of others to rape victims: Effects on concurrent victim adjustment. *American Journal of Community Psychology, 19,* 443–451.

Davis, R. C., Taylor, B., & Bench, S. (1995). Impact of sexual and nonsexual assault on secondary victims. *Violence and Victims, 10,* 73–84.

Denzin, N. K., & Lincoln, Y. S. (2000). *Handbook of qualitative research* (2nd ed.). Thousand Oaks, CA: Sage.

Dines, G., Russo, A., & Jensen, R. J. (1998). *Pornography: The production and consumption of inequality.* New York: Routledge.

Disch, E. (2001). Research as clinical practice: Creating a positive research experience for survivors of sexual abuse by professionals. *Sociological Practice, 3,* 221–239.

DiVasto, P., Kaufman, A., Jackson, R., Ballen, L., Symour, D., & Duphorne, P. (1980). Caring for rape victims: Its impact on providers. *Journal of Community Health, 5,* 204–208.

Dokecki, P. R. (2004). *The clergy sexual abuse crisis: Reform and renewal in the Catholic community.* Washington, DC: Georgetown University Press.

Donovan, R. (2007). To blame or not to blame: Influences of target race and observer sex on rape blame attributions. *Journal of Interpersonal Violence, 22,* 722–736.

Donovan, R., & Williams, M. (2002). Living at the intersection: The effects of racism and sexism on Black rape survivors. *Women & Therapy, 25,* 95–105.

Dubow, E. F., Lovko, K. R., & Kausch, D. F. (1990). Demographic differences in adolescents' health concerns and perceptions of helping agents. *Journal of Clinical Child Psychology, 19,* 44–54.

DuMont, J., Miller, K. L., & Myhr, T. L. (2003). The role of "real rape" and "real victim" stereotypes in the police reporting practices of sexually assaulted women. *Violence Against Women, 9,* 466–486.

Dunkel-Schetter, C., & Skokan, L. (1990). Determinants of social support provision in personal relationships. *Journal of Social and Personal Relationships, 7,* 437–450.

Dunmore, E. C., Clark, D. M., & Ehlers, A. (2001). A prospective investigation of the role of cognitive factors in persistent posttraumatic stress disorder (PTSD) after physical or sexual assault. *Behaviour Research and Therapy, 39,* 1063–1084.

Dunn, P. C., Vail-Smith, K., & Knight, S. M. (1999). What date/acquaintance rape victims tell others: A study of college student recipients of disclosure. *Journal of American College Health, 47,* 213–219.

Dussich, J. (2001). Decisions not to report sexual assault: A comparative study among women living in Japan who are Japanese, Korean, Chinese, and English-speaking. *International Journal of Offender Therapy and Comparative Criminology, 45,* 278–301.

Echols, A., & Willis, E. (1989). *Daring to be bad: Radical feminism in America, 1967–1975.* Minneapolis: University of Minnesota Press.

Ehrlich, S. (2001). *Representing rape: Language and sexual consent.* New York: Routledge.

Eliasson, M. (2002). Progress and backlash: Research on male violence to women. *Feminism & Psychology, 12,* 389–398.

Elliott, D. M., Mok, D. S., & Briere, J. (2004). Adult sexual assault: Prevalence, symptomatology, and sex differences in the general population. *Journal of Traumatic Stress, 17,* 203–211.

Erez, E., & Roberts, J. (2007). Victim participation in the criminal justice system. In R. C. Davis, A. J. Lurigio, & S. Herman (Eds.), *Victims of crime* (3rd ed., pp. 277–298). Thousand Oaks, CA: Sage.

Ericksen, J., Dudley, C., McIntosh, G., Ritch, L., Shumay, S., & Simpson, M. (2002). Clients' experiences with a specialized sexual assault service. *Journal of Emergency Nursing, 28,* 86–90.

Estrich, S. (1987). *Real rape.* Cambridge, MA: Harvard University Press.

Fairbrother, N., & Rachman, S. (2006). PTSD in victims of sexual assault: Test of a major component of the Ehlers–Clark theory. *Journal of Behavior Therapy and Experimental Psychiatry, 37,* 74–93.

Faludi, S. (1991). *Backlash: The undeclared war against American women.* New York: Doubleday.

Farley, M. (2003). *Prostitution, trafficking, and traumatic stress.* Binghamton, NY: Haworth Press.

Feldman-Summers, S., & Norris, J. (1984). Differences between rape victims who report and those who don't report to a public agency. *Journal of Applied Social Psychology, 14,* 562–573.

Field, H. S. (1978). Attitudes toward rape: A comparative analysis of police, rape crisis counselors, and citizens. *Journal of Personality and Social Psychology, 36,* 156–179.

Figley, C. R. (1995). *Compassion fatigue: Coping with secondary traumatic stress disorder in those who treat the traumatized.* Bristol, PA: Brunner/Mazel.

Filipas, H. H., & Ullman, S. E. (2001). Social reactions to sexual assault victims from various support sources. *Violence and Victims, 16,* 673–692.

Finch, E., & Munro, V. (2005). Juror stereotypes and blame attribution in rape cases involving intoxicants. *British Journal of Criminology, 45,* 25–38.

Fine, M. (1983). Coping with rape: Critical perspectives on consciousness. *Imagination, Cognition and Personality, 3,* 249–264.

Finkelhor, D. (2003). The legacy of the clergy abuse scandal. *Child Abuse & Neglect, 27,* 1225–1229.

Firestone, S. (1970). *The dialectic of sex: The case for feminist revolution.* New York: Bantam.

Fisher, B. S., & Cullen, F. T. (2000). Measuring the sexual victimization of women: Evolution, current controversies, and future research. In D. Duffee (Ed.). *Measurement and analysis of crime and justice: Criminal Justice 2000* (Vol. 4, pp. 317–390). Washington, DC: U.S. Department of Justice.

Fisher, B. S., Daigle, L. E., Cullen, F. T., & Turner, M. G. (2003a). Acknowledging sexual victimization as rape: Results from a national-level study. *Justice Quarterly, 20,* 535–574.

Fisher, B. S., Daigle, L. E., Cullen, F. T., & Turner, M. G. (2003b). Reporting sexual victimization to the police and others: Results from a national-level study of college women. *Criminal Justice and Behavior, 30,* 6–38.

Fisher, G. J. (1987). Latina and majority student attitudes toward forcible date rape as a function of differences in attitudes toward women. *Sex Roles, 17,* 93–101.

Foa, E. B., & Rothbaum, B. O. (1998). *Treating the trauma of rape: Cognitive–behavioral therapy for PTSD.* New York: Guilford Press.

Folkman, S., & Moskowitz, J. T. (2004). Coping: Pitfalls and promises. *Annual Review of Psychology, 55,* 745–774.

Follette, V. M., Polusny, M., Bechtle, A. E., & Naugle, A. E. (1996). Cumulative trauma: The impact of child sexual abuse, adult sexual assault, and spouse abuse. *Journal of Traumatic Stress, 9,* 25–35.

Follette, V. M., & Ruzek, J. I. (2006). *Cognitive–behavioral therapies for trauma* (2nd ed.). New York: Guilford Press.

Ford, T. M., Liwag-McLamb, M. G., & Foley, L. A. (1998). Perceptions of rape based on sex and sexual orientation of victim. *Journal of Social Behavior and Personality, 13,* 253–262.

Foshee, V. A., Bauman, K. E., Ennett, S. T., Linder, G. F., Benefield, T., & Suchindran, C. (2004). Assessing the long-term effects of the Safe Dates program and a booster in preventing and reducing adolescent dating violence victimization and perpetration. *American Journal of Public Health, 94,* 619–624.

Foubert, J. D. (2000). The longitudinal effects of a rape-prevention program on fraternity men's attitudes, behavioral intent, and behavior. *Journal of American College Health, 48,* 158–163.

Foubert, J. D., Newberry, J. T., & Tatum, J. L. (2007). Behavior differences seven months later: Effects of a rape prevention program on first-year men who join fraternities. *NASPA Journal, 44,* 728–749.

Francisco, P. W. (1999). *Telling: A memoir of rape and recovery.* New York: Harper-Collins.

Franiuk, R., Seefelt, J. L., Cepress, S. L., & Vandello, J. A. (2008). Prevalence and effects of rape myths in print journalism: The Kobe Bryant case. *Violence Against Women, 14,* 287–309.

Frattaroli, J. (2006). Experimental disclosure and its moderators: A meta-analysis. *Psychological Bulletin, 132,* 823–865.

Frazier, P. A., & Burnett, J. W. (1994). Immediate coping strategies among rape victims. *Journal of Counseling and Development, 72,* 633–639.

Frazier, P. A., & Haney, B. (1996). Sexual assault cases in the legal system: Police, prosecutor, and victim perspectives. *Law and Human Behavior, 20,* 607–628.

Frese, B., Moya, M., & Megias, J. L. (2004). Social perception of rape: How rape myth acceptance modulates the influence of situational factors. *Journal of Interpersonal Violence, 19,* 143–161.

Freyd, J. J., Klest, B., & Allard, C. B. (2005). Betrayal trauma: Relationship to physical health, psychological distress, and a written disclosure intervention. *Journal of Trauma & Dissociation, 6,* 83–104.

Frisina, P. G., Borod, J. C., & Lepore, S. J. (2004). A meta-analysis of the effects of written emotional disclosure on the health outcomes of clinical populations. *Journal of Nervous and Mental Disease, 192,* 629–634.

Funk, R. E. (1993). *Stopping rape: A challenge for men.* Philadelphia: New Society.

Garcia, L., Hurwitz, J., & Kraus, J. (2005). Acculturation and reported intimate partner violence among Latinas in Los Angeles. *Journal of Interpersonal Violence, 20,* 569–590.

Gavey, N. (2005). *Just sex: The cultural scaffolding of rape.* New York: Routledge.

Gavey, N. (2007). *Rape, recognition, and refusal.* Distinguished publication award address delivered to the Association for Women in Psychology, San Francisco.

Gelles, R. J. (2005). Protecting children is more important than preserving families. In D. R. Loseke, R. J. Gelles, & M. M. Cavanaugh (Eds.), *Current controversies on family violence* (2nd ed., pp. 311–328). Newbury Park, CA: Sage.

George, L. K., Winfield, I., & Blazer, D. G. (1992). Sociocultural factors in sexual assault: Comparison of two representative samples of women. *Journal of Social Issues, 48,* 105–125.

Getman, K. A. (1984). Sexual control in the slaveholding South: The implementation and maintenance of a racial caste system. *Harvard Women's Law Journal, 7,* 115–152.

Ghahramanlou, M., & Brodbeck, C. (2000). Predictors of secondary trauma in sexual assault trauma counselors. *International Journal of Emergency Mental Health, 2,* 229–240.

Giacopassi, D. J., & Dull, T. R. (1986). Gender and racial differences in the acceptance of rape myths within a college population. *Sex Roles, 15,* 63–75.

Gidycz, C. A., Dowdall, C. L., & Marioni, N. L. (2003). Interventions to prevent rape and sexual assault. In J. Petrak & B. Hedge (Eds.), *The trauma of adult sexual assault: Treatment, prevention, and policy* (pp. 235–259). New York: Wiley.

Gidycz, C. A., Rich, C. L., Orchowski, L. M., King, C., & Miller, A. (2006). The evaluation of a sexual assault self-defense and risk-reduction program for college women: A prospective study. *Psychology of Women Quarterly, 30,* 173–186.

Gilbert, N. (2005). Advocacy research overstates the incidence of date and acquaintance rape. In D. R. Loseke, R. J. Gelles, & M. M. Cavanaugh (Eds.), *Current controversies on family violence* (2nd ed., pp. 329–340). Newbury Park, CA: Sage.

Gilfus, M. E. (1999). The price of the ticket: A survivor-centered appraisal of trauma theory. *Violence Against Women, 5,* 1238–1257.

Glass, N., Perrin, N., Campbell, J., & Soeken, K. (2007). The protective role of tangible support on PTSD symptoms in urban female survivors of violence. *Research in Nursing and Health, 30,* 558–568.

Golding, J. M., Siegel, J. M., Sorenson, S. B., Burnam, M. A., & Stein, J. A. (1989). Social support sources following sexual assault. *Journal of Community Psychology, 17,* 92–107.

Golding, J. M., Stein, J. A., Siegel, J. M., Burnam, M. A., & Sorenson, S. B. (1988). Sexual assault history and use of health and mental health services. *American Journal of Community Psychology, 16,* 625–643.

Gonzales, J. (1999). Native American survivors. In *Support for survivors manual* (pp. 257–259). Sacramento: California Coalition Against Sexual Assault.

Goodman, L. A., & Epstein, D. (2008). *Listening to battered women: A survivor-centered approach to advocacy, mental health, and justice.* Washington, DC: American Psychological Association.

Gordon, M. T., & Riger, S. (1989). *The female fear: The social cost of rape.* New York: Free Press.

Grauerholz, L. (2000). An ecological approach to understanding sexual revictimization: Linking personal, interpersonal, and sociocultural factors and processes. *Child Maltreatment, 5,* 5–17.

Greenberg, M. S., & Ruback, R. B. (1992). *After the crime: Victim decision making.* New York: Plenum Press.

Greenfield, L. A., & Smith, S. K. (1999). *American Indians and crime* (Report No. NCJ 173386). Washington, DC: Bureau of Justice Statistics.

Guay, S., Billette, V., & Marchand, A. (2006). Exploring the links between post-traumatic stress disorder and social support: Processes and potential research avenues. *Journal of Traumatic Stress, 19*, 327–338.

Hagan, J., Simpson, J., & Gillis, A. R. (1987). Class in the household: A power–control theory of gender and delinquency. *American Journal of Sociology, 92*, 788–816.

Hammer, R. (2002). *Antifeminism and family terrorism: A critical feminist perspective.* New York: Rowman & Littlefield.

Hanson, R. F., Kievit, L. W., Saunders, B. E., Smith, D. W., Kilpatrick, D. G., Resnick, H. S., et al. (2003). Correlates of adolescent reports of sexual assault: Findings from the National Survey of Adolescents. *Child Maltreatment, 8*, 1–12.

Hanson, R. F., Resnick, H. S., Saunders, B. E., Kilpatrick, D. G., & Best, C. L. (1999). Factors related to the reporting of childhood rape. *Child Abuse & Neglect, 23*, 559–569.

Hawkins, S. R. (2005). *Evaluation findings: Men can stop rape, Men of Strength Club 2004–2005.* Retrieved April 11, 2008, from http://www.mencanstoprape.org/usr_doc/2005_MOST_Club_Evaluation_download.pdf

Heberle, R. (1996). Deconstructive strategies and the movement against sexual violence. *Hypatia, 11*, 63–76.

Heise, L. L. (1998). Violence against women: An integrated ecological framework. *Violence Against Women, 4*, 262–290.

Herbert, T., & Dunkel-Schetter, C. (1992). Negative social reactions to victims: An overview of responses and their determinants. In L. Montada, S. Fillipp, & M. J. Lerner (Eds.), *Life crises and experiences of loss in adulthood* (pp. 147–518). Hillsdale, NJ: Erlbaum.

Herek, G. (2009). Hate crimes and stigma-related experiences among sexual minority adults in the United States: Prevalence estimates from a national probability sample. *Journal of Interpersonal Violence, 24*, 54–74.

Hertz, R. (1997). *Reflexivity and voice.* Thousand Oaks, CA: Sage.

Hlavka, H. R., Kruttschnitt, C., & Carbone-Lopez, K. (2007). Revictimizing the victims? Interviewing women about interpersonal violence. *Journal of Interpersonal Violence, 22*, 894–920.

Hobfoll, S., Hall, B. J., Canetti-Nisim, D., Galea, S., Johnson, R. J., & Palmieri, P. (2007). Refining our understanding of traumatic growth in the face of terrorism: Moving from meaning cognitions to doing what is meaningful. *Applied Psychology: An International Review, 56*, 345–366.

Hollander, J. (2002). Resisting vulnerability: The social construction of gender in inter-action. *Social Problems, 49*, 474–496.

hooks, b. (1981). *Ain't I a woman: Black women and feminism.* Boston: South End Press.

hooks, b. (1984). *Feminist theory: From margin to center.* Boston, South End Press.

Horwitz, A. (2002). *Creating mental illness.* Chicago: University of Chicago Press.

House, J. S. (1981). *Work stress and social support.* Reading, MA: Addison-Wesley.

Howard, J. A. (1988). A structural approach to sexual attitudes: Interracial patterns in adolescent judgments about sexual intimacy. *Sociological Perspectives, 31,* 88–121.

INCITE! Women of Color Against Violence. (2006). *Color of violence: The INCITE! anthology.* Cambridge, MA: South End Press.

Ingram, K., Betz, N. E., Mindes, E. J., Schmitt, M. M., & Smith, N. G. (2001). Unsupportive responses from others concerning a stressful life event: Development of the unsupportive social interactions inventory. *Journal of Social and Clinical Psychology, 20,* 173–207.

Jaccard, J., & Dittus, P. J. (1991). *Parent–teen communication: Toward the prevention of unintended pregnancies.* New York: Springer-Verlag.

Janoff-Bulman, R. (1992). *Shattered assumptions: Towards a new psychology of trauma.* New York: Free Press.

Jansen, H., Watts, C., Ellsberg, M., Heise, L., & Garcia-Moreno, C. (2004). Interviewer training in the WHO multi-country study on women's health and domestic violence. *Violence Against Women, 10,* 831–849.

Jimenez, J. A., & Abreu, J. M. (2003). Race and sex effects on attitudinal perceptions of acquaintance rape. *Journal of Counseling Psychology, 50,* 252–256.

Jordan, J. (2002). Will any woman do? Police, gender, and rape victims. *Policing: An International Journal of Police Strategies and Management, 25,* 319–344.

Jordan, J. (2004). Beyond belief: Police, rape, and women's credibility. *Criminal Justice, 4,* 29–59.

Kalof, L., & Wade, B. H. (1995). Sexual attitudes and experiences with sexual coercion: Exploring the influence of race and gender. *Journal of Black Psychology, 21,* 224–238.

Kaniasty, K. (2005). Social support and traumatic stress. *PTSD Research Quarterly, 16,* 1–8.

Kaniasty, K., & Norris, F. H. (1992). Social support and victims of crime: Matching event, support, and outcome. *American Journal of Community Psychology, 20,* 211–241.

Kassing, L. R., Beesley, D., & Frey, L. L. (2005). Gender role conflict, homophobia, age, and education as predictors of male rape myth acceptance. *Journal of Mental Health Counseling, 27,* 311–328.

Kastigurirangan, A., Krishnan, S., & Riger, S. (2004). The impact of culture and minority status on women's experiences of domestic violence. *Trauma, Violence, & Abuse, 5,* 318–332.

Kellogg, N. D., & Huston, R. L. (1995). Unwanted sexual experiences in adolescents: Patterns of disclosure. *Clinical Pediatrics, 34,* 306–312.

Kilpatrick, D. G., Edmunds, C. N., & Seymour, A. K. (1992). *Rape in America: A report to the nation.* Arlington, VA: National Victim Center.

Kilpatrick, D. G., Resnick, H. S., Ruggiero, K. J., Conoscenti, L. M., & McCauley, J. (2007). *Drug-facilitated, incapacitated, and forcible rape: A national study. Final report* (Report No. NCJRS 219181). Washington, DC: U.S. Department of Justice.

Kimerling, R., Rellini, A., Kelly, V., Judson, P. L., & Learman, L. A. (2002). Gender differences in victim and crime characteristics of sexual assaults. *Journal of Interpersonal Violence, 17,* 526–532.

Koss, M. P. (1985). The hidden rape victim: Personality, attitudinal and situational characteristics. *Psychology of Women Quarterly, 9,* 192–212.

Koss, M. P. (1993). Detecting the scope of rape: A review of prevalence research methods. *Journal of Interpersonal Violence, 8,* 198–222.

Koss, M. P. (2000). Blame, shame, and community justice responses to violence against women. *American Psychologist, 48,* 16–26.

Koss, M. P. (2006). Restoring rape survivors: Justice, advocacy, and a call to action. In F. L. Denmark, H. H. Krauss, & E. Halpern (Eds.), *Annals of the New York Academy of Sciences: Vol. 1087. Violence and exploitation against women and girls* (pp. 206–234). New York: New York Academy of Sciences.

Koss, M. P., & Achilles, M. (2008). *Restorative justice responses to sexual assault.* Retrieved March 3, 2008, from http://www.vawnet.org

Koss, M. P., Dinero, T. E., Seibel, C. A., & Cox, S. L. (1988). Stranger and acquaintance rape: Are there differences in the victim's experience? *Psychology of Women Quarterly, 12,* 1–24.

Koss, M. P., Figueredo, J., & Prince, R. J. (2002). Cognitive mediation of rape's mental, physical, and social health impact: Tests of four models in cross-sectional data. *Journal of Consulting and Clinical Psychology, 76,* 926–941.

Koss, M. P., Gidycz, C. A., & Wisniewski, N. (1987). The scope of rape: Incidence and prevalence of sexual aggression and victimization in a national sample of students in higher education. *Journal of Consulting and Clinical Psychology, 55,* 162–170.

Lamb S. (1999). *New versions of victims: Feminists struggle with the concept.* New York: New York University Press.

Lamb, S., & Edgar-Smith, S. (1994). Aspects of disclosure: Mediators of outcome of child sexual abuse. *Journal of Interpersonal Violence, 9,* 307–326.

Lanza, A. F., Cameron, A. E., & Revenson, T. A. (1995). Perceptions of helpful and unhelpful support among married individuals with rheumatic diseases. *Psychology & Health, 10,* 449–462.

Layman, M., Gidycz, C. A., & Lynn, S. J. (1996). Unacknowledged versus acknowledged rape victims: Situational factors and posttraumatic stress. *Journal of Abnormal Psychology, 105,* 124–131.

Lazarus, R. S., & Folkman, S. (1984). *Stress, appraisal, and coping.* New York: Springer.

Ledray, L. (1999). *SANE development and operation guide.* New York: National Criminal Justice Reference Service.

Lee, J., Pomeroy, E. C., Yoo, S., & Rheinboldt, K. T. (2005). Attitudes towards rape: A comparison between Asian and Caucasian college students. *Violence Against Women, 11*, 177–196.

Leonard, D. J. (2007). Innocent until proven innocent. *Journal of Sport & Social Issues, 31*, 25–44.

Lepore, S. J., Ragan, J. D., & Jones, S. (2000). Talking facilitates cognitive–emotional processes of adaptation to an acute stressor. *Journal of Personality and Social Psychology, 78*, 499–508.

Liang, B., Goodman, L., Tummala-Narra, P., & Weintraub, S. (2005). A theoretical framework for understanding help-seeking processes among survivors of intimate partner violence. *American Journal of Community Psychology, 36*, 71–84.

Little, K. (2001). Sexual assault nurse examiner programs: Improving the community response to sexual assault victims. *Office for Victims of Crime Bulletin, 4*, 1–19.

Littleton, H., Axsom, D., Breitkopf, C. R., & Berenson, A. (2006). Rape acknowledgment and postassault experiences: How acknowledgment status relates to disclosure, coping, worldview, and reactions received from others. *Violence and Victims, 21*, 761–778.

Littleton, H. T., Grills-Taquechel, A., & Axsom, D. (2009). Sexual assault victims' acknowledgment status and revictimization risk. *Psychology of Women Quarterly, 33*, 34–42.

Littleton, H., & Henderson, C. (2009). If she is not a victim, does that mean she was not traumatized? Evaluation of predictors of PTSD symptomatology among college rape victims. *Violence Against Women, 15*, 148–167.

Littleton, H., Rhatigan, D. L., & Axsom, D. (2007). Unacknowledged rape: How much do we know about the hidden rape victim? *Journal of Aggression, Maltreatment & Trauma, 14*, 57–74.

Lizotte, A. J. (1985). The uniqueness of rape: Reporting assaultive violence to the police. *Crime & Delinquency, 31*, 169–190.

Logan, T. K., Evans, L., Stevenson, E., & Jordan, C. (2005). Barriers to services for rural and urban rape survivors. *Journal of Interpersonal Violence, 20*, 591–616.

Long, L., Ullman, S. E., Starzynski, L., Long, S., & Mason, G. (2007). Age and educational differences in African American women's sexual assault experiences. *Feminist Criminology, 2*, 117–136.

Long, S., Ullman, S. E., Long, L., Mason, G., & Starzynski, L. (2007). Women's experiences of male-perpetrated sexual assault by sexual orientation. *Violence and Victims, 22*, 684–701.

Lonsway, K. A., Banyard, V. L., Berkowitz, A. D., Gidycz, C. A., Koss, M. P., Schewe, P. A., et al. (2009, January). Sexual assault prevention and risk reduction: A review of the research literature for practitioners. *Sexual Assault Report*, 1–20.

Lonsway, K. A., & Fitzgerald, L. (1994). Rape myths: In review. *Psychology of Women Quarterly, 18,* 133–164.

Low, G., & Organista, K. C. (2000). Latinas and sexual assault: Towards culturally sensitive assessment and intervention. *Journal of Multicultural Social Work, 8,* 131–157.

Lyon, T. D. (2009). Abuse disclosure: What adults can tell. In B. L. Bottoms, C. J., Najdowski, & G. S. Goodman (Eds.), *Children as victims, witnesses, and offenders: Psychological science and the law* (pp. 19–35). New York: Guilford Press.

MacKinnon, C. A. (1987). *Feminism unmodified: Discourses on life and law.* Cambridge, MA: Harvard University Press.

Madigan, L., & Gamble, N. (1991). *The second rape: Society's continued betrayal of the victim.* New York: Lexington Books.

Maercker, A., & Muller, J. (2004). Social acknowledgment as a victim or survivor: A scale to measure a recovery factor of PTSD. *Journal of Traumatic Stress, 17,* 345–351.

Major, B., Zubek, J., Cooper, L., Cozzarelli, C., & Richards, C. (1997). Mixed messages: implications of social conflict and social support within close relationships for adjustment to a stressful life event. *Journal of Personality and Social Psychology, 72,* 1349–1363.

Malamuth, N. M., & Check, J. V. P. (1985). The effects of aggressive pornography on beliefs in rape myths: Individual differences. *Journal of Research in Personality, 19,* 299–320.

Malamuth, N. M., & Dean, K. E. (1991). Attraction to sexual aggression. In A. Parrot & L. Bechhofer (Eds.), *Acquaintance rape: The hidden crime* (pp. 229–247). New York: Wiley.

Maracek, J. (1999). Trauma talk in feminist clinical practice. In S. Lamb (Ed.), *New versions of victims: Feminists struggle with the concept* (pp. 158–182). New York: New York University Press.

Marcus, S. (1992). Fighting bodies: Fighting words. In J. Butler & J. W. Scott (Eds.), *Feminists theorize the political* (pp. 385–403). New York: Routledge.

Mardorossian, C. M. (2002). Towards a new feminist theory of rape. *Signs, 27,* 743–775.

Martin, P. Y. (2005). *Rape work: Victims, gender, and emotions in organization and community context.* New York: Routledge.

Martin, P. Y., & Powell, R. M. (1994). Accounting for the "second assault": Legal organizations' framing of rape. *Law & Social Inquiry, 19,* 853–890.

Mason, S. E., & Clemans, S. E. (2008). Participatory research for rape survivor groups. *Affilia, 23,* 66–76.

Matthews, N. (1994). *Confronting rape: The feminist anti-rape movement and the state.* London: Routledge.

McCann, I. L., & Pearlman, L. A. (1990). Vicarious traumatization: A framework for understanding the psychological effects of working with victims. *Journal of Traumatic Stress, 3,* 131–149.

McCaughey, M. (1997). *Real knockouts: The physical feminism of women's self-defense.* New York: New York University Press.

McGoldrick, M., Walsh, F., & Anderson, C. (1989). *Women in families: A framework for family therapy.* New York: Norton.

McNair, L. D., & Neville, H. A. (1996). African American women survivors of sexual assault: The intersection of race and class. *Women & Therapy, 18,* 107–118.

Meili, T. (2003). *I am the Central Park Jogger: A story of hope and possibility.* New York: Simon & Schuster.

Menard, K. S. (2005). *Reporting sexual assault: A social ecology perspective.* El Paso, TX: LFB Scholarly Publishing.

Men Can Stop Rape. (1987). *Mobilizing male youth to prevent men's violence against women.* Retrieved April 10, 2008, from http://www.mencanstoprape.org/index.htm

Messman-Moore, T. L., & Long, P. J. (2000). Child sexual abuse and revictimization in the form of adult sexual abuse, adult physical abuse, and adult psychological maltreatment. *Journal of Interpersonal Violence, 15,* 489–502.

Michigan Sexual Assault Systems Response Team Task Force. (2001). *The response to sexual assault: Removing barriers to services and justice.* Lansing: Author.

Moorti, S. (2002). *The color of rape: Gender and race in television's public sphere.* Albany: State University of New York Press.

Moraga, C., & Anzaldua, G. (1981). *This bridge called my back: Writings by radical women of color.* Watertown, MA: Kitchen Table Women of Color Press.

Morgan, R. (1970). *Sisterhood is powerful: An anthology of writings from the women's liberation movement.* New York: Random House.

Mori, L., Bernat, J., Glenn, P., Selle, L., & Zarate, M. (1995). Attitudes toward rape: Gender and ethnic differences across Asian and Caucasian college students. *Sex Roles, 32,* 457–467.

Moss, M., Frank, E., & Anderson, B. (1990). The effects of marital status and partner support on rape trauma. *American Journal of Orthopsychiatry, 60,* 379–391.

Muehlenhard, C. L., Friedman, D. E., & Thomas, C. M. (1985). Is date rape justifiable? *Psychology of Women Quarterly, 9,* 297–309.

Nagel, B., Matsuo, H., McIntyre, K. P., & Morrison, N. (2005). Attitudes toward victims of rape: Effects of gender, race, religion, and social class. *Journal of Interpersonal Violence, 20,* 725–737.

Najavits, L. M. (2002). *Seeking safety: A treatment manual for PTSD and substance abuse.* New York: Guilford Press.

Neville, H. A., & Heppner, M. J. (1999). Contextualizing rape: Reviewing sequelae and proposing a culturally inclusive ecological model of sexual assault recovery. *Applied and Preventive Psychology, 8,* 41–62.

Neville, H. A., & Pugh, A. O. (1997). General and culture-specific factors influencing African American women's reporting patterns and perceived social support following sexual assault. *Violence Against Women, 3,* 361–381.

Norris, F. H., Foster, J., & Weisshaar, D. L. (2002). The epidemiology of sex differences in PTSD across developmental, societal, and research contexts. In R. Kimerling, P. Ouimette, & J. Wolfe (Eds.), *Gender and PTSD* (pp. 3–42). New York: Guilford Press.

Norris, F. H., Kaniasty, K. Z., & Scheer, D. A. (1990). Use of mental health services among victims of crime: Frequency, correlates, and subsequent recovery. *Journal of Consulting and Clinical Psychology, 58*, 538–547.

Norris, J., & Cubbins, L. A. (1992). Dating, drinking, and rape: Effects of victim's and assailant's alcohol consumption on judgments of their behavior and traits. *Psychology of Women Quarterly, 16*, 179–191.

Orchowski, L. M., Gidycz, C. A., & Raffle, H. (2008). Evaluation of a sexual assault risk reduction and self-defense program: A prospective analysis of a revised protocol. *Psychology of Women Quarterly, 32*, 204–218.

Orcutt, J. D., & Faison, R. (1988). Sex-role attitude change and reporting of rape victimization, 1973–1985. *Sociological Quarterly, 29*, 589–604.

Orton, R. S. (1993). Outside in: A man in the movement. In E. Buchwald, P. Fletcher, & M. Roth (Eds.), *Transforming a rape culture* (pp. 237–246). Minneapolis, MN: Milkweed Press.

Outcault, S. D., Dilalla, D. L., & Weston, R. (2006, August). *Friends as support providers to sexual assault survivors: Interference of rape myth acceptance.* Poster presented at the 114th Annual Convention of the American Psychological Association, New Orleans, LA.

Ozer, E. J., Best, S. R., Lipsey, T. L., & Weiss, D. S. (2003). Predictors of PTSD and symptoms in adults: A meta-analysis. *Psychological Bulletin, 129*, 52–73.

Padgett, D. K., Harman, C. P., Burns, B. J., & Schlesinger, H. J. (1994). Women and outpatient mental health services: Use by Black, Latina, and White women in a national insured population. *Journal of Mental Health Administration, 21*, 347–360.

Paglia, C. (1991). *Sexual personae: Art and decadence from Nefertiti to Emily Dickinson.* New York: Vintage.

Park, C. L., & Blumberg, C. J. (2002). Disclosing trauma through writing: Testing the meaning-making hypothesis. *Cognitive Therapy and Research, 26*, 597–616.

Parks, K. A., Pardi, A. M., & Bradizza, C. M. (2006). Collecting data on alcohol use and alcohol-related victimization: A comparison of telephone and web-based survey methods. *Journal of Studies on Alcohol, 67*, 318–323.

Paul, P. (2005). *Pornified: How the culture of porn is changing our lives, our relationships, and our families.* New York: Macmillan.

Payne, D. L., Lonsway, K. A., & Fitzgerald, L. F. (1999). Rape myth acceptance: Exploration of its structure and its measurement using the Illinois Rape Myth Acceptance Scale. *Journal of Research in Personality, 53*, 27–68.

Pearlman, L. A., & Mac Ian, P. S. (1995). Vicarious traumatization: An empirical study of the effects of trauma work on trauma therapists. *Professional Psychology: Research and Practice, 26*, 558–565.

Pearlman, L. A., & Saakvitne, K. W. (1995). *Trauma and the therapist: Countertransference and vicarious traumatization in psychotherapy with incest survivors*. New York: Norton.

Pennebaker, J. W. (1997). Writing about emotional experiences as a therapeutic process. *Psychological Science, 8*, 162–166.

Pennebaker, J. W., Kiecolt-Glaser, J. K., & Glaser, R. (1988). Disclosure of traumas and immune function: Health implications for psychotherapy. *Journal of Consulting and Clinical Psychology, 56*, 239–245.

Phillips, L. (2000). *Flirting with danger: Young women's reflections on sexuality and domination*. New York: New York University Press.

Pierce-Baker, C. (1998). *Surviving the silence: Black women's stories of rape*. New York: Norton.

Pollard, P. (1992). Judgments about victims and attackers in depicted rapes: A review. *British Journal of Social Psychology, 31*, 307–326.

Popiel, D. A., & Susskind, E. C. (1985). The impact of rape: Social support as a moderator of stress. *American Journal of Community Psychology, 13*, 645–676.

Potter, S. J., Moynihan, M. M., Stapleton, J. G., & Banyard, V. L. (2009). Empowering bystanders to prevent campus violence against women: A preliminary evaluation of a poster campaign. *Violence Against Women, 15*, 106–121.

Potter, S. J., Stapleton, J. G., & Moynihan, M. M. (2008). Designing, piloting, and evaluating a violence against women media campaign for bystanders. *Journal of Prevention & Intervention in the Community, 36*, 39–55.

Raine, N. V. (1998). *After silence: Rape and my journey back*. New York: Crown.

Ream, A. (2004). *The voices and faces project*. Retrieved May 1, 2008, from http://www.voicesandfaces.org

Regehr, C., & Alaggia, R. (2006). Perspectives on the justice system for victims of sexual violence. *Victims & Offenders, 1*, 33–46.

Reinharz, S. (1994). Toward an ethnography of "voice" and "silence." In E. Trickett & R. Watts (Eds.), *Human diversity: Perspectives on people in context* (pp. 178–200). San Francisco: Jossey-Bass.

Reinharz, S., & Chase, S. E. (2002). Interviewing women. In J. F. Gubrium & J. A. Holstein (Eds.), *Handbook of interview research: Context and method* (pp. 73–90). Thousand Oaks, CA: Sage.

Rennison, C. M. (2002). *Rape and sexual assault: Reporting to police and medical attention, 1992–2000* (Report No. NCJ 194530). Washington, DC: U.S. Department of Justice.

Rennison, C. M. (2007). Reporting to the police by Latina victims of violence. *Violence and Victims, 22*, 754–772.

Resick, P. A. (1983). The rape reaction: Research findings and implications for intervention. *The Behavior Therapist, 6*, 129–132.

Resick, P. A. (1993). The psychological impact of rape. *Journal of Interpersonal Violence, 8*, 223–255.

Resick, P. A., Galovski, T. E., Uhlmansiek, M. O., Scher, C. D., Clum, G. A., & Young-Xu, Y. (2008). A randomized clinical trial to dismantle components of cognitive processing therapy for PTSD in female victims of interpersonal violence. *Journal of Consulting and Clinical Psychology, 76*, 243–258.

Resick, P. A., & Schnicke, M. K. (1992). Cognitive processing therapy for sexual assault victims. *Journal of Consulting and Clinical Psychology, 60*, 748–756.

Rich, A. (1980). Compulsory heterosexuality and lesbian existence. *Signs, 5*, 631–660.

Rich, R. F., & Sampson, R. J. (1990). Public perceptions of criminal justice policy: Does victimization make a difference? *Violence and Victims, 5*, 109–118.

Richardson, D., & Campbell, J. L. (1982). Alcohol and rape: The effect of alcohol on attributions of blame for rape. *Personality and Social Psychology Bulletin, 8*, 468–476.

Richie, B. E. (2000). A black feminist reflection on the antiviolence movement. *Signs, 25*, 1133–1137.

Rickert, V. I., Wiemann, C. M., & Vaughan, R. D. (2005). Disclosure of date/acquaintance rape: Who reports and when. *Journal of Pediatric and Adolescent Gynecology, 18*, 17–24.

Riger, S. (1993). What's wrong with empowerment? *American Journal of Community Psychology, 21*, 279–292.

Roesler, T. A., & Wind, T. W. (1994). Telling the secret: Adult women describe their disclosures of incest. *Journal of Interpersonal Violence, 9*, 327–338.

Roiphe, K. (1993). *The morning after: Sex, fear, and feminism on campus.* Boston: Little, Brown.

Rook, K. S. (1984). The negative side of social interaction: Impact on psychological well-being. *Journal of Personality and Social Psychology, 46*, 1097–1108.

Rosenbaum, D. P. (1987). Coping with victimization: The effects of police intervention on victims' psychological adjustment. *Crime & Delinquency, 33*, 502–519.

Rossi, A. S. (1973). *The feminist papers: From Adams to De Beauvoir.* Boston: Northeastern University Press.

Rossman, B. B., & Rosenberg, M. (1998). *Multiple victimization of children: Conceptual, development, research, and treatment issues.* Philadelphia: Haworth Press.

Rozee, P., & Koss, M. P. (2001). Rape: A century of resistance. *Psychology of Women Quarterly, 25*, 295–311.

Ruch, L., & Chandler, S. (1983). Sexual assault trauma during the acute phase: An exploratory model and multivariate analysis. *Journal of Health and Social Behavior, 24*, 174–185.

Ruggiero, K. J., Smith, D. W., Hanson, R. F., Resnick, H. S., Saunders, B. E., Kilpatrick, D. G., et al. (2004). Is disclosure of childhood rape associated with mental health outcome? Results from the National Women's Study. *Child Maltreatment, 9*, 62–77.

Russell, D. E. H. (1974). *The politics of rape: The victim's perspective.* New York: Stein & Day.

Russell, D. E. H. (1982). *Rape in marriage*. New York: Macmillan.

Russell, D. E. H., & Bolen, R. M. (2000). *The epidemic of rape and child sexual abuse in the United States*. Thousand Oaks, CA: Sage.

Saakvitne, K. W., & Pearlman, L. A. (1996). *Transforming the pain: A workbook on vicarious traumatization*. New York: Norton.

Sabin-Farrell, R., & Turpin, G. (2003). Vicarious traumatization: Implications for the mental health of workers? *Clinical Psychology Review, 23*, 449–480.

Sales, E., Baum, M., & Shore, B. (1984). Victim readjustment following assault. *Journal of Social Issues, 40*, 17–36.

Salston, M., & Figley, C. R. (2003). Secondary traumatic stress effects of working with survivors of criminal victimization. *Journal of Traumatic Stress, 16*, 167–174.

Sampson, R. (1995). The community. In J. Q. Wilson & J. Petersilia (Eds.), *Crime* (pp. 193–216). San Francisco: ICS Press.

Santello, M., & Leitenberg, H. (1993). Sexual aggression by an acquaintance: Methods of coping and later psychological adjustment. *Violence and Victims, 8*, 91–104.

Sapp, M., Farrell, W. C., Johnson, J. H., Jr., & Hitchcock, K. (1999). Attitudes toward rape among African American male and female college students. *Journal of Counseling and Development, 77*, 204–208.

Schauben, L. J., & Frazier, P. A. (1995). Vicarious trauma: The effects on female counselors of working with sexual violence survivors. *Psychology of Women Quarterly, 19*, 49–64.

Scherer, M. (1992). *Still loved by the sun: A rape survivor's journal*. New York: Simon & Schuster.

Schewe, P. A. (2002). *Preventing violence in relationships: Interventions across the life span*. Washington, DC: American Psychological Association.

Schewe, P. A. (2006). Interventions to prevent sexual violence. In L. Doll, S. Bonzo, J. Mercy, & D. Sleet (Eds.), *Handbook of injury and violence prevention* (pp. 223–240). New York: Springer.

Schuller, R. A., & Stewart, A. (2000). Police responses to sexual assault complaints: The role of perpetrator/complainant intoxication. *Law and Human Behavior, 24*, 535–550.

Schuller, R. A., & Wall, A. M. (1998). The effects of defendant and complainant intoxication on mock jurors' judgments of sexual assault. *Psychology of Women Quarterly, 22*, 555–573.

Schwartz, M., & DeKeseredy, W. (1997). *Sexual assault on the college campus: The role of male peer support*. Thousand Oaks, CA: Sage.

Scott, E. K. (1998). Creating partnerships for change: Alliances and betrayals in the racial politics of two feminist organizations. *Gender & Society, 12*, 400–423.

Sebold, A. (1999). *Lucky*. New York: Simon & Schuster.

Shaw, C., & McKay, H. (1942). *Juvenile delinquency and urban areas*. Chicago: University of Chicago Press.

Sheldon, J. P., & Parent, S. L. (2002). Clergy's attitudes and attributions of blame toward female rape victims. *Violence Against Women, 8,* 233–256.

Shipherd, J. C., & Beck, J. G. (1999). The effects of suppressing trauma-related thoughts on women with rape-related PTSD. *Behaviour Research and Therapy, 37,* 99–112.

Sims, B., Yost, B., & Abbott, C. (2006). The efficacy of victim services programs: Alleviating the psychological suffering of crime victims? *Criminal Justice Policy Review, 17,* 387–406.

Sinclair, B. B., & Gold, S. R. (1997). The psychological impact of withholding disclosure of child sexual abuse. *Violence and Victims, 12,* 137–145.

Singleton, R., & Straits, D. (2005). The nature of science. In R. Singleton & D. Straits (Eds.), *Approaches to social research* (4th ed., pp. 14–40). New York: Oxford University Press.

Skogan, W. G. (2006). *Police and community in Chicago: A tale of three cities.* New York: Oxford University Press.

Smith, D. W., Letourneau, E. J., Saunders, B. E., Kilpatrick, D. G., Resnick, H. S., & Best, C. L. (2000). Delay in disclosure of childhood rape: Results from a national survey. *Child Abuse & Neglect, 24,* 273–287.

Smith, M. E. (2005). Female sexual assault: The impact on the male significant other. *Issues in Mental Health Nursing, 26,* 149–167.

Smith, S. G., & Cook, S. L. (2008). Disclosing sexual assault to parents: The influence of parental messages about sex. *Violence Against Women, 14,* 1326–1348.

Sommers, C. H. (1994). *Who stole feminism? How women have betrayed women.* New York: Simon & Schuster.

Sorenson, S. B., & Siegel, J. M. (1992). Gender, ethnicity, and sexual assault: Findings from a Los Angeles study. *Journal of Social Issues, 48,* 93–104.

Sorenson, S. B., Stein, J. A., Siegel, J. M., Golding, J. M., & Burnam, M. A. (1987). The prevalence of adult sexual assault: The Los Angeles Epidemiologic Catchment Area Project. *American Journal of Epidemiology, 126,* 1154–1164.

Sorsoli, L., Kia-Keating, M., & Grossman, F. K. (2008). "I keep that hush-hush": Male survivors of sexual abuse and the challenges of disclosure. *Journal of Counseling Psychology, 55,* 333–345.

Stamm, B. H. (1995). *Secondary traumatic stress: Self-care issues for clinicians, researchers, and educators.* Lutherville, MD: Sidran Foundation.

Stanko, E. A. (1997). "I second that emotion": Reflections on feminism, emotionality, and research on sexual violence. In M. D. Schwartz (Ed.), *Researching sexual violence against women: Methodological and personal perspectives* (pp. 74–85). Thousand Oaks, CA: Sage.

Stark, E. (2007). *Coercive control: The entrapment of women in personal life.* New York: Oxford University Press.

Starzynski, L. L., Ullman, S. E., Filipas, H. H., & Townsend, S. M. (2005). Correlates of women's sexual assault disclosure to informal and formal support sources. *Violence and Victims, 20*, 415–431.

Starzynski, L. L., Ullman, S. E., Townsend, S. M., Long, L. L., & Long, S. (2007). What factors predict women's disclosure of sexual assault to mental health professionals? *Journal of Community Psychology, 35*, 619–638.

Stevens, L. (2007, December). *Screening for sexual violence: Gaps in research and recommendations for change*. Harrisburg, PA: VAWnet. Retrieved May 11, 2008, from http://www.vawnet.org

Stewart, B. D., Hughes, C., Frank, E., Anderson, B., Kendall, K., & West, D. (1987). The aftermath of rape: Profiles of immediate and delayed treatment seekers. *Journal of Nervous and Mental Disease, 175*, 90–94.

Stoltenberg, J. (1999). *Refusing to be a man: Essays on social justice*. New York: Routledge.

Sudderth, L. K. (1998). "It'll come right back at me": The interactional context of discussing rape with others. *Violence Against Women, 4*, 572–594.

Sue, D. (1994). Asian American mental health and help-seeking behavior: Comment on Solberg et al. (1994), and Tata and Leong (1994). *Journal of Counseling Psychology, 41*, 292–295.

Symonds, M. E. (1980). The "second injury" to victims. *Evaluation and Change, 4*, 36–38.

Tang, S., Freyd, J., & Wang, M. (2007). What do we know about gender in the disclosure of child sexual abuse? *Journal of Psychological Trauma, 6*, 1–26.

Tarrier, N., & Humphreys, A. L. (2003). PTSD and the social support of the interpersonal environment: The development of social cognitive behavior therapy. *Journal of Cognitive Psychotherapy, 17*, 187–198.

Tarrier, N., Sommerfield, C., & Pilgrim, H. (1999). The effect of the relatives' level of expressed emotion (EE) on the outcome of psychological treatment of PTSD patients. *Psychological Medicine, 29*, 801–811.

Taylor, S. E. (1983). Adjustment to threatening events: A theory of cognitive adaptation. *American Psychologist, 38*, 1161–1173.

Taylor, S. E. (2007). Social support. In H. S. Friedman & R. C. Silver (Eds.), *Foundations of health psychology* (pp. 145–171). New York: Oxford University Press.

Taylor, S. E., & Brown, J. D. (1988). Illusion and well-being: A social psychological perspective on mental health. *Psychological Bulletin, 103*, 193–210.

Temkin, J., & Krahe, B. (2008). *Sexual assault and the justice gap: A question of attitude*. Oxford, England: Hart.

Thompson, M., Sitterle, B., Clay, G., & Kingree, J. (2007). Reasons for not reporting victimizations to the police: Do they vary for physical and sexual incidents? *Journal of American College Health, 55*, 277–282.

Tjaden, P., & Thoennes, N. (1998). *Prevalence, incidence, and consequences of violence against women: Findings from the National Violence Against Women Survey* (Report

No. NCJ-172837). Washington, DC: U.S. Department of Justice, National Institute of Justice.

Tjaden, P., & Thoennes, N. (2000). *Full report of prevalence, incidence, and consequences of violence against women: Findings from the National Violence Against Women Survey* (Report No. NCJ 183781). Washington, DC: U.S. Department of Justice, National Institute of Justice.

Tjaden, P., & Thoennes, N. (2006). *Extent, nature, and consequences of rape victimization: Findings from the National Violence Against Women Survey* (Report No. NCJ 210346). Washington, DC: U.S. Department of Justice, National Institute of Justice.

Townsend, S. M., & Campbell, R. M. (2008). Identifying common practices in community-based rape prevention programs. *Journal of Prevention & Intervention in the Community, 36*, 121–135.

Trippany, R. L., Kress, V. E., & Wilcoxon, S. A. (2004). Preventing vicarious trauma: What counselors should know when working with trauma survivors. *Journal of Counseling and Development, 82*, 31–37.

Turner, R. J. (1983). Direct, indirect, and moderating effects of social support on psychological distress and associated conditions. In H. B. Kaplan (Ed.), *Psychosocial stress: Trends in theory and research* (pp. 105–155). New York: Academic Press.

Tyler, T. R., & Huo, Y. J. (2002). *Trust in the law: Encouraging public cooperation with the police and courts.* New York: Russell Sage Foundation.

Uji, M., Shono, M., Shikai, N., & Kitamura, T. (2007). Case illustrations of negative sexual experiences among university women in Japan: Victimization disclosure and reactions of the confidant. *International Journal of Offender Therapy and Comparative Criminology, 51*, 227–242.

Ullman, S. E. (1996a). Correlates and consequences of adult sexual assault disclosure. *Journal of Interpersonal Violence, 11*, 554–571.

Ullman, S. E. (1996b). Do social reactions to sexual assault victims vary by support provider? *Violence and Victims, 11*, 143–156.

Ullman, S. E. (1996c). Social reactions, coping strategies, and self-blame attributions in adjustment to sexual assault. *Psychology of Women Quarterly, 20*, 505–526.

Ullman, S. E. (1999). Social support and recovery from sexual assault: A review. *Aggression and Violent Behavior, 4*, 343–358.

Ullman, S. E. (2000). Psychometric characteristics of the Social Reactions Questionnaire: A measure of reactions to sexual assault victims. *Psychology of Women Quarterly, 24*, 257–271.

Ullman, S. E. (2003). Social reactions to child sexual abuse disclosures: A critical review. *Journal of Child Sexual Abuse, 12*, 89–121.

Ullman, S. E. (2005). Interviewing clinicians and advocates who work with sexual assault survivors: A personal perspective on moving from quantitative to qualitative methods. *Violence Against Women, 11*, 1–27.

Ullman, S. E. (2007a). Mental health service seeking in sexual assault victims: A review of the literature. *Women & Therapy, 30,* 61–84.

Ullman, S. E. (2007b). A 10-year update on "Review and Critique of Empirical Studies of Rape Avoidance." *Criminal Justice and Behavior, 34,* 411–429.

Ullman, S. E., & Brecklin, L. (2002). Sexual assault history, PTSD, and mental health service seeking in a national sample of women. *Journal of Community Psychology, 30,* 1–19.

Ullman, S. E., & Filipas, H. H. (2001a). Correlates of formal and informal support seeking in sexual assault victims. *Journal of Interpersonal Violence, 16,* 1028–1047

Ullman, S. E., & Filipas, H. H. (2001b). Predictors of PTSD symptom severity and social reactions in sexual assault victims. *Journal of Traumatic Stress, 14,* 369–389.

Ullman, S. E., & Filipas, H. H. (2005). Gender differences in social reactions to abuse disclosures, post-abuse coping, and PTSD of child sexual abuse survivors. *Child Abuse & Neglect, 29,* 767–782.

Ullman, S. E., Filipas, H. H., Townsend, S. M., & Starzynski, L. L. (2007). Psychosocial correlates of PTSD symptom severity in sexual assault survivors. *Journal of Traumatic Stress, 20,* 821–831.

Ullman, S. E., & Najdowski, C. J. (2009). *Prospective changes in attributions of self-blame and social reactions to women's disclosures of adult sexual assault.* Manuscript submitted for publication.

Ullman, S. E., & Siegel, J. M. (1993). Victim–offender relationship and sexual assault. *Violence and Victims, 8,* 121–134.

Ullman, S. E., & Siegel, J. M. (1995). Sexual assault, social reactions, and physical health. *Women's Health: Research on Gender, Behavior, and Policy, 1,* 289–308.

Ullman, S. E., & Townsend, S. M. (2007). Barriers to working with sexual assault survivors: A qualitative study of rape crisis center workers. *Violence Against Women, 13,* 412–443.

Ullman, S. E., & Townsend, S. M. (2008). What is an empowerment approach to working with sexual assault survivors? *Journal of Community Psychology, 36,* 299–312.

Ullman, S. E., Townsend, S. M., Filipas, H. H., & Starzynski, L. L. (2007). Structural models of the relations of assault severity, social support, avoidance coping, self-blame, and PTSD among sexual assault survivors. *Psychology of Women Quarterly, 31,* 23–37.

Ullrich, P. M., & Lutgendorf, S. K. (2002). Journaling about stressful events: Effects of cognitive processing and emotional expression. *Annals of Behavioral Medicine, 24,* 244–250.

U.S. Department of Justice. (2004). *A national protocol for sexual assault medical forensic examinations: Adults/adolescents.* Washington, DC: Author.

Valentiner, D., Foa, E., Riggs, D., & Gershuny, B. (1996). Coping strategies and PTSD in female victims of sexual and nonsexual assault. *Journal of Abnormal Psychology, 105,* 455–458.

Varelas, N., & Foley, L. A. (1998). Blacks' and Whites' perceptions of interracial and intraracial date rape. *Journal of Social Psychology, 138*, 392–400.

Vicary, J. R., Klingaman, L. R., & Harkness, W. L. (1995). Risk factors associated with date rape and sexual assault of adolescent girls. *Journal of Adolescence, 18*, 289–306.

Vidal, M. E., & Petrak, J. (2007). Shame and adult sexual assault: A study with a group of female survivors recruited from an East London population. *Sexual and Relationship Therapy, 22*, 159–171.

Wakelin, A., & Long, K. M. (2003). Effects of victim gender and sexuality on attributions of blame to rape victims. *Sex Roles, 49*, 477–487.

Walker, R. (1992, January–February). Becoming the third wave. *Ms., 39–41.*

Walker, L. (1979). *The battered woman.* New York: Harper & Row.

Wall, A. M., & Schuller, R. A. (2000). Sexual assault and defendant/victim intoxication: Jurors' perceptions of guilt. *Journal of Applied Social Psychology, 30*, 253–274.

Ward, C. A. (1988). The Attitudes Toward Rape Victims Scale. *Psychology of Women Quarterly, 12*, 127–146.

Ward, C. A. (1995). *Attitudes toward rape: Feminist and social psychological perspectives.* Thousand Oaks, CA: Sage.

Wasco, S. M. (2003). Conceptualizing the harm done by rape: Applications of trauma theory to experiences of sexual assault. *Trauma, Violence, & Abuse, 4*, 309–322.

Wasco, S. M., & Campbell, R. M. (2002). Emotional reactions of rape victim advocates: A multiple case study of anger and fear. *Psychology of Women Quarterly, 26*, 120–130.

Washington, P. A. (2001). Disclosure patterns of Black female sexual assault survivors. *Violence Against Women, 7*, 1254–1283.

Washington Coalition of Sexual Assault Programs. (2004). Vicarious trauma and its impact on advocates, therapists, and friends. *Research and Advocacy Digest, 6*, 1–16.

West, C. M. (2006). *Sexual violence in the lives of African American women.* Harrisburg, PA: VAWnet. Retrieved May 20, 2008, from http://www.vawnet.org.

White, B. H., & Kurpius, S. E. (2002). Effects of victim sex and sexual orientation on perceptions of rape. *Sex Roles, 46*, 191–200.

Widom, C. S. (1997). *Accuracy of adult recollections of early childhood abuse.* New York: Plenum Press.

Williams, J. E. (1979). Sex role stereotypes: Women's liberation and rape. A cross-cultural analysis of attitudes. *Sociological Symposium, 25*, 61–97.

Williams, J. E., & Holmes, K. A. (1981). *The second assault: Rape and public attitudes.* Westport, CT: Greenwood Press.

Williams, L. S. (1984). The classic rape: When do victims report? *Social Problems, 31*, 459–467.

Winerman, L. (2006). Helping others, helping ourselves. *Monitor on Psychology, 37*, 38–41.

Winkler, C. (2002). *One night: Realities of rape*. Walnut Creek, CA: AltaMira Press.

Wollstonecraft, M. (1967). *A vindication of the rights of women*. New York: Norton. (Original work published 1792)

Wood, G. G., & Roche, S. E. (2001). Representing selves, reconstructing lives: Feminist group work with women survivors of male violence. *Social Work With Groups, 23*, 5–23.

Wortman, C. B. (2004). Posttraumatic growth: Progress and problems. *Psychological Inquiry, 15*, 81–90.

Wyatt, G. E. (1992). The sociocultural context of African American and White American women's rape. *Journal of Social Issues, 48*, 77–91.

Wyatt, G. E., Notgrass, C. M., & Newcomb, M. (1990). Internal and external mediators of women's rape experiences. *Psychology of Women Quarterly, 14*, 153–176.

Yassen, J., & Glass, L. (1984, May–June). Sexual assault survivor groups: A feminist practice perspective. *Social Work*, 252–257.

Yllo, K. (2005). Through a feminist lens: Gender, diversity, and violence: Extending the feminist framework. In D. R. Loseke, R. J. Gelles, & M. Cavanaugh (Eds.), *Current controversies on family violence* (2nd ed., pp. 19–34). Thousands Oaks, CA: Sage.

Ziegenmeyer, N. (1992). *Taking back my life*. New York: Summit.

Zoellner, L. A., Foa, E. B., & Brigidi, B. D. (1999). Interpersonal friction and PTSD in female victims of sexual and nonsexual assault. *Journal of Traumatic Stress, 12*, 689–700.

Zweig, J., & Burt, M. (2007). Predicting women's perceptions of domestic violence and sexual assault agency helpfulness. *Violence Against Women, 13*, 1149–1178.

INDEX

ABOUT THE AUTHOR

Sarah E. Ullman, PhD, is a professor of criminology, law, and justice at the University of Illinois at Chicago. She received her doctorate in social/developmental psychology from Brandeis University and completed a post-doctoral fellowship in health psychology at the University of California, Los Angeles. Dr. Ullman's research interests focus on violence against women, in particular the sexual victimization of women in adulthood, including the impact of rape on women's mental and physical health, which can include posttraumatic stress disorder, suicidal behavior, problem drinking, and mental health services-seeking. She has studied women's resistance strategies and self-defense training in rape situations and the role of alcohol in sexual assault incidents. Dr. Ullman recently completed a longitudinal study funded by the National Institute on Alcohol Abuse and Alcoholism of survivors of sexual assault that examined how social reactions from formal and informal support sources affect women's coping and recovery from sexual assault, including their posttraumatic stress disorder and substance abuse outcomes. She has also interviewed both survivors and service providers (advocates and clinicians) about their disclosure and help-seeking experiences and is developing an informal support network intervention for survivors and their social network members.